FUNNY BOY

FUNNY BOY

a novel

Shyam Selvadurai

William Morrow and Company, Inc.
NEW YORK

Originally published in 1994 by McClelland & Stewart Ltd. (Toronto), Jonathan Cape (London), and Penguin Books (Bombay)

Lines from "The Best School of All" are from *Book of Lively Verse, Part 2*, compiled by Alan Sauvain (University Tutorial Press, 1937).

"Pigs Can't Fly" appeared in the *Toronto South Asian Review* and in *Meanwhile, in Another Part of the Forest: Gay Stories from Alice Munro to Yukio Mishima*, edited by Alberto Manguel and Craig Stephenson (Knopf Canada).

Library of Congress Cataloging-in-Publication Data

Salvadurai, Shyam, 1965–
    Funny boy : a novel / Shyam Selvadurai.
        p.   cm.
    ISBN 0-688-14595-7 (hardcover)
    I. Title.
PR9440.9.S42F86   1996
823—dc20   95-30685
                                                          CIP

Printed in the United States of America

First U.S. Edition

1 2 3 4 5 6 7 8 9 10

To my parents,
Christine and David Selvadurai,
for believing that pigs can fly

Contents

FUNNY BOY

Pigs Can't Fly

B esides Christmas and other festive occasions, spend-the-
days were the days most looked forward to by all of us,
cousins, aunts, and uncles.

For the adults a spend-the-day was the one Sunday of the
month they were free of their progeny. The eagerness with
which they anticipated these days could be seen in the way
Amma woke my brother, my sister, and me extra early when
they came. Unlike on school days, when Amma allowed us
to dawdle a little, we were hurried through our morning
preparations. Then, after a quick breakfast, we would be
driven to the house of our grandparents.

The first thing that met our eyes on entering our grand-parents' house, after we carefully wiped our feet on the door-mat, would be the dark corridor running the length of it, on one side of which were the bedrooms and on the other the drawing and dining rooms. This corridor, with its old pho-tographs on both walls and its ceiling so high that our foot-steps echoed, scared me a little. The drawing room into which we would be ushered to pay our respects to our grandparents was also dark and smelt like old clothes that had been locked away in a suitcase for a long time. There my grandparents Ammachi and Appachi sat, enthroned in big reclining chairs. Appachi usually looked up from his paper and said vaguely, "Ah, hello, hello," before going back behind it, but Ammachi always called us to her with the beckoning movement of her middle and index fingers. With our legs trembling slightly, we would go to her, the thought of the big canes she kept behind her tall clothes almariah strongly imprinted upon our minds. She would grip our faces in her plump hands, and one by one kiss us wetly on both cheeks and say, "God has blessed me with fifteen grandchildren who will look after me in my old age." She smelt of stale coconut oil, and the diamond mukkuthi in her nose always pressed painfully against my cheek.

When the aunts and uncles eventually drove away, wav-ing gaily at us children from car windows, we waved back at the retreating cars with not even a pretense of sorrow. For one glorious day a month we were free of parental control and the ever-watchful eyes and talebearing tongues of the house servants.

We were not, alas, completely abandoned, as we would

have so liked to have been. Ammachi and Janaki were supposedly in charge. Janaki, cursed with the task of having to cook for fifteen extra people, had little time for supervision and actually preferred to have nothing to do with us at all. If called upon to come and settle a dispute, she would rush out, her hands red from grinding curry paste, and box the ears of the first person who happened to be in her path. We had learned that Janaki was to be appealed to only in the most dire emergencies. The one we understood, by tacit agreement, never to appeal to was Ammachi. Like the earth-goddess in the folktales, she was not to be disturbed from her tranquillity. To do so would have been the cause of a catastrophic earthquake.

In order to minimize interference by either Ammachi or Janaki, we had developed and refined a system of handling conflict and settling disputes ourselves. Two things formed the framework of this system: territoriality and leadership.

Territorially, the area around my grandparents' house was divided into two. The front garden, the road, and the field that lay in front of the house belonged to the boys, although included in their group was my female cousin Meena. In this territory, two factions struggled for power, one led by Meena, the other by my brother, Varuna, who, because of a prevailing habit, had been renamed Diggy-Nose and then simply Diggy.

The second territory was called "the girls'," included in which, however, was myself, a boy. It was to this territory of "the girls'," confined to the back garden and the kitchen porch, that I seemed to have gravitated naturally, my earliest memories of those spend-the-days always belonging in the back garden of my grandparents' home. The pleasure the boys had standing for hours on a cricket field under the sweltering sun, watching the batsmen run from crease to crease, was incomprehensible to me.

For me, the primary attraction of the girls' territory was the potential for the free play of fantasy. Because of the force of my imagination, I was selected as leader. Whatever the game, be it the imitation of adult domestic functions or the enactment of some well-loved fairy story, it was I who discovered some new way to enliven it, some new twist to the plot of a familiar tale. Led by me, the girl cousins would conduct a raid on my grandparents' dirty-clothes basket, discovering in this odorous treasure trove saris, blouses, sheets, curtains with which we invented costumes to complement our voyages of imagination.

The reward for my leadership was that I always got to play the main part in the fantasy. If it was cooking-cooking we were playing, I was the chef; if it was Cinderella or Thumbelina, I was the much-beleaguered heroine of these tales.

Of all our varied and fascinating games, bride-bride was my favorite. In it I was able to combine many elements of the other games I loved, and with time bride-bride, which had taken a few hours to play initially, became an event that spread out over the whole day and was planned for weeks in advance. For me the culmination of this game, and my ultimate moment of joy, was when I put on the clothes of the bride. In the late afternoon, usually after tea, I, along with the older girl cousins, would enter Janaki's room. From my sling-bag I would bring out my most prized possession, an old white sari, slightly yellow with age, its border torn and missing most of its sequins. The dressing of the bride would now begin, and then, by the transfiguration I saw taking place in Janaki's cracked full-length mirror—by the sari being wrapped around my body, the veil being pinned to my head, the rouge put on my cheeks, lipstick on my lips, kohl around my eyes—I was able to leave the constraints of my self and ascend into another, more brilliant, more beautiful self, a self to whom this day was dedicated, and around whom the world, represented by my cousins putting flowers in my hair, draping the palu, seemed to revolve. It was a self magnified, like the goddesses of the Sinhalese and Tamil cinema, larger than life; and like them, like the Malini Fonsekas and the Geetha Kumarasinghes, I was an icon, a graceful, benevolent, perfect being upon whom the adoring eyes of the world rested.

Those spend-the-days, the remembered innocence of childhood, are now colored in the hues of the twilight sky. It is a picture made even more sentimental by the loss of all that was associated with them. By all of us having to leave Sri Lanka years later because of communal violence and forge a new home for ourselves in Canada.

Yet those Sundays, when I was seven, marked the beginning of my exile from the world I loved. Like a ship that leaves a port for the vast expanse of sea, those much-looked-forward-to days took me away from the safe harbor of childhood towards the precarious waters of adult life.

The visits at my grandparents' began to change with the return from abroad of Kanthi Aunty, Cyril Uncle, and their daughter, Tanuja, whom we quickly renamed "Her Fatness," in that cruelly direct way children have.

At first we had no difficulty with the newcomer in our midst. In fact we found her quite willing to accept that, by reason of her recent arrival, she must necessarily begin at the bottom.

In the hierarchy of bride-bride, the person with the least importance, less even than the priest and the pageboys, was the groom. It was a role we considered stiff and boring, that held no attraction for any of us. Indeed, if we could have dispensed with that role altogether we would have, but alas it was an unfortunate feature of the marriage ceremony. My younger sister, Sonali, with her patient good nature, but also sensing that I might have a mutiny on my hands if I asked anyone else to play that role, always donned the long pants and tattered jacket, borrowed from my grandfather's clothes chest. It was now deemed fitting that Her Fatness should take over the role and thus leave Sonali free to wrap a bedsheet around her body, in the manner of a sari, and wear araliya flowers in her hair like the other bridesmaids.

For two spend-the-days, Her Fatness accepted her role without a murmur and played it with all the skilled unobtrusiveness of a bit player. The third spend-the-day, however, everything changed. That day turned out to be my grandmother's birthday. Instead of dropping the children off and driving away as usual, the aunts and uncles stayed on for lunch, a slight note of peevish displeasure in their voices.

We had been late, because etiquette (or rather my father) demanded that Amma wear a sari for the grand occasion of her mother-in-law's sixtieth birthday. Amma's tardiness and her insistence on getting her palu to fall to exactly above her knees drove us all to distraction (especially Diggy, who quite rightly feared that in his absence Meena would try to persuade the better members of his team to defect to her side). Even I, who usually loved the ritual of watching Amma get dressed, stood in her doorway with the others and fretfully asked if she was ever going to be ready.

When we finally did arrive at Ramanaygam Road, everyone else had been there almost an hour. We were ushered into the drawing room by Amma to kiss Ammachi and present her with her gift, the three of us clutching the present. All the uncles and aunts were seated. Her Fatness stood in between Kanthi Aunty's knees, next to Ammachi. When she saw us, she gave me an accusing, hostile look and pressed farther between her mother's legs. Kanthi Aunty turned away from her discussion with Mala Aunty, and, seeing me, she smiled and said in a tone that was as heavily sweetened as undiluted rose syrup, "So, what is this I hear, aah? Nobody will play with my little daughter."

I looked at her and then at Her Fatness, shocked by the lie. All my senses were alert.

Kanthi Aunty wagged her finger at me and said in a playful, chiding tone, "Now, now, Arjie, you must be nice to my little daughter. After all, she's just come from abroad and everything." Fortunately, I was prevented from having to answer. It was my turn to present my cheek to Ammachi, and, for the first time, I did so willingly, preferring the prick of the diamond mukkuthi to Kanthi Aunty's honeyed admonition.

Kanthi Aunty was the fourth oldest in my father's family.

First there was my father, then Ravi Uncle, Mala Aunty, Kanthi Aunty, Babu Uncle, Seelan Uncle, and finally Radha Aunty, who was much younger than the others and was away, studying in America. Kanthi Aunty was tall and bony, and we liked her the least, in spite of the fact that she would pat our heads affectionately whenever we walked past or greeted her. We sensed that beneath her benevolence lurked a seething anger, tempered by guile, that could have deadly consequences if unleashed in our direction. I had heard Amma say to her sister, Neliya Aunty, that Poor Kanthi was bitter because of the humiliations she had suffered abroad. "After all, darling, what a thing, forced to work as a servant in a whitey's house to make ends meet."

Once Ammachi had opened the present, a large silver serving tray, and thanked us for it (and insisted on kissing us once again), my brother, my sister, and I were finally allowed to leave the room. Her Fatness had already disappeared. I hurried out the front door and ran around the side of the house.

When I reached the back garden I found the girl cousins squatting on the porch in a circle. They were so absorbed in what was happening in the center that none of them even heard my greeting. Lakshmi finally became aware of my presence and beckoned me over excitedly. I reached the circle, and the cause of her excitement became clear. In the middle, in front of Her Fatness, sat a long-legged doll with shiny gold hair. Her dress was like that of a fairy queen, the gauze skirt sprinkled with tiny silver stars. Next to her sat her male counterpart, dressed in a pale-blue suit. I stared in wonder at the marvelous dolls. For us cousins, who had grown up under a government that strictly limited all foreign imports, such toys were unimaginable. Her Fatness turned to the other cousins and asked them if they wanted to hold the dolls for a moment. They nodded eagerly, and the dolls passed from hand to hand. I moved closer to get a better look. My gaze involuntarily rested on Her Fatness, and she gave me a smug look. Immediately her scheme became evident to me. It was with these dolls that my cousin from abroad hoped to seduce the other cousins away from me.

Unfortunately for her, she had underestimated the power of bride-bride. When the other cousins had all looked at the dolls, they bestirred themselves and, without so much as a backward glance, hurried down the steps to prepare for the marriage ceremony. As I followed them, I looked triumphantly at Her Fatness, who sat on the porch, clasping her beautiful dolls to her chest.

When lunch was over, my grandparents retired to their room for a nap. The other adults settled in the drawing room to read the newspaper or doze off in the huge armchairs. We, the bride-to-be and the bridesmaids, retired to Janaki's room for the long-awaited ritual of dressing the bride.

We were soon disturbed, however, by the sound of booming laughter. At first we ignored it, but when it persisted, getting louder and more drawn out, my sister, Sonali, went to the door and looked out. Her slight gasp brought us all out onto the porch. There the groom strutted, up and down, head thrown back, stomach stuck out. She sported a huge bristly mustache (torn out of the broom) and a cigarette (of rolled paper and talcum powder), which she held between her fingers and puffed on vigorously. The younger cousins, instead of getting dressed and putting the final touches to the altar, sat along the edge of the porch and watched with great amusement.

"Aha, me hearties!" the groom cried on seeing us. She opened her hands expansively. "Bring me my fair maiden, for I must be off to my castle before the sun settest."

We looked at the groom, aghast at the change in her behavior. She sauntered towards us, then stopped in front of me, winked expansively, and, with her hand under my chin, tilted back my head.

"Ahh!" she exclaimed. "A bonny lass, a bonny lass in-deed."

"Stop it!" I cried, and slapped her hand. "The groom is not supposed to make a noise."

"Why not?" Her Fatness replied angrily, dropping her hearty voice and accent. "Why can't the groom make a noise?"

"Because."

"Because of what?"

"Because the game is called bride-bride, not groom-groom."

Her Fatness seized her mustache and flung it to the ground dramatically. "Well, I don't want to be the groom anymore. I want to be the bride."

We stared at her in disbelief, amazed by her impudent challenge to my position.

"You can't," I finally said.

"Why not?" Her Fatness demanded. "Why should you

always be the bride? Why can't someone else have a chance too?"

"Because . . ." Sonali said, joining in. "Because Arjie is the bestest bride of all."

"But he's not even a girl," Her Fatness said, closing in on the lameness of Sonali's argument. "A bride is a girl, not a boy." She looked around at the other cousins and then at me. "A boy cannot be the bride," she said with deep conviction. "A girl must be the bride."

I stared at her, defenseless in the face of her logic.

Fortunately, Sonali, loyal to me as always, came to my rescue. She stepped in between us and said to Her Fatness, "If you can't play properly, go away. We don't need you."

"Yes!" Lakshmi, another of my supporters, cried.

The other cousins, emboldened by Sonali's fearlessness, murmured in agreement.

Her Fatness looked at all of us for a moment and then her gaze rested on me.

"You're a pansy," she said, her lips curling in disgust.

We looked at her blankly.

"A faggot," she said, her voice rising against our uncomprehending stares.

"A sissy!" she shouted in desperation.

It was clear by this time that these were insults.

"Give me that jacket," Sonali said. She stepped up to Her Fatness and began to pull at it. "We don't like you anymore."

"Yes!" Lakshmi cried. "Go away, you fatty-boom-boom!"

This was an insult we all understood, and we burst out

laughing. Someone even began to chant, "Hey fatty-boom-boom. Hey fatty-boom-boom."

Her Fatness pulled off her coat and trousers. "I hate you all," she cried. "I wish you were all dead." She flung the groom's clothes on the ground, stalked out of the back garden, and went around the side of the house.

We returned to our bridal preparations, chuckling to ourselves over the new nickname we had found for our cousin.

When the bride was finally dressed, Lakshmi, the maid of honor, went out of Janaki's room to make sure that everything was in place. Then she gave the signal and the priest and choirboys began to sing, with a certain want of harmony and correct lyrics, "The voice that breathed on Eeeden, the first and glorious day. . . ." Solemnly, I made my way down the steps towards the altar that had been set up at one end of the back garden. When I reached the altar, however, I heard the kitchen door open. I turned to see Her Fatness with Kanthi Aunty. The discordant singing died out.

Kanthi Aunty's benevolent smile had completely disappeared and her eyes were narrowed with anger.

"Who's calling my daughter fatty?" Kanthi Aunty said. She came to the edge of the porch.

We stared at her, no one daring to own up.

Her gaze fell on me and her eyes widened for a moment. Then a smile spread across her face.

"What's this?" she said, the honey seeping back into her voice. She came down a few steps and crooked her finger at me. I looked down at my feet and refused to go to her.

"Come here, come here," she said.

Unable to disobey her command any longer, I went to

her. She looked me up and down for a moment, and then gingerly, as if she were examining raw meat at the market, turned me around.

"What's this you're playing?" she asked.

"It's bride-bride, Aunty," Sonali said.

"Bride-bride," she murmured.

Her hand closed on my arm in a tight grip.

"Come with me," she said.

I resisted, but her grip tightened, her nails digging into my elbow. She pulled me up the porch steps and towards the kitchen door.

"No," I cried. "No, I don't want to."

Something about the look in her eyes terrified me so much I did the unthinkable and I hit out at her. This made her hold my arm even more firmly. She dragged me through the kitchen, past Janaki, who looked up, curious, and into the corridor and towards the drawing room. I felt a heaviness begin to build in my stomach. Instinctively I knew that Kanthi Aunty had something terrible in mind.

As we entered the drawing room, Kanthi Aunty cried out, her voice brimming over with laughter, "See what I found!"

The other aunts and uncles looked up from their papers or bestirred themselves from their sleep. They gazed at me in amazement as if I had suddenly made myself visible, like a spirit. I glanced at them and then at Amma's face. Seeing her expression, I felt my dread deepen. I lowered my eyes. The sari suddenly felt suffocating around my body, and the hairpins that held the veil in place pricked at my scalp.

Then the silence was broken by the booming laugh of Cyril Uncle, Kanthi Aunty's husband. As if she had been hit,

Amma swung around in his direction. The other aunts and uncles began to laugh too, and I watched as Amma looked from one to the other like a trapped animal. Her gaze finally came to rest on my father, and for the first time I noticed that he was the only one not laughing. Seeing the way he kept his eyes fixed on his paper, I felt the heaviness in my stomach begin to push its way up my throat.

"Ey, Chelva," Cyril Uncle cried out jovially to my father, "looks like you have a funny one here."

My father pretended he had not heard and, with an inclination of his head, indicated to Amma to get rid of me.

She waved her hand in my direction and I picked up the edges of my veil and fled to the back of the house.

That evening, on the way home, both my parents kept their eyes averted from me. Amma glanced at my father occasionally, but he refused to meet her gaze. Sonali, sensing my unease, held my hand tightly in hers.

Later, I heard my parents fighting in their room.

"How long has this been going on?" my father demanded.

"I don't know," Amma cried defensively. "It was as new to me as it was to you."

"You should have known. You should have kept an eye on him."

"What should I have done? Stood over him while he was playing?"

"If he turns out funny like that Rankotwera boy, if he turns out to be the laughingstock of Colombo, it'll be your fault," my father said in a tone of finality. "You always spoil him and encourage all his nonsense."

"What do I encourage?" Amma demanded.

"You are the one who allows him to come in here while you're dressing and play with your jewelry."

Amma was silent in the face of the truth.

Of the three of us, I alone was allowed to enter Amma's bedroom and watch her get dressed for special occasions. It was an experience I considered almost religious, for, even though I adored the goddesses of the local cinema, Amma was the final statement in female beauty for me.

When I knew Amma was getting dressed for a special occasion, I always positioned myself outside her door. Once she had put on her underskirt and blouse, she would ring for our servant, Anula, to bring her sari, and then, while taking it from her, hold the door open so I could go in as well. Entering that room was, for me, a greater boon than that granted by any god to a mortal. There were two reasons for this. The first was the jewelry box which lay open on the dressing table. With a joy akin to ecstasy, I would lean over and gaze inside, the faint smell of perfume rising out of the box each time I picked up a piece of jewelery and held it against my nose or ears or throat. The second was the pleasure of watching Amma drape her sari, watching her shake open the yards of material, which, like a Chinese banner caught by the wind, would linger in the air for a moment before drifting gently to the floor; watching her pick up one end of it, tuck it into the waistband of her skirt, make the pleats, and then

with a flick of her wrists invert the pleats and tuck them into
her waistband; and finally watching her drape the palu across
her breasts and pin it into place with a brooch.

When Amma was finished, she would check to make sure
that the back of the sari had not risen up with the pinning of
the palu, then move back and look at herself in the mirror.
Standing next to her or seated on the edge of the bed, I, too,
would look at her reflection in the mirror, and, with the
contented sigh of an artist who has finally captured the exact
effect he wants, I would say, "You should have been a film
star, Amma."

"A film star?" she would cry and lightly smack the side
my head. "What kind of a low-class-type person do you think
I am?"

One day, about a week after the incident at my grandparents', I positioned myself outside my parents' bedroom
door. When Anula arrived with the sari, Amma took it and
quickly shut the door. I waited patiently, thinking Amma had
not yet put on her blouse and skirt, but the door never
opened. Finally, perplexed that Amma had forgotten, I
knocked timidly on the door. She did not answer, but I could
hear her moving around inside. I knocked a little louder and
called out "Amma" through the keyhole. Still no response,
and I was about to call her name again when she replied
gruffly, "Go away. Can't you see I am busy?"

I stared disbelievingly at the door. Inside I could hear the
rustle of the sari as it brushed along the floor. I lifted my hand
to knock again when suddenly I remembered the quarrel I
had heard on the night of that last spend-the-day. My hand
fell limply by my side.

I crept away quietly to my bedroom, sat down on the edge of my bed, and stared at my feet for a long time. It was clear to me that I had done something wrong, but what it was I couldn't comprehend. I thought of what my father had said about turning out "funny." The word "funny" as I understood it meant either humorous or strange, as in the expression "That's funny." Neither of these fitted the sense in which my father had used the word, for there had been a hint of disgust in his tone.

Later, Amma came out of her room and called Anula to give her instructions for the evening. As I listened to the sound of her voice, I realized that something had changed forever between us.

A little while after my parents had left for their dinner party, Sonali came looking for me. Seeing my downcast expression, she sat next to me, and, though unaware of anything that had passed, slipped her hand in mine. I pushed it away roughly, afraid that if I let her squeeze my hand I would start to cry.

The next morning Amma and I were like two people who had had a terrible fight the night before. I found it hard to look her in the eye and she seemed in an unusually gay mood.

The following spend-the-day, when Amma came to awaken us, I was already seated in bed and folding my bride-bride sari. Something in her expression, however, made me hurriedly return the sari to the bag.

"What's that?" she said, coming towards me, her hand

outstretched. After a moment I gave her the bag. She glanced at its contents briefly. "Get up, it's spend-the-day," she said. Then, with the bag in her hand, she went to the window and looked out into the driveway. The seriousness of her expression, as if I had done something so awful that even the usual punishment of a caning would not suffice, frightened me.

I was brushing my teeth after breakfast when Anula came to the bathroom door, peered inside, and said with a sort of grim pleasure, "Missie wants to talk to you in her room." Seeing the alarm in my face, she nodded and said sagely, "Up to some kind of mischief as usual. Good-for-nothing child."

My brother, Diggy, was standing in the doorway of our parents' room, one foot scratching impatiently against the other. Amma was putting on her lipstick. My father had already gone for his Sunday squash game, and, as usual, she would pick him up after she had dropped us off at our grandparents'.

Amma looked up from the mirror, saw me, and indicated with her tube of lipstick for both of us to come inside and sit down on the edge of the bed. Diggy gave me a baleful look, as if it were my fault that Amma was taking such a long time to get ready. He followed me into the room, his slippers dragging along the floor.

Finally Amma closed her lipstick, pressed her lips together to even out the color, then turned to us.

"Okay, mister," she said to Diggy, "I am going to tell you something, and this is an order."

We watched her carefully.

"I want you to include your younger brother on your cricket team."

Diggy and I looked at her in shocked silence, then he cried, "Ah! Come on, Amma!"

And I, too, cried out, "I don't want to play with them. I hate cricket!"

"I don't care what you want," Amma said. "It's good for you."

"Arjie's useless," Diggy said. "We'll never win if he's on our team."

Amma held up her hand to silence us. "That's an order," she said.

"Why?" I asked, ignoring her gesture. "Why do I have to play with the boys?"

"Why?" Amma said. "Because the sky is so high and pigs can't fly, that's why."

"Please, Amma! Please!" I held out my arms to her.

Amma turned away quickly, picked up her handbag from the dressing table, and said, almost to herself, "If the child turns out wrong, it's the mother they always blame, never the father." She clicked the handbag shut.

I put my head in my hands and began to cry. "Please, Amma, please," I said through my sobs.

She continued to face the window.

I flung myself on the bed with a wail of anguish. I waited for her to come to me as she always did when I cried, waited for her to take me in her arms, rest my head against her breasts, and say in her special voice, "What's this, now? Who's the little man who's crying?"

But she didn't heed my weeping any more than she had heeded my cries when I knocked on her door.

Finally I stopped crying and rolled over on my back.

Diggy had left the room. Amma turned to me, now that I had become quiet, and said cheerfully, "You'll have a good time, just wait and see."

"Why can't I play with the girls?" I replied.

"You can't, that's all."

"But why?"

She shifted uneasily.

"You're a big boy now. And big boys must play with other boys."

"That's stupid."

"It doesn't matter," she said. "Life is full of stupid things and sometimes we just have to do them."

"I won't," I said defiantly. "I won't play with the boys."

Her face reddened with anger. She reached down, caught me by the shoulders, and shook me hard. Then she turned away and ran her hand through her hair. I watched her, gloating. I had broken her cheerful facade, forced her to show how much it pained her to do what she was doing, how little she actually believed in the justness of her actions.

After a moment she turned back to me and said in an almost pleading tone, "You'll have a good time."

I looked at her and said, "No, I won't."

Her back straightened. She crossed to the door and stopped. Without looking at me she said stiffly, "The car leaves in five minutes. If you're not in it by then, watch out."

I lay back on the bed and gazed at the mosquito net swinging gently in the breeze. In my mind's eye, I saw the day that stretched ahead of me. At the thought of having to waste the most precious day of the month in that field in front of my grandparents' house, the hot sun beating on my head, the perspiration running down the sides of my face, I felt a sense of despair begin to take hold of me. The picture of what would take place in the back garden became clear. I saw Her Fatness seizing my place as leader of the girls, claiming for herself the rituals I had so carefully invented and planned. I saw her standing in front of Janaki's mirror as the other girls fixed her hair, pinned her veil, and draped her sari. The thought was terrible. Something had to be done. I could not give up that easily, could not let Her Fatness, whose sneaking to Kanthi Aunty had forced me into the position I was now in, so easily take my place. But what could I do?

As if in answer, an object that rested just at the periphery of my vision claimed my attention. I turned my head slightly and saw my sling-bag. Then a thought came to me. I reached out, picked up the bag, and hugged it close to my chest. Without the sari in that bag, it was impossible for the girls to play bride-bride. I thought of Her Fatness with triumph. What would she drape around her body? A bedsheet like the bridesmaids? No! Without me and my sari she would not be able to play bride-bride properly.

There was, I realized, an obstacle that had to be overcome first. I would have to get out of playing cricket. Amma had laid down an order, and I knew Diggy well enough to know that, in spite of all his boldness, he would never dare to disobey an order from Amma.

I heard the car start up, and its sound reminded me of another problem that I had not considered. How was I going to smuggle the sari into the car? Amma would be waiting in the car for me, and if I arrived with the sling-bag she would make me take it back. I could not slip it in without her no-

ticing. I sat still, listening to the whir of the engine at coun-
terpoint to the clatter of Anula clearing the breakfast table,
and suddenly a plan revealed itself to me.

I took the sari out of the bag, folded the bag so that it
looked like there was something in it, and left it on the bed.
Taking the sari with me, I went to the bedroom door and
peered out. The hall was empty. I went into Sonali's room,
which was next to my parents', and I crouched down on one
side of the doorway. I took off my slippers and held them
with the sari in my arms. The curtain in the open doorway
of Sonali's room blew slightly in the breeze, and I moved
farther away from it so that I would not be seen. After what
seemed like an interminable amount of time, I heard Amma
coming down the hallway to fetch me from her room. I
crouched even lower as the sound of her footsteps got closer.
From below the curtain, I saw her go into her room. As she
entered, I stood up, pushed aside the curtain, and darted down
the hallway. She came out of her room and called to me, but
I didn't stop, and ran outside.

Thankfully the rear door of the car was open. I jumped
in, quickly stuffed the sari into Sonali's sling-bag, and lay back
against the seat, panting. Diggy and Sonali were looking at
me strangely but they said nothing.

Soon Amma came out and got into the car. She glared at
me, and I gave her an innocent look. I smiled at Sonali conspiratorially. Sonali, my strongest ally, was doing her best to
keep the bewilderment out of her face. By way of explanation, I said, with pretend gloominess, "I can't play with you
today. Amma says that I must play with the boys."

Sonali looked at me in amazement and then turned to

Amma. "Why can't he play with the girls?" she said.

"Why?" Amma said and started up the car. "Because the sky is so high and pigs can't fly."

Amma sounded less sure of herself this time and a little weary. Looking in front, I saw that Diggy had turned in his seat and was regarding me morosely. I was reminded that the sari in the bag was worth nothing if I couldn't get out of the long day of cricket that lay ahead of me.

All the way to my grandparents' house, I gazed at the back of Diggy's head, hoping inspiration would come. The sound of his feet kicking irritably against the underside of the glove compartment confirmed that, however bad the consequences, he would follow Amma's orders. The sound of that ill-natured kicking made me search my mind all the more desperately for a way to escape playing cricket with the boys.

When the car turned down Ramanaygam Road, I still had not thought of anything. Meena was standing on top of the garden wall, her legs apart, her hands on her hips, her panties already dirty underneath her short dress. The boy cousins were on the wall on either side of her.

As we walked up the path to pay our respects to Ammachi and Appachi, I whispered to Sonali to keep the sari hidden and to tell no one about it. When we went into the drawing room, Her Fatness, who was as usual between Kanthi Aunty's knees, gave me a victorious look. A feeling of panic began to rise in me that no plan of escape had yet presented itself.

Once we had gone through the ritual of presenting our cheeks to our grandparents, we followed Amma outside to say goodbye.

"You children be good," Amma said before she got into

the car. She looked pointedly at me. "I don't want to hear that you've given Ammachi and Appachi any trouble."

I watched her departing car with a sense of sorrow.

Diggy grabbed my arm. I followed reluctantly as he hurried across the road, still holding on to me, as if afraid I would run away.

The wickets had already been set up in the field in front of the house, and the boys and Meena were seated under a guava tree. When they saw us come towards them, they stopped talking and stared at us.

Muruges, who was on Diggy's team, stood up.

"What's he doing here?" he demanded, waving his half-eaten guava at me.

"He's going to play."

"What?" the others cried in amazement.

They looked at Diggy as if he had lost his mind.

"He's not going to play on our team, is he?" Muruges said, more a threat than a question.

"He's quite good," Diggy answered halfheartedly.

"If he's going to be on our team, I'm changing sides," Muruges declared, and some of the others murmured in agreement.

"Come on, guys," Diggy said with desperation in his voice, but they remained stern.

Diggy turned to Meena. "I'll trade you Arjie for Sanjay."

Meena spat out the seeds of the guava she was eating. "Do you think I'm mad or something?"

"Ah, come on," Diggy said in a wheedling tone. "He's good. We've been practicing the whole week."

"If he's so good, why don't you keep him yourself?

Maybe with him on your team you might actually win."

"Yeah," Sanjay cried, insulted that I was considered an equal trade for him. "Why don't you keep the girlie-boy?"

At the new nickname "girlie-boy," everyone roared with laughter, and even Diggy grinned.

I should have felt humiliated and dejected that nobody wanted me on their team, but instead I felt the joy of relief begin to dance inside of me. The escape I had searched for was offering itself without any effort on my part. If Diggy's best team members were threatening to abandon him he would have no alternative but to let me go. I looked at my feet so that no one would see the hope in my eyes.

Unfortunately, the nickname "girlie-boy" had an effect which I had not predicted. The joke at my expense seemed to clear the air. After laughing heartily, Muruges withdrew his threat. "What the hell," he said benevolently. "It can't hurt to have another fielder. But," he added, as a warning to Diggy, "he can't bat."

Diggy nodded as if he had never even considered letting me bat. Since each side had only fifty overs, it was vital to send the best batsmen in first, and often the younger cousins never got a chance.

I glared at Muruges, and he, thinking that my look was a reaction to the new nickname, said "girlie-boy" again.

Diggy now laughed loudly, but in his laugh I detected a slight note of servility and also relief that the catastrophe of losing his team had been averted. I saw that the balance he was trying to maintain between following Amma's orders and keeping his team members happy was extremely precarious. All was not lost. Such a fragile balance would be easy to upset.

The opportunity to do this arose almost immediately.

Our team was to go first. In deciding the batting order, there was a certain system that the boys always followed. The captain would mark numbers in the sand with hyphens next to each and then cover the numbers with a bat. The players, who had been asked to turn their backs, would then come over and choose a hyphen. What was strange to me about this exercise was its redundancy, for when the numbers were uncovered, no matter what the batting order, the older and better players always went first, the younger cousins assenting without a murmur.

When Diggy uncovered the numbers, I was first, Diggy was second. Muruges had one of the highest numbers and would bat towards the end, if at all. "Well," Muruges said to Diggy in a tone that spoke of promises already made, "I'll take Arjie's place."

Diggy nodded vigorously as if Muruges had read his very thoughts.

Unfortunately for him, I had other plans.

"I want to go first," I said firmly, and waited for my request to produce the necessary consequences.

Muruges was crouched down, fixing his pads, and he straightened up slowly. The slowness of his action conveyed his anger at my daring to make such a suggestion and at the same time challenged Diggy to change the batting order.

Meena, unexpectedly, came to my defense. "He is the first!" she said. "Fair is fair!" In a game of only fifty overs, a bad opening bat would be ideal for her team.

"Fair is fair," I echoed Meena. "I picked first place and I should be allowed to play!"

"You can't," Diggy said desperately. "Muruges always goes first."

Meena's team, encouraged by her, also began to cry out, "Fair is fair!"

Diggy quickly crossed over to Muruges, put his arm around his shoulder, turned him away from the others, and talked earnestly to him. But Muruges shook his head, unconvinced by whatever Diggy was saying. Finally Diggy dropped his hand from Muruges's shoulder and cried out in exasperation at him, "Come on, men!" In response, Muruges began to unbuckle his pads. Diggy put his hand on his shoulder, but he shrugged it off. Diggy, seeing that Muruges was determined, turned to me.

"Come on, Arjie," he said, pleading. "You can go later in the game."

"No," I said stubbornly, and, just to show how determined I was, I picked up the bat.

Muruges saw my action and threw the pads at my feet.

"I'm on your team now," he announced to Meena.

"Ah, no! Come on, men!" Diggy shouted in protest.

Muruges began to cross over to where Meena's team was gathered.

Diggy turned towards me now and grabbed the bat.

"*You* go!" he cried. "We don't need *you*." He pulled the bat out of my hands and started to walk with it towards Muruges.

"You're a cheater, cheater pumpkin-eater! I chose to bat first!" I yelled.

But I had gone too far. Diggy turned and looked at me. Then he howled as he realized how he had been tricked.

Instead of giving Muruges the bat, he lifted it above his head and ran towards me. I turned and fled across the field towards my grandparents' gate. When I reached it, I lifted the latch, went inside the garden, and quickly put the latch back into place. Diggy stopped when he reached the gate. Safe on my side, I made a face at him through the slats. He came close and I retreated a little. Putting his head through the slats, he hissed at me, "If you ever come near the field again, you'll be sorry."

"Don't worry," I replied tartly. "I never will."

And with that, I forever closed any possibility of entering the boys' world again. But I didn't care, and just to show how much I didn't care I made another face, turned my back on Diggy, and walked up the front path to the house. As I went through the narrow passageway between the house and the side wall that led to the back, I could hear the girls' voices as they prepared for bride-bride, and especially Her Fatness's, ordering everyone around. When I reached the back garden, I stopped when I saw the wedding cake. The bottom layer consisted of mud pies molded from half a coconut shell. They supported the lid of a biscuit tin, which had three mud pies on it. On these rested the cover of a condensed-milk tin with a single mud pie on top. This was the three-tiered design that *I* had invented. Her Fatness had copied my design exactly. Further, she had taken upon herself the sole honor of decorating it with florets of gandapahana flowers and trails of antigonon, in the same way I had always done.

Sonali was the first to become aware of my presence. "Arjie!" she said, pleased.

The other cousins now noticed me, and they also exclaimed in delight. Lakshmi called out to me to come and join them, but before I could do so Her Fatness rose to her feet.

"What do you want?" she said.

I came forward a bit and she immediately stepped towards me, like a female mongoose defending her young against a cobra. "Go away!" she cried, holding up her hand. "Boys are not allowed here."

I didn't heed her command.

"Go away," she cried again. "Otherwise I'm going to tell Ammachi!"

I looked at her for a moment, but fearing that she would see the hatred in my eyes, I glanced down at the ground.

"I want to play bride-bride, please," I said, trying to sound as pathetic and inoffensive as possible.

"Bride-bride," Her Fatness repeated mockingly.

"Yes," I said, in a shy whisper.

Sonali stood up. "Can't he play?" she said to Her Fatness. "He'll be very good."

"Yes, he'll be very good," the others murmured in agreement.

Her Fatness considered their request.

"I have something that you don't have," I said quickly, hoping to sway her decision.

"Oh, what is that?"

"The sari!"

"The sari?" she echoed. A look of malicious slyness flickered across her face.

"Yes," I said. "Without the sari you can't play bride-bride."

"Why not?" Her Fatness said with indifference.

Her lack of concern about the sari puzzled me. Fearing that it might not have the same importance for her as it did for me, I cried out, "Why not?" and pretended to be amazed that she would ask such a question. "What is the bride going to wear, then? A bedsheet?"

Her Fatness played with a button on her dress. "Where is the sari?" she asked very casually.

"It's a secret," I said. I was not going to give it to her until I was firmly entrenched in the girls' world again. "If you let me play, I will give it to you when it's time for the bride to get ready."

A smile crossed her face. "The thing is, Arjie," she said in a very reasonable tone, "we've already decided what every-one is going to be for bride-bride and we don't need anyone else."

"But there must be some parts you need people for," I said and then added, "I'll play any part."

"Any part," Her Fatness repeated. Her eyes narrowed and she looked at me appraisingly.

"Let him play," Sonali and the others said.

"I'll play *any* part," I reiterated.

"You know what?" Her Fatness said suddenly, as if the idea had just dawned on her. "We don't have a groom."

That Her Fatness wanted me to swallow the bitter pill of humiliation was clear, and so great was my longing to be part of the girls' world again that I swallowed it.

"I'll take it," I said.

"Okay," Her Fatness said as if it mattered little to her whether I did or not.

The others cried out in delight and I smiled, happy that my goal had been at least partially achieved. Sonali beckoned to me to come and help them. I went towards where the preparations were being made for the wedding feast, but Her Fatness quickly stepped in front of me.

"The groom cannot help with the cooking."

"Why not?" I protested.

"Because grooms don't do that."

"They do."

"Have you ever heard of a groom doing that?"

I couldn't say I had, so I demanded with angry sarcasm, "What do grooms do then?"

"They go to office."

"Office?" I said.

Her Fatness nodded and pointed to the table on the back porch. The look on her face told me she would not tolerate any argument.

"I can't go to office," I said quickly. "It's Sunday."

"We're pretending it's Monday," Her Fatness replied glibly.

I glared at her. Not satisfied with the humiliation she had forced me to accept, she was determined to keep my participation in bride-bride to a minimum. For an instant I thought to refuse her, but, seeing the warning look in her eyes, I finally acquiesced and went up the porch steps.

From there, I watched the other cousins getting ready for the wedding. Using a stone, I began to bang on the table as if stamping papers. I noted, with pleasure, that the sound irritated Her Fatness. I pressed an imaginary buzzer and made a loud noise. Getting no response from anyone, I did so again.

Finally the other cousins looked up. "Boy," I called out imperiously to Sonali, "come here, boy."

Sonali left her cooking and came up the steps with the cringing attitude of the office peons at my father's bank.

"Yes sir, yes sir," she said breathlessly. Her performance was so accurate that the cousins stopped to observe her.

"Take this to the bank manager in Bambalapitiya," I said. Bowing again, she took the imaginary letter and hurried down the steps. I pressed my buzzer again. "Miss," I called to Lakshmi. "Miss, can you come here and take some dictation."

"Yes, sir, coming, sir," Lakshmi said, fluttering her eyelashes, with the exaggerated coyness of a Sinhala comic actress. She came up the steps, wriggling her hips for the amusement of her audience. Everyone laughed except Her Fatness.

When Lakshmi finished the dictation and went down the steps, the other cousins cried out, "Me! Me!" and clamored to be the peon I would call next. But, before I could choose one of them, Her Fatness stormed up the steps.

"Stop that!" she shouted at me. "You're disturbing us."

"No!" I cried back, now that I had the support of everyone else.

"If you can't behave, go away."

"If I go away, you won't get the sari."

Her Fatness looked at me a long moment and then smiled.

"What sari?" she said. "I bet you don't even have the sari."

"Yes, I do," I said in an earnest tone.

"Where?"

"It's a secret."

"You are lying. I know you don't have it."

"I do! I do!"

"Show me."

"No."

"You don't have it and I'm going to tell Janaki you are disturbing us."

I didn't move, wanting to see if she would carry out her threat. She crossed behind the table and walked towards the kitchen door. When she got to the door and I was sure she was serious, I jumped up.

"Where is it?" I said urgently to Sonali.

She pointed to Janaki's room.

I ran to Janaki's door, opened it, and went inside. Sonali's bag was lying on the bed, and I picked it up and rushed back out onto the porch. Her Fatness had come away from the kitchen door.

"Here!" I cried.

Her Fatness folded her arms. "Where?" she said tauntingly. I opened the bag, put my hand inside, and felt around for the sari. I touched a piece of clothing and drew it out. It was only Sonali's change of clothes. I put my hand inside again and this time brought out an Enid Blyton book. There was nothing else in the bag.

"Where is the sari?" Her Fatness demanded.

I glanced at Sonali, and she gave me a puzzled look.

"Liar, liar on the wall, who's the liarest one of all?" Her Fatness cried.

I turned towards Janaki's door, wondering if the sari had fallen out. Then I saw a slight smirk on Her Fatness's face and the truth came to me. She'd known all along about the sari. She must have discovered it earlier and hidden it. I realized I had been duped and felt a sudden rush of anger. Her Fatness saw the comprehension in my eyes, and her arms dropped by her sides as if in readiness. She inched back towards the kitchen door for safety. But I was not interested in her for the moment. What I wanted was the sari.

I rushed into Janaki's room.

"I'm going to tell Janaki you're in her room!" Her Fatness cried.

"Tell and catch my long fat tail!" I shouted back.

I looked around Janaki's room. Her Fatness must have hidden it here. There was no other place. I lifted Janaki's mattress. There was nothing under it, save a few Sinhala love comics. I went to Janaki's suitcase and began to go through the clothes she kept neatly folded inside it. As silent as a shadow, Her Fatness slipped into the room. I became aware of her presence and turned. But too late. She took the sari from the shelf where she had hidden it and ran out the door. Leaving the suitcase still open, I ran after her. The sari clutched to her chest, she rushed for the kitchen door. Luckily Sonali and Lakshmi were blocking her way. Seeing me coming at her, she jumped off the porch and began to head towards the front of the house. I leapt off the porch and chased after her. If she got to the front of the house, she would go straight to Ammachi.

Just as she reached the passageway, I managed to get hold of her arm. She turned, desperate, and struck out at me. Ducking her blow, I reached for the sari and managed to get some of it in my hand. She tried to take it back from me, but

I held on tightly. Crying out, she jerked away from me with her whole body, hoping to wrest the sari from my grip. With a rasping sound, the sari began to tear. I yelled at her to stop pulling, but she jerked away again and the sari tore all the way down. There was a moment of stunned silence. I gazed at the torn sari in my hand, at the long threads that hung from it. Then, with a wail of anguish, I rushed at Her Fatness and grabbed hold of her hair. She screamed and flailed at me. I yanked her head so far to one side that it almost touched her shoulder. She let out a guttural sound and struck out desperately at me. Her fist caught me in the stomach and she managed to loosen my grip.

She began to run towards the porch steps, crying out for Ammachi and Janaki. I ran after her and grabbed the sleeve of her dress before she went up the porch steps. She struggled against my grip and the sleeve ripped open and hung down her arm like a broken limb. Free once again, she stumbled up the steps towards the kitchen door, shouting at the top of her voice.

Janaki rushed out of the kitchen. She raised her hand and looked around for the first person to wallop, but when she saw Her Fatness with her torn dress, she held her raised hand to her cheek and cried out in consternation, "Buddu Ammo!"

Now Her Fatness began to call out only for Ammachi.

Janaki came hurriedly towards her. "Shhh! Shhhh!" she said, but Her Fatness only increased the volume of her cry.

"What's wrong? What's wrong?" Janaki cried impatiently.

Her Fatness pointed to me.

"Janakiii! See what that boy did," she replied.

"I didn't do anything," I yelled, enraged that she was trying to push the blame onto me.

I ran back to where I had dropped the sari, picked it up, and held it out to Janaki.

"Yes!" Sonali cried, coming to my defense. "She did it and now she's blaming him."

"It's her fault!" Lakshmi said, also taking my side.

Now all the voices of the girl cousins rose in a babble supporting my case and accusing Her Fatness.

"Quiet!" Janaki shouted in desperation. "Quiet!"

But nobody heeded her. We all crowded around her, so determined to give our version of the story that it was a while before we became aware of Ammachi's presence in the kitchen doorway. Gradually, like the hush that descends on a garrison town at the sound of enemy guns, we all became quiet. Even Her Fatness stopped her wailing.

Ammachi looked at all of us and then her gaze came to rest on Janaki. "How many times have I told you to keep these children quiet?" she said, her tone awful.

Janaki, always so full of anger, now wrung her hands like a child in fear of punishment. "I told them . . ." she started to say, but Ammachi raised her hand for silence. Her Fatness began to cry again, more out of fear than anything else. Ammachi glared at her, and, as if to deflect her look, Her Fatness held up her arm with the ripped sleeve.

"Who did that?" Ammachi said after a moment.

Her Fatness pointed at me, and her crying got even louder.

Ammachi looked at me sternly and then beckoned me with her index finger.

"Look!" I cried and held out the sari as if in supplication. "Look at what she did!"

But Ammachi was unmoved by the sight of the sari and continued to beckon me.

As I looked at her, I could almost hear the singing of the cane as it came down through the air, and then the sharp crack, which would be followed by searing pain. The time Diggy had been caned for climbing the roof came back to me, his pleas for mercy, his shouts of agony and loud sobs.

Before I could stop myself, I cried out angrily at Ammachi, "It's not fair! Why should I be punished?"

"Come here," Ammachi said.

"No. I won't."

Ammachi came to the edge of the porch, but rather than backing away I remained where I was.

"Come here, you vamban," she said to me sharply.

"No!" I cried back. "I hate you, you old fatty."

The other cousins and even Janaki gasped at my audacity. Ammachi began to come down the steps. I stood my ground for a few moments but then my courage gave out. I turned, and, with the sari still in my hands, I fled. I ran from the back garden to the front gate and out. In the field across the way, the boys were still at their cricket game. I hurried down the road towards the sea. At the railway lines I paused briefly, went across, then scrambled over the rocks to the beach. Once there, I sat on a rock and flung the sari down next to me. "I hate them, I hate them all," I whispered to myself. "I wish I was dead."

I put my head down and felt the first tears begin to wet my knees.

★ ★ ★

After a while I was still. The sound of the waves, their regular rhythm, had a calming effect on me. I leaned back against the rock behind me, watching them come in and go out. Soon the heat of the rocks became unbearable and I stood up, removed my slippers, and went down the beach to the edge of the water.

I had never seen the sea this color before. Our visits to the beach were usually in the early evening when the sea was a turquoise blue. Now, under the midday sun, it had become hard silver, so bright that it hurt my eyes.

The sand burned my feet, and I moved closer to the waves to cool them. I looked down the deserted beach, whose white sand almost matched the color of the sea, and saw tall buildings shimmering in the distance like a mirage. This daytime beach seemed foreign compared with the beach of the early evening, which was always crowded with strollers and joggers and vendors. Now both the beach and the sea, once so familiar, were like an unknown country into which I had journeyed by chance.

I knew then that something had changed. But how, I didn't altogether know.

The large waves, impersonal and oblivious to my despair, threw themselves against the beach, their crests frothing and hissing. Soon I would have to turn around and go back to my grandparents' house, where Ammachi awaited me with her thinnest cane, the one that left deep impressions on the backs of our thighs, so deep that sometimes they had to be treated with gentian violet. The thought of that cane as it cut through the air, humming like a mosquito, made me wince even now, so far away from it.

I glanced at the sari lying on the rock where I had thrown it, and I knew that I would never enter the girls' world again. Never stand in front of Janaki's mirror, watching a transformation take place before my eyes. No more would I step out of that room and make my way down the porch steps to the altar, a creature beautiful and adored, the personification of all that was good and perfect in the world. The future spend-the-days were no longer to be enjoyed, no longer to be looked forward to. And then there would be the loneliness. I would be caught between the boys' and the girls' worlds, not belonging or wanted in either. I would have to think of things with which to amuse myself, find ways to endure the lunches and teas when the cousins would talk to one another about what they had done and what they planned to do for the rest of the day.

The bell of St. Fatima's Church rang out the Angelus, and its melancholy sound seemed like a summoning. It was time to return to my grandparents' house. My absence at the lunch table would be construed as another act of defiance and eventually Janaki would be sent to fetch me. Then the punishment I received would be even more severe.

With a heavy heart, I slowly went back up the beach, not caring that the sand burned the soles of my feet. I put my slippers on, picked up my sari, and climbed up the rocks. I paused and looked back at the sea one last time. Then I turned, crossed the railway lines, and began my walk up Ramanaygam Road to the future that awaited me.

Radha Aunty

—◆—

A proposal arrived for Radha Aunty even before she
returned from America.

I was in my grandparents' drawing room, dusting all their
teak furniture, when I heard Ammachi telling the aunts and
uncles about it. The Nagendras were the family interested in
Radha Aunty. At the mention of the name, the aunts let out
little sounds of pleasure and admiration. Old Mr. Nagendra
had been at Cambridge with Appachi, and the families were
known to each other. His son, Rajan, had met Radha Aunty
at a dinner party in America, and he had been so taken with
her that he had written to his parents asking them to make a

proposal on his behalf. Ammachi had phoned Radha Aunty and, according to her, Radha Aunty seemed very amenable to the idea. Rajan would be returning to Sri Lanka a few months after Radha Aunty was to come back.

"What kind of a man is he?" one of the uncles asked.

"An engineer," Ammachi replied. "Works for a big company in America. Very well off."

"An engineer!" one of the aunts cried. "How wonderful for Radha."

"And such a good family, too," another added.

"What about his character?" a third asked.

"Excellent," Ammachi replied. "Doesn't drink or womanize. And we know for a fact that there is no insanity in the family."

As I listened to them, I felt an excitement stir in me, an excitement that had died with my expulsion from the world of the girls. There was going to be a wedding in the family! A real wedding, in a real church with a real bride. I had been at other weddings, but had never had a chance to take part in the preparations that went into the marriage ceremony. Now it would be my turn to experience all those delights. I looked around the drawing room. In a few months this room would be transformed by the preparations for a wedding. I saw it all in my mind: the buying of the sari, the making of the confetti, the wrapping of the cake, the delicious pala harams, the jasmine garlands, the bridesmaids.

Radha Aunty, who was the youngest in my father's family, had left for America four years ago when I was three, and I

could not remember what she looked like. I went into the
corridor to look at the family photographs that were hung
there. But all the pictures were old ones, taken when Radha
Aunty was a baby or a young girl. Try as I might, I couldn't
get an idea of what she looked like now. My imagination,
however, was quick to fill in this void. Since my idea of
romance and marriage was inseparable from Sinhala films and
Janaki's love comics, the picture I formed of Radha Aunty
bore a strong resemblance to that goddess of the Sinhala
screen Malini Fonseka. The Radha Aunty of my mind was
plump with big rounded hips. She had a fair complexion and
large kohl-rimmed eyes. Her hair was straight and made into
an elaborate coiffure on top of her head, and she wore a Manipuri sari with a gold border.

I was so engrossed in my daydream of this lovely creature
that I didn't notice that the aunts and uncles had left and
Ammachi had come out into the corridor.

"Ah, ah!" she cried angrily when she saw me. "What are
you doing here?"

Without replying, I turned and ran back into the drawing
room.

"I'm coming to check your work soon," Ammachi called
out warningly. I began to dust her furniture fervently.

Since that fateful spend-the-day a few months ago, when
Her Fatness and I had fought, Ammachi had undertaken to
master what she considered my "devil's temperament." In
addition to the caning which I had received, a caning so severe that she broke the cane while administering it, I was
assigned a task each spend-the-day which would keep me
occupied and "out of mischief." The tasks were unpleasant,

and what made them unbearable was Ammachi's constant supervision, the high standard of excellence she demanded, and the cuffs I received on the side of my head for any mistakes I made.

The only respite I had was in the afternoon, when Ammachi retired to bed for an hour. Janaki had taken pity on me and, during the time my grandmother rested, she would allow me to read her Sinhala love comics in the open corridor that joined the kitchen to the main house. That afternoon, her love comics took on a new significance. My favorite was the love story of Mani-lal and Sakuntala, and as I reread, I saw instead Rajan Nagendra and Radha Aunty. I imagined them standing under an araliya tree, Radha Aunty leaning against its trunk with her head bent modestly, a slight tear in her eye; Rajan Nagendra, his hand pressed against the tree, his face serious as he implored her to marry him. Now Sakuntala started to cry, just as I imagined Radha Aunty would. I turned the page, and, there, Mani-lal had taken her in his arms. He would ask her parents for their consent. Sakuntala now nodded meekly. I turned the pages rapidly. The part about asking the parents and their refusing didn't interest me. I wanted to read the inevitable end, about the wedding. Sakuntala smiling through her tears, Mani-lal, a look of fierce pride on his face. I closed the comic book. My feelings were so stirred up that I couldn't sit still any longer. I went down the steps into the side garden and began to walk along the edge of the drain that ran along the ground under the kitchen window. I could hardly believe that all I had read in those comics was going to come true. Soon Radha Aunty would return, followed by Rajan Nagendra. Then they would be married, and I would find myself in the midst of a real-life love story.

I waited anxiously for Radha Aunty's return. She was to arrive in four weeks, and, as the time drew nearer, I felt the same kind of excitement I had felt when my parents returned from their trip to Europe the year before. Then, all I had thought about were the toys and chocolate and chewing gum they would bring. Now all I thought about was the world of weddings.

Finally she arrived. I begged my parents to take me when they went to see her, but it was late in the evening and they refused. I had to wait for the next spend-the-day.

That Sunday, I woke up earlier than usual. I lay in bed, listening for the sounds of the morning to begin—the sparrows, the mynahs, the Milk Board van, Anula putting out the coffee cups, my father clearing his throat. Now that the day had finally arrived, I felt nervous. Soon I would be in the presence of a grand person, someone who was separated from everyday people, because she inhabited the realm of romance and marriage.

When we arrived outside my grandparents' house, I was the first one out of the car. As I opened the gate, I was surprised to hear the sound of Ammachi's piano. In all the years I had come here, I had never heard it. Someone was playing "Chopsticks." The player hit a painfully wrong note and then the piano was silent. In that instant, I realized who it was. Amma, Diggy, Sonali, and I started to walk up the driveway. "Chopsticks" started again, haltingly now. As I listened to the music, I felt disoriented. This was not in keeping with my Radha Aunty. I had imagined her doing a number of things, going for walks on the beach with Rajan, getting dressed to go out with him, even cooking and cleaning for him, but I had never imagined her playing "Chopsticks" on the piano. I hurried up the driveway and into the house.

When we went into the drawing room, there she was, seated at the piano. Radha Aunty. She had begun to play another tune. I stared at her in shock. She couldn't have been more different from the way I had pictured her. The first and biggest difference between the imagined Radha Aunty and the real one was the color of her skin. She was a karapi, as dark as a laborer. Worse, her long hair was frizzy like Ammachi's and it seemed about to burst out of the clip that held it in place at the back of her neck. She was thin, not plump, and, as Amma would have said, "flat like a boy." Instead of a sari, she wore a halter top and strange trousers that were tight to the knee and then became wider. Further, the heels on her shoes were odd because they ran the length of each shoe. I had never seen shoes or trousers like these before.

It was my turn to greet Ammachi. After I had done so, Ammachi told me my chore for the day. I was to clean all the brass ornaments in the drawing room. As she spoke I nodded distractedly, for I was still looking at Radha Aunty.

She ended the tune on a wrong note, shook her head, and cried out, "Oh, God, I'm so terrible." She laughed. Then she noticed me staring at her and wrinkled her forehead, imitating the look on my face.

"Hello," she said cheerfully. "Which one are you?"

"Arjie," I said.

She held out her hand to me. "What? I don't get a kiss or anything?"

I went to her and offered my cheek to be kissed.

Radha Aunty turned back to the piano and began to play "Somewhere My Love."

I sat down behind her and opened the can of Brasso. I tipped some out onto a rag and glanced at Radha Aunty petulantly. I felt that in some way she had let me down, cheated me. As I began to polish a lamp, I eyed her and thought of Sakuntala and the other heroines of Janaki's love comics. This was not how a bride-to-be was supposed to behave. It was unthinkable that a woman who was on the brink of marriage could look like this and play the piano so badly.

Ammachi came over to me, interrupting my reverie. I began to busily polish the lamp. Then she took it from me. "Chah!" she said. "This is terrible. Do it again."

Radha Aunty stopped playing the piano and regarded us with interest. Ammachi returned the lamp to me and I began to polish it vigorously. "Harder," she commanded. "Rub harder."

I rubbed as intensely as I could, feeling my palm heat up against the brass.

"More Brasso," she said. "Put more Brasso."

I reached for the tin.

"Quick, quick," she cried. "Otherwise it will dry."

"Honestly, Amma," Radha Aunty suddenly said, "you treat him like a servant boy."

I glanced at Ammachi, wondering how she would react to this criticism from her daughter.

"No," she said, "I'm just trying to teach him a skill."

Radha Aunty laughed. "What?" she said. "Are you planning to set him up on Galle Road as a brass karaya?"

Ammachi didn't reply. She bent down to examine my

work again, but this time she said nothing. After a few moments, she left.

Radha Aunty swung around on her stool and watched me polishing the lamp. "Why aren't you playing with the others?" she asked.

"Because . . ." I said, and my voice trailed off. I did not want to tell her the truth for fear that she would laugh at me in the way the other adults had done. "Because I don't want to," I added quickly. She looked at me keenly and smiled as if she didn't believe me.

She turned back to the piano and began to play. I studied her again, but with a slight change of attitude. Yes, it was true that she was a disappointment, but she had come to my rescue. If she had not said anything, I would surely have received a blow across the side of my head. As I looked at her I began to realize that she was different from other adults. There was a cheerfulness about her that none of the other aunts and uncles had, not even the nice ones like Mala Aunty. Further, she had not pressed me to tell her why I was not playing with the others. She lacked that terrible curiosity other adults had which made them insist on knowing things you were uncomfortable telling, and she had not cared about my obvious fib.

That afternoon there were no chores to do, so I sat in the open corridor with a love comic. Radha Aunty passed by on her way to the kitchen, and she looked at me, curious. When she came back out of the kitchen, she stopped and said, "What? All alone?"

I nodded and smiled slightly.

"Never mind," Radha Aunty said. "Come to my bedroom and play." I looked at her in surprise, feeling suddenly shy in her presence.

"Come on," she said, and I picked up my comic and followed her as she went into the main part of the house.

Her room consisted of a single bed, an almariah, and a dressing table. I had been in this room before, but now it was transformed by her personal effects. The greatest change was the dressing table, for the surface was covered with her makeup. I gazed at the various shades of lipstick and nail polish. A glass jar contained a selection of shiny stars and circles. I leaned over to examine them more closely. "They're pottus," Radha Aunty said. She picked one up and stuck it in the middle of her forehead to demonstrate what it looked like. I gazed at her forehead, enchanted by the pottu, so different from the colored pencils Amma used. I turned and looked covetously at the jar. "You want to try it?" Radha Aunty asked, sounding both surprised and amused.

I nodded shyly.

She picked up a star, smeared a little Vaseline on it, and then stuck it on my forehead. I gazed at my reflection. Radha Aunty sat on the dressing-table stool and looked at me with a mischievous glint in her eyes. Then she picked up a tube of lipstick. "Open your mouth," she said.

Through the corner of my eye, I watched Radha Aunty work. She painted my eyelids with blue shadow, put rouge on my cheeks, and even darkened a birthmark above my lip. When she was done, I grinned at my reflection in the mirror.

She looked at me and laughed. "Gosh," she said. "You would have made a beautiful girl." Then she took me by the hand and led me out to the kitchen. "Look!" she cried to Janaki.

Janaki smiled in spite of herself. "You'd better not let the parents see him like that," she said.

"Nonsense," Radha Aunty replied. "It's all in good fun."

For the rest of the afternoon, Radha Aunty allowed me to play with her makeup and jewelry while she lay on her bed reading. By now I had lost my earlier shyness. I donned several of her chains and bangles and studied the effect in the mirror. Then I decided to paint my nails. I opened the bottle of nail polish and paused for a moment to breathe in its heady smell before I drew the brush out. While I colored my nails, I watched Radha Aunty's reflection in the dressing-table mirror. She became aware that I was looking at her and lowered her book.

"Radha Aunty," I said, "when are you going to marry Rajan Nagendra?"

"Who?" she asked.

"You know," I said, and smiled to show that I knew she was playing with me. I waved my hand and blew on it in the same way Amma did when she wanted her nails to dry.

"Why are you asking?"

"Because."

"Do you think I should?"

She was still teasing me, but I decided to treat her question with seriousness. I nodded vigorously.

"Why?"

I looked at her, taken aback. I searched my mind for an answer and then, remembering what the adults had said, I replied, "Because he's an engineer and he doesn't have insanity in his family." Radha Aunty looked at me in astonishment. Then she began to laugh.

"Why are you laughing?" I cried, suddenly feeling shy again.

She reached out and hugged me, still laughing. "Where did you hear that?" she asked.

I told her, and this made her laugh all the more. Since she was in such good humor, I decided to go further. "You must get married, soon," I said. "Please, please. You will be the bestest bride ever," I added insincerely.

"The bestest bride," she said. "You think so?"

I nodded. "And you must have a long, long veil."

"Oh, dear," she said. "But won't it be too heavy for my head?"

"No," I replied. "You must have many bridesmaids to carry it."

"How many?"

"Ten."

Radha Aunty laughed and I laughed, too, with excitement.

"And how many flower girls should I have?"

"Seven."

"And pageboys?"

"Seven."

"Will you be one?"

"Yes!"

I reached out and hugged her. "Can Sonali, my sister, be a flower girl?"

She nodded.

"But not Tanuja," I added, determined to keep Her

Fatness out of the fun. "She'll spoil everything."

"Okay," Radha Aunty replied.

Since she was amenable to suggestion, I recommended that the bridesmaids wear pink saris with shiny sequins, the flower girls pink maxis and flowered hair bands, and the page-boys black waistcoats with gold buttons. Radha Aunty laughed at my suggestions, but I pleaded with her until she finally lifted her hands in surrender. I was ecstatic now, all my earlier disappointment forgotten. Things were working out better than I had anticipated. I had never imagined that I would actually have a hand in deciding what the bridal party would look like. The most I had expected was to be allowed to view the wedding preparations without being chased away. Radha Aunty had turned out to be different from what I had expected, but better. She was definitely my favorite aunt.

That afternoon Her Fatness came to tea dressed up as the bride. She talked loudly about what they planned to do at the bridal ceremony after tea. I glanced disdainfully at the bed-sheet wrapped around her body and the curtain on her head. Except for the bedsheet, she was wearing exactly what I used to when I was the bride. Now I marveled to think that I had actually found this costume beautiful. How pitiful that curtain, discolored with age, looked attached to her head, its borders sticking out awkwardly. The garland of flowers pinned to it appeared ill-made and sparse. I glanced across at Radha Aunty and imagined what she would be like in her expensive Manipuri sari and long, long veil. I pictured her entourage in the garments I had chosen for them and I felt a glow of pride as if they stood before me. As Her Fatness spoke of the girls' plans for the rest of the afternoon, she looked at me, searching for envy in my face. I looked at her with contempt. I had better things to worry about than her silly game. I kept my fingers prominently spread out on the table so that she would notice my nails. When she saw them, her face became clouded with jealousy.

⟻⟨◆⟩⟶

One day, not long after Radha Aunty had returned from America, Amma said to me, "How would you like to be in a play?" I looked at her in astonishment. She told me that Radha Aunty was in a play called *The King and I* and the director was looking for young people to play the children of the King of Siam. The rehearsals would be on Saturdays and Sundays and one evening during the week.

"Well, do you want to?" Amma asked.

I nodded, thrilled at the prospect of being in a play. Last year, Amma had taken us to see a production of *The Pied Piper of Hamelin*. Although the play was boring, I found myself envying the children who were in it, because they got to wear makeup and costumes and dance around the stage.

I asked Amma if she knew *The King and I*. She said she had seen the film a long time ago. As far as she remembered, it was the story of an English governess who goes to the court of Siam to teach English and other Western subjects to the king's children and wives.

"Does she marry the king in the end?" I asked eagerly.

"Marry the king?" Amma repeated. She laughed. "You must be mad."

"Why?" I cried, disappointed that the story didn't end with a marriage.

"Because at that time people didn't marry outside their race."

"And now?" I asked, determined to get a happy ending out of the story. "If it was now, would they have married?"

Amma looked at me, irritated by my persistence. "I don't know," she said. "Probably not."

"But *why* not?"

"Because most people marry their own kind," Amma said in a tone that warned me not to ask further questions.

I found my enthusiasm for *The King and I* ebbing. I couldn't see the point of a play where the hero and heroine didn't get married at the end. Amma must have read my mind, because she said, "You'll have a good time. The songs in *The King and I* are very catchy."

The next Saturday, I went for my first rehearsal. Amma drove me to my grandparents' house, and from there I went by bus with Radha Aunty. When rehearsals were over, I was to come back to my grandparents' house for dinner, and then Amma would pick me up.

The rehearsals were held at St. Theresa's Girls' Convent. Sonali attended the school, but I had never been there myself. The high spiked gates were covered with sheets of takaran so no one could look in or out. Today, they were slightly ajar. We took a path that led to a netball court, crossed it, and then went down a corridor towards the rehearsal hall. Now I could hear the sound of a piano, and a lady singing. We entered the hall and stood at the back. The only people on the stage were a white lady and a white boy. Before they could finish their song, another lady rose from a chair in the middle of the hall and cried out, "Stop. Stop." She began to walk towards the stage, calling out directions to the actors. Radha Aunty took this opportunity to introduce me. This lady, whom she called Aunty Doris, looked me over and smiled. "What a lovely boy," she said. "Should have been a girl with those eyelashes." Aunty Doris had fair skin like a foreigner, and yet she spoke English as we did, with a Sri Lankan accent. She wore big round glasses and there were deep dark circles under her eyes.

Since we would not be needed for a while, Radha Aunty took me outside into the courtyard. Some children were playing a game in one corner, but I stayed with Radha Aunty. A group of men and women were seated on some steps, and when they saw Radha Aunty they called to her to come and join in an argument they were having. They were discussing a song in the play which said that man was like a bee and woman like a blossom. A man, whose name I learned was Anil, had started the discussion. He agreed with this sentiment and all the men supported him.

They began to argue, each side yelling with joy when they scored a point. Radha Aunty was soon the leader of the girls, and she and Anil exchanged comments back and forth until Radha Aunty said, "I would rather wither and drop off my stem than be pollinated by a bee like you."

At this retort even the boys cheered, and Anil bowed slightly to concede to her the victory.

As we walked towards the hall a little later, one of the girls gestured towards Anil and said to Radha Aunty, "I think that bee is dying to pollinate your blossom."

The other girls who had heard this comment screamed

with laughter. Radha Aunty was not amused. "You're mad," she said. "Utterly mad."

Although I didn't altogether understand the joke, I knew that it was something bad, because Radha Aunty looked very annoyed.

After rehearsal that day, we were walking to the bus stop when Anil drove up in his car and stopped. He rolled down his window and said, "Do you want a lift?"

"No," Radha Aunty replied.

"But I'm going in your direction, and the buses are very slow and it's too late to be standing at the bus stop alone."

Radha Aunty hesitated for a moment and then accepted. On the way, she was silent and he didn't say much either. I began to wonder if that argument between them had been more serious than it had appeared. He offered to drop us at my grandparents' gate, but she insisted that he leave us at the top of the road.

When we came into the drawing room, Ammachi looked up in surprise from her newspaper and said, "How did you get home so quickly?"

"We got a bus right away," Radha Aunty replied.

I glanced at her, puzzled, and she gave me a warning look. When we went down the corridor to her room, I waited for her to give me an explanation for her lie, but she declined to say anything.

After the next rehearsal, Anil offered us a lift and Radha Aunty accepted a little more graciously this time, though once again she insisted that he drop us off at the top of the road.

When we came back to my grandparents' house, Ammachi was waiting for us in the front garden. Radha Aunty greeted her, but in return Ammachi glared at us.

"Who is this boy you're taking lifts from?" Ammachi asked.

Radha Aunty paused for a moment, then she lifted the latch of the gate and we went into the garden. "What boy?" she said.

"Don't lie to me. I know you've been taking lifts."

"So?" Radha Aunty shrugged as if she couldn't understand what all the fuss was about.

"Who is he?" Ammachi demanded.

"A boy. From the play."

"What is his name?"

"Why?"

"What is his name?"

"Anil."

"Anil who?"

Radha Aunty was silent.

"What is his last name."

"Jayasinghe," she replied finally.

Ammachi let out a small cry that was both triumphant and despairing. "A Sinhalese! I knew it!"

Appachi came out onto the front porch, drawn by the sound of her voice. Ammachi turned to him. "What did I tell you? She was getting a lift from a Sinhalese. Only a Sinhalese would be impertinent enough to offer an unmarried girl a lift."

Appachi didn't say anything, but his expression showed that he regretted having come out. Radha Aunty sensed his sympathy and appealed to him. "He lives in the next road, that's why he offered us a lift. It was so much easier than taking the bus. What's so wrong with getting a lift from a boy I know?"

"What's wrong?" Ammachi said. "I'll tell you what's wrong." She paused for effect. "People will talk."

"So let them."

"And what if the Nagendras hear that you're gallivanting around with an unknown Sinhala boy?"

Radha Aunty was silent. She looked at the ground in front of her, a sullen expression on her face.

Ammachi came a little closer to Radha Aunty. "Is there something going on with this Sinhala boy?" she asked.

"No!" Radha Aunty cried, her eyes wide with hurt.

Ammachi studied her keenly and then her expression softened. "Anyway, don't do it again."

She tried to touch Radha Aunty's arm, but Radha Aunty gave her an angry look and went up the steps and in through the front door. I followed her. The intensity of Ammachi's reaction had shaken me. I wondered why Anil's being Sinhalese upset her so. I was in a Sinhala class at school and my friends were Sinhalese. My parents' best friends were, too. Even our servant was Sinhalese, and, in fact, we spoke with her only in Sinhalese. So what did it matter whether Anil was Sinhalese or not?

Janaki was waiting for us at the end of the corridor. She had been listening. "It's that banana seller at the top of the road who told," she said to Radha Aunty. "I have a mind to get my sister's husband to give him a sound thrashing."

"She's such a racist," Radha Aunty said to me.

I looked at Radha Aunty. I did not understand the meaning of the word "racist," but I could tell that it was not a nice thing.

"Radha, baba, you mustn't forget what happened," said Janaki.

Radha Aunty clicked her tongue against her teeth impatiently. "Oh, I'm so tired of that," she said. "Why can't we just put it behind us?"

Janaki sighed and said, "You were too young to remember when they brought the body home. You should have seen it. It was as if someone had taken the lid of a tin can and cut pieces out of him."

I stared at Janaki in shock.

"I know, I know," Radha Aunty said, brushing aside Janaki's remarks. "But is that a reason to hate every Sinhalese?"

Janaki glanced down the corridor, for Ammachi had come in through the front door. She turned and hurried away to the kitchen, and Radha Aunty went into her room. I didn't follow her. Instead I stood there, as Ammachi came towards me. Familiar as her face was—especially the disapproving expression with which she looked at me before asking why I had not gone to wash my face and hands before dinner—I somehow saw her differently now.

At first I could not think of anyone who would explain the word "racist" to me and tell me the story of that body. Then it came to me that my father was very approachable once he was comfortably seated in the garden each evening, the second glass of whiskey in his hand.

So, one evening, I waited until I saw that dreamy, philosophical expression soften his features, then I approached him.

"Appa?" I said.

"Hmmm?"

"What is a racist?"

He turned in his chair and studied me. "Where did you hear that word?" he asked.

I told him and he was silent for a moment, nursing his glass of whiskey.

"Appa, who was that person who was killed?" I asked.

"It was Ammachi's father," he replied, after a moment. "Your great-grandfather."

I stared at him. I thought about the photograph of my great-grandfather which hung at the center of all the pictures in the corridor at my grandparents' house and I found it impossible to connect him with the dead man Janaki had described.

"Why?" I finally asked. "Why did somebody do that?"

"Because he was Tamil."

"But you're Tamil and I'm Tamil and nobody's killing us."

"This was twenty years ago, in the fifties, son. At that time, some Sinhalese people killed Tamil people."

"But why?"

He shifted in his chair. "It's too hard to explain. You'll understand when you're older."

"But I want to know now."

He looked at me, irritated. "It had to do with some laws," he said. "The Sinhalese wanted to make Sinhala the only national language, and the Tamils did not like this. So there was a riot and many Tamils were killed."

From then on I began to listen carefully to the conversation of the adults to discover more about the quarrels between the Sinhalese and the Tamils. What I learned made me very uneasy, because I realized these problems were not a thing of the past.

There was a group in Jaffna called the Tamil Tigers. They wanted a separate country, and the Sinhalese were very angry about this. Ammachi often talked about the Tigers. She was on their side and declared that if they did get a separate state, which they would call Eelam, she would be the first to go and live in it. My father told her she was mad. This made Ammachi even more angry, and they had many disputes about the Tigers. Now I understood why they had quarreled so bitterly when I started school a year ago and my father had put me in a Sinhalese class. Ammachi had said he was betraying the Tamils, but my father had said that there was no use in putting me in a Tamil class when Sinhalese was "the real language of the future."

I began to notice other things as well. In school, it was customary for classes to challenge each other to a game of cricket. Sometimes, instead of playing against other Sinhalese classes, the boys in our class played the Tamil class. When this happened, there was none of the usual joking and laughing, and when the match was over the players parted without shaking hands or patting each other on the back.

The next rehearsal was on the morning of spend-the-day. It was only for the children and wives of the King of Siam. Anil was not there and we were spared the embarrassment of having to refuse his lift.

When we came back for lunch, Janaki was waiting for us, a grim expression on her face. She asked Radha Aunty to follow her to the kitchen. When I attempted to go with them, she shooed me away and shut the kitchen door, so I ran into the side garden and stood beneath the kitchen window.

"What's wrong?" I heard Radha Aunty ask.

"You'll never believe, baba. This morning your Amma went to see the Jayasinghes to make sure that boy stops giving you lifts."

Radha Aunty drew in her breath. "What happened?" she asked.

"When she came back she said she had fixed everything."

"How embarrassing!" Radha Aunty cried. "I can never face that boy again!"

After a moment, Radha Aunty spoke again. "I must go there and apologize, Janaki."

"Baba!" Janaki exclaimed. "Are you mad or something?"

"I must do it. Today."

"You know, baba," Janaki said, "this evening I am taking the children for a sea bath. Come with us and then you can go and see him."

"But what if the children tell?"

Janaki was silent for a moment. "Best thing is to take that Arjie with you. The children will think you have gone back to the house together."

When we went for a sea bath that evening, I could hardly contain my excitement. I knew that I had to act normal, otherwise the cousins, and especially Sonali, might suspect that something was wrong. The feeling of fear that we might get caught and the thrill of doing something forbidden made me want to squeeze Radha Aunty's hand as we walked down to the beach. Radha Aunty seemed very calm, and had I not overheard her conversation with Janaki, I would have never suspected that she was planning anything.

Once we were on the beach, the cousins left their slippers and clothes by the rocks and ran to the water, shouting with glee. Janaki, who was helping the smallest cousin out of her clothes, called to them to wait for her, but they ignored her. Instead of joining the other cousins, I stayed by Radha Aunty. Finally, the little cousin was naked, and she ran screaming with delight towards the water. As Janaki rushed after her, she gave Radha Aunty a quick look to tell her that it was all right for us to leave. Radha Aunty grabbed my hand and said, "Come, let's go for a walk." Now I saw that she was nervous.

We climbed up the rocks and crossed the railway tracks. "We're dropping in at Anil's house," she said to me, trying to sound casual.

"Yes," I replied.

"What do you mean, yes?" She looked at me carefully and then shook her finger at me. "You listened to our conversation, didn't you?"

Since she didn't really seem annoyed, I nodded.

"Honestly, you're something else."

She took my hand and we walked along the railway tracks until we came to the road on which Anil lived.

Anil's house was about the same size as my grandparents'. When Radha Aunty lifted the latch of the gate and banged it

down a few times, a golden retriever ran down the driveway
and barked at us. After a moment, Anil came out onto the
front steps. He was wearing a sarong and a banyan. When he
saw us, he stood still in surprise. I looked anxiously at his face
to see if he was angry.

"Hello," Radha Aunty said cheerfully, as if nothing out
of the ordinary had happened. Yet as she spoke she gripped
my hand tightly.

Anil came down to the gate without replying.

"What are you doing here?" He sounded more concerned than angry.

"I wanted to see you," she said. "May I come in?"

He nodded and opened the gate. At the sound of the gate
opening, a man called out from inside the house, asking who
it was.

"Nobody," Anil cried back. "Just a friend."

As we walked up the driveway, the man came to the front
door and looked at us. I could tell it was Anil's father because
he was fair-skinned and slim, like Anil, but much shorter. His
face was thin and sharp and he was balding. "Who is this?"
he said to Anil, nodding towards Radha Aunty.

"A friend," Anil replied, embarrassed by his father's rude-
ness.

Anil's father scrutinized his face for a moment and then
said to him, "Have you no manners? Go and put on a shirt."

Anil hurried into the house. Once he had gone, his father
said to Radha Aunty, "You are Miss Chelvaratnam, no?"

Radha Aunty looked at him in surprise.

"I know all Anil's other friends," he said.

He indicated for us to follow him inside. As we entered,

Anil came out of his bedroom buttoning his shirt. He glanced anxiously at his father and then at us, as if he expected something to have happened. "Come and sit down," he said.

When we were settled in the drawing room, Radha Aunty said, "I came to apologize for what happened this morning."

Anil waved away her apology. "It was nothing."

"What do you mean, nothing?" his father said to him. "It was downright insulting."

"My mother gets—" Radha Aunty started to say, but Anil's father interrupted her.

"Coming here and accusing my son of this and that and the other. As if my son was desperate for a bride or something."

Anil threw him a warning look, which he ignored. "We are from a good family as well. High-country Sinhalese, we are. Last thing we also want is for our son to marry some non-Sinhalese."

"I understand," Radha Aunty said and looked at her hands.

"No, you don't understand," he said, and wagged his finger at her. "It was very high-handed of your mother to come here and do that."

"Thatha," Anil said firmly, "this is not your concern."

"Oh, yes, it is," he replied. "Our family name has been insulted. I shall not take this lying down."

Anil turned in his chair and called down the hall for his mother. I noticed that someone was standing behind the curtained doorway at the end of the hall.

"Menik!" Anil's mother called out sharply from behind it. "Come here!"

Anil's father became silent.

"Menik! Come here. Soon!"

Anil's father rose reluctantly from his chair. Before he left us, he raised his finger and said, "Be careful. We Sinhalese are losing patience with you Tamils and your arrogance."

Anil leaned back in his chair and groaned in mortification. His father walked down the hall. I felt relieved to see him go, for I was beginning to feel frightened of him.

Anil looked at Radha Aunty and said, "I'm so sorry."

Radha Aunty smiled bravely. "It's all right."

"Can I get you anything to drink?"

She shook her head and stood up. "Have to get back. I just came to apologize, that's all."

We walked down the driveway in silence. When we were at the gate, Anil said, "I didn't know that you were engaged."

"I'm not," Radha Aunty replied.

"Your mother said . . ."

"She lied."

"Oh," he said, and then was silent.

Radha Aunty lifted the latch.

"But there is someone?"

"Yes."

Radha Aunty pushed open the gate and we went out.

"And you will marry him?"

Radha Aunty paused and then put the latch back into place. "Yes. I think I might."

As we went towards the beach again, I thought of all that had happened at Anil's house. Now I was beginning to understand why Ammachi had been so angry. Part of her anger was because Anil was Sinhalese, but another part, I now saw, had to do with her fear that Anil and Radha Aunty were in

love with each other. I felt she was wrong. Anil and Radha
Aunty didn't act like people in love. They were more like
friends. I found myself thinking of Anil. He didn't fit my idea
of what a lover looked like. He was fairly tall and, though
not thin, his body was angular and a little awkward. With his
large eyes, full lips, and thick, curly hair, which hung almost
to his shoulders, he looked like someone too young to be a
lover. Also, he was not serious enough.

At the next rehearsal, when we came in through the gates of
St. Theresa's, Anil was leaning against the wall of a building
as if waiting for someone. We greeted him, and from the way
Radha Aunty and Anil smiled at each other, I could tell they
were thinking about that day we had gone to his house.

"Did you get into trouble for seeing me?" Anil asked.

Radha Aunty shook her head. "My mother doesn't have
any spies on your road."

We walked together towards the rehearsal hall.

"Why does she hate the Sinhalese so much?" Anil asked.

"Her father was killed in the 'fifty-eight riots."

He was silent for a moment. "And you? Are you anti-
Sinhalese?"

"No."

"Would you allow your child to marry a Sinhalese?"

"Yes, definitely."

"And yourself?"

"What?"

"Would you marry a Sinhalese?"

Radha Aunty glanced quickly at him and then looked
away. "Probably not."

"Why?"

"Because."

"So then you are anti-Sinhalese."

"No!"

"But you just said—"

"What I meant was that, yes, in principle I would. But now . . ."

"There is someone."

She nodded.

They were both silent. They didn't seem as friendly anymore.

It was a full day of rehearsal, and a lot of people went to Green Cabin for lunch. There were only two vehicles to take us to the restaurant—a minivan belonging to one of the girls and Anil's car. By the time Radha Aunty and I got to the gates of St. Theresa's, the minivan was full. Radha Aunty grabbed my hand and hurried back inside the gates again. "Let's sit down for a while," she said to me and pointed to some steps.

"But we'll miss the ride."

"Never mind. We'll take a bus."

I looked at the fixed expression on her face and I saw there was no point in arguing, but I couldn't see why she would give up the comfort of a lift to Green Cabin to stand in the midday sun and wait for a bus.

When we arrived at the restaurant, all the tables were taken and the cast occupied the row of open-air booths that were detached from the main part of the restaurant. Radha Aunty held on to my hand as she went from one booth to the other, looking for a place. Anil was in the last booth with a group of his male friends. When he saw us, he moved a little and indicated that there was enough space for both of us. Radha Aunty hesitated, and then quickly ushered me into the booth ahead of her, so that I was seated between them. As Radha Aunty looked at the menu, I saw Anil's friends glance at him and smile. He returned their looks with a stern expression.

When the waiter had brought their food, he began to take Radha Aunty's order. Anil insisted that Radha Aunty have his lamprais, but she pretended she had not heard him and ordered one from the waiter. She also ordered a plate of pastries for me and two glasses of lime juice. Once the waiter had gone, Anil repeated his request, but she shook her head.

"Then I shall wait till your lamprais comes," he said stubbornly.

"Why is that?" Radha Aunty asked rudely.

His friends had begun to eat, and they looked at each other in amusement.

"Because you are a lady and it would be impolite."

Radha Aunty shrugged dismissively. "Think of me as a friend, not a lady."

One of the boys at the table made a noise that sounded like a suppressed laugh. Radha Aunty fixed her eyes on him. "You should be careful," she said. "There are bones in the chicken and we wouldn't want you to choke."

At this all the boys started to laugh helplessly and even Radha Aunty grinned. "Honestly, you all are quite mad," she said.

After this, the atmosphere eased and Radha Aunty chatted with them until our food arrived. By now, the boys had almost finished, but Anil was still waiting to eat with us. Radha Aunty had scarcely begun to eat her lamprais when the waiter brought the finger bowls and bill for the other boys. Radha Aunty looked at them in alarm and said, "You're not going?"

They nodded. "Have to go and do an errand for the pater," one of them said.

Another one put his hand on Anil's shoulder, gave him a steady look, and said, "Anil, machan, we will see you later."

The others grinned. They went into the main part of the restaurant and we heard them laughing. The other cast members were getting up to leave as well. Radha Aunty called to some of the girls to come and sit with us, but they shook their heads and said they were going across the road to Sharaz to do some shopping. Soon the only ones left were the three of us. Radha Aunty began to eat quickly now, as if she, too, had to do something before rehearsals began.

"So," Anil said after a silence, "where does he live?"

"Who?"

"Your intended."

"I don't have an intended."

"You know what I mean."

Radha Aunty ate in silence for a while and then said, "America."

"You met him there?"

She nodded.

"Was it love at first sight?"

She glared at him as if to say it was none of his business.

"Sorry," he said, "I am just curious."

She didn't respond. I looked at Radha Aunty. Today, it seemed her moods changed constantly.

"Do you know why I am curious?"

Radha Aunty shrugged, her mouth full, as if she had no interest in his curiosity.

"I think you know why," he said.

Radha Aunty gave him a furious look and inclined her head in my direction.

"I don't care," he said. "This is the only chance I have to say it to you."

Radha Aunty took a sip from her glass of lime juice and called to the waiter, who was passing by, to bring our bill.

"Hurry up," she said to me. "We haven't got the whole day."

"What are you scared of?" he asked.

Instead of answering him, Radha Aunty suddenly frowned and stared ahead of her.

"What's wrong?" Anil asked.

"Shhh," she said.

I stopped eating and my eyes followed her gaze. Then I saw what had stopped her. Mala Aunty and Kanthi Aunty were in the main part of Green Cabin buying some pastries.

"Who is it?" Anil whispered.

Radha Aunty held her finger to her lips.

Now they had paid for their pastries and collected them. But instead of going out through the front door they started to come towards the side exit where our booth was. We watched, in horror, as they approached. They saw us and stopped.

"Radha?" Kanthi Aunty said, as if she was not sure that it was her.

Radha Aunty looked down at her plate. Both aunts now

stared at Anil. Kanthi Aunty gathered herself together, like a hen rustling her feathers. "What are you doing here?" she asked sternly.

"Come," Mala Aunty whispered to Kanthi Aunty and took her by the arm. She resisted for a moment, then she marched out with Mala Aunty.

Radha Aunty continued to eat, her head bent over her plate. After a few moments, she sniffed and rubbed the back of her hand across her cheeks. Anil and I both looked at her in distress.

"Please," he said, "don't do that."

He took out his handkerchief and offered it to her. She waved it away angrily and took one out of her bag.

"Well, at least it's out in the open now. We can stop pretending."

Radha Aunty didn't reply. Instead she blew her nose.

"Look," he said, "I'll come and explain to your family."

She stared at him in amazement and cried out, "Are you mad or something?"

"Why not?" he asked.

"It's enough that you've got me into trouble—now you want to make it even worse?"

"What did I do wrong?"

"You shouldn't have stayed here with me. I'm practically married . . ."

"You said you weren't even engaged."

"Doesn't matter. You shouldn't have sat with me."

He leaned back against the seat of the booth and looked at her for a moment. "Do you like me?" he asked.

She glared at him, then glanced over at me.

He smiled as if she had said she liked him.

"Don't you see, Radha?" he said. "If we like each other we can work out the rest."

She was silent.

"Other Sinhalese and Tamil people have got married," he said.

"Other people didn't have a mother like mine or a father like yours."

"I'm sure your mother is not as bad as you think. I know that my father will give in, despite all he has said.

"Think about it," he said after a moment. "If you really like me, together we can make our parents accept us."

The waiter brought our bill at this moment, and Anil took it from him. Radha Aunty protested but finally allowed him to pay for us.

As we left Green Cabin, I studied Radha Aunty and Anil. It was clear to me now that Anil wanted to marry Radha Aunty, but I couldn't tell what she wanted. Besides, there was Rajan. How did he fit in?

When we got off the bus that evening and began to walk down Ramanaygam Road, I saw that Mala Aunty's car was parked outside my grandparents' gate, and my heart sank. As we neared the house, Radha Aunty gripped my hand tightly.

I had expected to find Ammachi and the aunts waiting for us in the garden or at least hear the sound of excited voices from the drawing room. Instead, a hush lay over the house and garden as if there were a funeral. The squeaking of the gate as we opened it was loud in the stillness. Radha Aunty beckoned to me and we crept around the side of the house and entered by the kitchen.

Janaki saw us as we came in, and her eyes widened with apprehension. She looked towards the dining room and whispered, "They are at the table."

Radha Aunty sighed. "How bad is it?" she asked Janaki.

Janaki made a face to show that it was not good.

Radha Aunty sighed again. "It was all so innocent, really. We were just having lunch together."

Janaki didn't say anything. After a moment, she went back to her work.

Radha Aunty left the kitchen and went into the main part of the house. At the sound of her footsteps in the corridor, Ammachi called out, "Who is that?"

"It's me," Radha Aunty said, unlocking her bedroom door.

"When did you come in?"

"Just now, through the back."

"Like a thief," Kanthi Aunty said.

Radha Aunty went inside her room without replying.

I remained out in the corridor. I heard the aunts and Ammachi discussing what they should do next. They decided to wait for her to join them at dinner. Janaki came out into the corridor and waved her hand, indicating for me to go to the dining room. When I entered, they all looked at me solemnly. I lowered my head and hurriedly took a seat next to Mala Aunty.

"Huh," Kanthi Aunty said. "Imagine implicating a child and all."

We heard Radha Aunty come out of her room.

"Now, Amma," Mala Aunty cautioned. "Please remain calm. Nothing will be gained by shouting at her."

Mala Aunty was a doctor, so her opinions were highly valued, even by Ammachi.

Radha Aunty came into the dining room briskly and took her seat. She looked around and smiled. "Well," she said. "Here I am."

They stared at her, nonplussed. She reached out and helped herself to some pittu.

"You think this is funny?" Ammachi said after a few moments. I could tell she was really trying to control herself.

"No," she replied brightly. "I think it's very serious."

"Let's see how serious it is when Amma puts an end to your acting in *The King and I*," Kanthi Aunty said.

Radha Aunty paused and then put down the plate of pittu.

"Oh," she said and waited.

"I'm going to call Doris this evening," Ammachi said.

"Call," Radha Aunty said. "I don't give a damn."

"Radha," Mala Aunty appealed to her. "Please!"

"What?" she said. "I haven't done anything."

"Haven't done anything?" Ammachi cried, unable to control herself any longer. "You flaunt your illicit relations in public and you dare to say you haven't done anything."

" 'Illicit relations,' " Radha Aunty said in an amused voice. "Honestly, Amma, you'd think I was a prostitute or something."

Abruptly, Ammachi stood up, reached across the table, and slapped Radha Aunty.

We all gasped. Radha Aunty stared at Ammachi in astonishment, then her face crumpled and she began to cry. Ammachi sat down. Even she seemed a little shocked at what she had just done. I looked at my plate, but the sound of those agonized sobs prevented me from touching my food. Finally Radha Aunty became still. All the vivacity and spirit had gone out of her face.

"Now that you are calm, let me tell you what we plan to do," Ammachi said, trying to sound stern again.

Radha Aunty turned her face away as if the sight of Ammachi was distasteful.

"We are sending you to Jaffna to stay with my cousin Nages. Hopefully, after a month you will come to your senses."

Radha Aunty curled her lip in contempt. She pushed back her chair and stood up. Then, without a word, she left the dining room.

Once she had gone, the tension eased slightly.

"Really, Amma," Mala Aunty said, "how could you?"

Ammachi said, "I did what was correct," but she sounded unsure.

"To slap a grown woman like that. It was completely uncalled-for."

"I am a good mother and I challenge any of you to say otherwise." Ammachi looked around the table, hoping someone would agree with her. No one said anything.

Mala Aunty got up and left the dining room. I heard her knocking on Radha Aunty's door and calling out her name softly. Finally Radha Aunty opened the door.

I got up from the table.

"Where are you going?" Ammachi asked.

"To do pee-pee," I replied meekly.

She waved her hand, dismissing me. She couldn't very well forbid me to use the toilet.

I hurried through the kitchen and into the side garden. I could hear the sound of voices as I approached Radha Aunty's window. I stood under it and listened.

"She had no business to do that!" Radha Aunty cried.

"I know, I know," Mala Aunty said softly.

"All this is ridiculous," Radha Aunty said.

"Are you in love with this boy?" Mala Aunty asked after a moment.

"No . . . I don't know," Radha Aunty said. Then she laughed. "The funny thing is I never thought of him like that until Amma started to make a fuss. It was only after she went to speak to his parents that I began to see him differently."

"So you are in love."

Radha Aunty didn't answer for a moment. "Until a few days ago I only thought of Rajan, but now I find myself thinking of Anil as well."

Mala Aunty sighed. "It'll never work."

"But other Sinhalese and Tamil people get married."

"I know," Mala Aunty replied, "but they have their parents' consent."

"If two people love each other, the rest is unimportant."

"No, it isn't. Ultimately, you have to live in the real world. And without your family you are nothing."

Radha Aunty was silent.

"And don't forget," Mala Aunty added, "things are getting worse between the Sinhalese and Tamils. These Tamil Tigers in Jaffna are very serious about a separate state. They're

determined to get this Eelam, even if they have to use violence to do it."

"Rubbish," Radha Aunty said. "Utter rubbish. All this
separation talk will come to nothing."

"I hope you're right," Mala Aunty replied. "Otherwise,
people in mixed marriages will find themselves in a terrible
dilemma."

Ammachi's plan to keep Radha Aunty away from Anil received a setback when she phoned Aunty Doris. Aunty Doris
refused to let Radha Aunty out of the play. "How can I find
someone at this late date?" we heard her shouting over the
phone. "You can't let me down now."

Finally, Ammachi had to give in, and she and Aunty Doris
reached a compromise. Radha Aunty would continue acting
in *The King and I* and Appachi would drive her to and from
rehearsals. In return, Aunty Doris would let Radha Aunty off
for a few weeks so that Ammachi could send her to Jaffna.

The next rehearsal was for only the wives and children of
the King of Siam, so Anil was not there. When we were
leaving the hall after rehearsal, Aunty Doris called out to
Radha Aunty to wait for her. She stood in the doorway as
Aunty Doris collected her scripts and put them in her bag.
By now the hall was empty. Radha Aunty nudged me and
pointed to Aunty Doris's bag. I offered to carry it, and she
thanked me. She took Radha Aunty's arm, and we began to
walk slowly to the gate.

"So, what's this I hear about you?" she said to Radha
Aunty. Before Radha Aunty could speak, she continued,

"Your mother was quite furious but I stuck to my guns." She laughed conspiratorially.

Radha Aunty turned to look at her in surprise.

"Yes, my dear," Aunty Doris said. "One less Siamese wife would have hardly affected the show."

"Why, Aunty?" she asked after a moment.

Aunty Doris was silent. Then she said, "Because I want you to get to know this boy. To be sure you are making the right decision." She turned to Radha Aunty. "Child, our families have been friends for a long time. I have known you since you were a baby." She paused. "I want you to think about this carefully. I don't want you to make the same mistake I did."

"But you and your husband . . ."

"Yes, we did fine. But sometimes I wonder. Paskaran was a lovely man. Kind and gentle and very handsome in his youth. We met on a ship, you know. He was returning from his studies in England and I, like any Burgher girl from a good family, was coming back from finishing school and a tour of Europe. I noticed him immediately. All the women did, even the British ones, although they pretended to be indifferent. Of course, my father had a fit; called him a black Tamil bugger and everything. In those days, Burghers thought they were a cut above other Sri Lankans. His family was not too pleased either. With a foreign education he was very eligible and could have got a Tamil girl with a big fat dowry. But in spite of all the fuss we married."

Aunty Doris let go of Radha Aunty's arm, and they walked in silence for a moment. Then Aunty Doris continued, "My father never did forgive me, and he forbade my mother and sisters to have anything to do with me. They emigrated to England without even telling me, left no address or anything. I was heartbroken, because I was very close to my mother and sisters." She was silent again for a moment. "My mother passed away and I didn't even know about it. Found out months later through a mutual friend. When my father finally died, my sisters and I were free to make contact again. But it was too late then. We had become strangers to each other. Now Paskaran is dead and I'm alone." She shrugged. "Of course, my sisters want me to come and settle in England with them. But what would I do there? I'm too old to start over again. . . . Anyway, this is my home. I am Sri Lankan." She sighed. "Sometimes I wonder if it was all worth it in the end. To have made all those sacrifices. Life is a funny thing, you know. It goes on, whatever decisions you make. Ultimately you have children or don't have children and then you grow old. Whether you married the person you loved or not seems to become less important as time passes. Sometimes I think that if I had gone to England with them maybe I would have met somebody else. . . ." She clicked her tongue against her teeth and laughed. "Anyway, there's no point in thinking about that—no?"

We had reached the gate, and Appachi was waiting for us in the car.

Aunty Doris took her bag from me. "These rehearsals are a good chance to make sure you really want to marry him. Promise me you'll think about it carefully?"

Radha Aunty nodded.

On the way home that day, I found myself thinking about Aunty Doris's story. I wondered what it would be like if I was forced to go away from Sonali or Amma for a long time, if I was only allowed to see them after many years had passed. Radha Aunty was staring out of the window, a brooding expression on her face. It was only then I realized that Aunty Doris's story had been a warning to her of what the future might hold if she decided to marry Anil. Now it came to me that if she did marry Anil I would never see her again. This thought was unbearable. Radha Aunty had become a very important part of my life; she was my only friend. The thought of returning to being alone was terrible. I looked at Radha Aunty again and, for the first time, I saw that she was beautiful. Her dark skin and frizzy hair were attractive in their own way. She had noticed I was watching her, and I took her hand.

In spite of the strict eye Ammachi kept on her, Radha Aunty still managed to see Anil outside of rehearsals. One of the times she met him was on my cousin Lakshmi's birthday. Mala Aunty took all the cousins to the zoo that day, enlisting Janaki's and Radha Aunty's help to keep us under control.

Part of the zoo was built on a slope into which had been cut a number of terraces. As you descended the steps you could make little detours along the terraces to look at the animals in their various cages. When we got to the bottom, where the giant tortoises were, Radha Aunty grabbed my hand and said to Mala Aunty, "Our friend"—meaning me—"has to use the toilet." She pressed my hand hard, warning me not to seem surprised.

"Oh dear, I guess he has to go," Mala Aunty said, distressed at losing Radha Aunty's help, even temporarily.

We climbed back up the steps until we were at the top; then we set out in the direction of the elephant-dance arena. Anil was waiting for us there. Radha Aunty bought me an ice palam and told me to sit in the arena and wait for her. She pressed some money into my hand so that I could buy some cashew nuts if I wished. I was there for quite a while and the arena had started to fill up for the next elephant dance when Radha Aunty returned. Anil was no longer with her. She hugged me and said, "You're such a good boy, Arjie. I shall make you chief pageboy at my wedding."

I looked at her and knew that this time she was talking about her wedding to Anil and not to Rajan.

She took my hand and we hurried back to where we had said we would meet the other cousins.

We had been gone almost an hour, and the cousins had grown quite unruly while waiting for us.

"Where have you been?" Mala Aunty cried out in annoyance.

"We got lost," Radha Aunty said.

Mala Aunty stared at her, and a look of alarm and suspicion crossed her face. "Hmmph," she said and turned away to call the cousins, who were leaning dangerously close to the bear cage. As we began to walk around the zoo again, Radha Aunty whispered to Janaki, "Everything is set. When I come back from Jaffna we're going to do it. I don't care what his parents or my parents say."

A few days later, Radha Aunty took a train north to Jaffna. I was to go without her to rehearsals, and now Amma drove me there. The first time she dropped me outside St. Theresa's,

I looked at the tall gates and felt lost and alone. Slowly, I made my way towards the netball court. The other children in the cast were playing rounders, and I stood watching them for a while, then made my way to the rehearsal hall. The men and women who were Radha Aunty's friends were talking outside the hall. Anil was not with them. Feeling that I didn't belong there either, I went into the hall. The actors were doing the scene where the king's chief wife sings to the English governess about the things she liked in her husband. I noticed Anil now. He was leaning on the piano, his hand under his chin. From the expression on his face I could tell that he, too, was missing Radha Aunty. I went and stood by him.

It was during Radha Aunty's absence that I began to really get to know Anil. I was struck by how different he was from men like my father and uncles. His friendliness towards me was casual and effortless, unlike the stiff formality other adults had when they felt compelled to make a gesture of cordiality towards us children.

A month passed, and soon it was time for Radha Aunty to come back. The day before she returned, however, we heard that there was trouble in Jaffna. The old market had been burned down and nobody was certain who had done it. A curfew would be set. Ammachi phoned Nages Aunty to find out if it was safe to send Radha Aunty by train. Nages Aunty said that the tension had died down and that she had arranged for a police friend of hers to escort Radha Aunty to the station. Radha Aunty was taking the night train, which would bring her to Colombo early the next day.

That morning, after rehearsal, Amma didn't come to pick me up. I sat on the steps by the gate and watched the other cast members leave. Anil saw me waiting and he offered to keep me company until Amma arrived. After half an hour had gone by, however, I became uneasy. The sun was very hot now and I was beginning to feel hungry. Finally, Anil offered to leave me at my grandparents' house on his way home. I wondered if he had offered to drop me at their house rather than my house because he hoped to get a glimpse of Radha Aunty.

When we turned down Ramanaygam Road, I was surprised to see all the aunts' and uncles' cars parked outside the house and my parents' as well. Anil saw me lean forward in my seat.

"What's wrong?" he asked.

"I don't know."

Diggy and some of the other cousins were seated on the wall. When they saw me, they jumped down and ran to the car.

"You'll never guess what!" Diggy cried. "Radha Aunty's train was attacked."

I looked at them, shocked. Anil turned off the ignition.

"What happened?" he asked.

"People attacked the Tamils on the train," Diggy said. "Radha Aunty was hurt and everything."

"But why?" Anil asked.

"Because there was trouble in Jaffna," Diggy explained. "When the train got to Anuradhapura, Sinhalese people began throwing stones and bottles at the train. Next thing you know, there was a big hullabaloo." He leaned forward into the car. "And now they say there's going to be trouble in Colombo too. The government is going to declare a curfew."

Anil looked worried. He opened the door on his side, and I got out as well.

As we walked up the driveway, I could hear the adults' voices in the drawing room. Some cousins were in the garden, and they stared at Anil. I went in to call Amma. When Amma saw me she cried out, "Oh, darling, I completely forgot about you."

"It's okay," I replied. "Anil drove me home."

"Who?" Amma asked.

Before I could reply, Mala Aunty said, "The Sinhala man. You know, the one who Radha . . ." Her voice trailed off, and the adults glanced at each other significantly.

"He's here," I said and pointed to the front porch.

Mala Aunty covered her mouth, and the other adults looked towards the porch.

"I'll deal with him," Ammachi said, and she stood up.

"No, no," Amma said hastily. "I'll talk to him. After all, he brought Arjie and everything."

She got up and followed me out onto the porch.

"Thank you for driving my son here," she said to Anil.

He waved his hand as if to say it was nothing.

"What's happened?" he asked.

"The train coming from Jaffna was attacked at the Anuradhapura station."

"And Radha . . . I mean your sister-in-law, how is she?"

Amma shook her head. "We don't know as yet. Mr.

Rasiah, a family friend of ours, was on the train and he was able to get her out of the station quickly."

Anil exhaled slowly. "Where is she now?" he asked.

"She's with Mr. Rasiah. He is bringing her back to Colombo."

"May I see her when she comes back?"

"I'm afraid I don't think that's a good idea." She smiled at Anil to indicate that the visit was over. He nodded, and after a moment he left.

When we went back into the drawing room, everyone looked at Amma expectantly.

"He wanted to find out what had happened," she said. "Poor man."

Kanthi Aunty made a derisive sound. "Don't start that 'poor man' nonsense. Especially not after what has happened."

Amma sent me to the bathroom to wash before lunch. As I walked down the corridor, I was suddenly brought up short by the photograph of my great-grandfather on the wall. I stared at it for a moment, and then the gravity of the looming crisis sank in. I shivered involuntarily as I recalled what my father had said about the fights between the Sinhalese and the Tamils in the fifties and how many Tamils had been killed. Was it happening all over again? Would we suffer a similar fate to that of my great-grandfather? I turned away from the photograph, not wanting to look at it anymore, not wanting to be reminded of what might await us.

The atmosphere at lunch was tense. The adults sat at the dining table and we children sat in the drawing room, our plates on our laps. No one spoke except to ask someone to pass a dish. The radio was on so we could listen for more news. Many places in Sri Lanka were already under curfew, and this evening there would be one in Colombo.

We were midway through the meal when we heard the sound of a car stopping outside our gate. We became silent. There was a banging on the gate and a man called out, asking if anyone was home. Radha Aunty had arrived. We all got up, left our plates, and hurried down the corridor to the front door. When we arrived on the porch, Radha Aunty and Mr. Rasiah were walking up the driveway. We stood still and watched them. Radha Aunty walked slowly, her hand resting on Mr. Rasiah's arm. She was wearing a scarf and she kept her head bent. When she was close to us, she lifted her head, and we all stared at her in horror. The right half of her face was dark and swollen. The scarf around her head covered a bloody bandage.

Ammachi made a small noise that sounded like a whimper and went to Radha Aunty. She put her arms around her and hugged her tightly. Radha Aunty stood there without responding. She seemed oblivious to all of us. Ammachi tried to lead her towards the house, but she made a protesting sound and clung to Mr. Rasiah's arm.

"She's still very shocked," Mr. Rasiah said by way of explaining her behavior. He gently disengaged her fingers from his arm so that Ammachi could lead Radha Aunty into the house. As she went past me I looked at her, unable to believe that she was the same Radha Aunty who had left for Jaffna a few weeks earlier. The uncles, my father, and Appachi invited Mr. Rasiah to sit down and have some lunch with them. The aunts, Amma, I, and all the cousins followed as

Ammachi led Radha Aunty down the corridor to Radha Aunty's room. We stood in the doorway and watched as Ammachi helped her to sit down on her bed.

Now Mala Aunty, being the doctor, took charge. She removed the scarf and began to examine the wound. When she tried to take off the bandage, Radha Aunty drew in her breath sharply and put her hand up to stop her.

"I have to take it off," Mala Aunty said. "We must see if you need stitches or not."

She found a pair of scissors in a drawer and began to snip at the bandage. Radha Aunty gripped the edges of the bed, a grimace on her face. Finally the bandage came undone and we saw the gash on her forehead. Mala Aunty tilted Radha Aunty's head back and examined the wound carefully. Then she nodded, indicating that stitches weren't needed. She sent me to get a new bandage from Appachi.

When I arrived in the dining room, Mr. Rasiah was in the middle of describing what had happened at the Anuradhapura station. I forgot about my errand for a moment and stood listening to him tell how Radha Aunty had been assaulted by two men, one carrying a stick and the other a belt, and how he had managed to save her because he spoke good Sinhalese and the men had believed he was Sinhalese.

When I returned with the bandage, Radha Aunty was lying on her bed and someone had drawn the curtains. Mala Aunty took the bandage from me and began to dress the wound. When she was done, all the aunts left, leaving the door slightly ajar behind them. The other cousins went down the corridor, talking excitedly about the size and bloodiness of Radha Aunty's wound. I waited till they had gone and then I entered Radha Aunty's room. She opened her eyes as I came in and stared at me, then she closed them again. I sat on the edge of the bed. In the dining room I could hear Mr. Rasiah finishing his story. I thought how rapidly our lives had changed. Yesterday, it would have been impossible to imagine these events. In a few hours curfew would begin, the night would descend, and there would be the anxiety of waiting till morning, wondering what would happen to us. As I sat there on Radha Aunty's bed, I thought of all Mr. Rasiah had said and found myself wondering how people could be so cruel, so terrible. The scene he had described, the bottles being flung, the beatings, seemed unreal. And yet they were real, as I could see before my very eyes.

My thoughts were disturbed by the sound of the doorbell ringing. I glanced towards the half-open door, wondering who was visiting us at this hour. Radha Aunty, too, was listening. Then we heard Anil asking for her. Radha Aunty sat up in bed.

"Radha is not in," we heard Kanthi Aunty say. "She had to go to the dispensary."

"When will she be back?" Anil asked.

Radha Aunty lowered her feet over the side of the bed and stood up.

"I don't know."

"May I wait?"

"No. It's very insensitive of you to come around at a time like this."

"I was only concerned about Radha . . ."

"There is no need for you to be concerned."

Radha Aunty stood in the middle of her room as if uncertain of what to do next. Now we heard Ammachi's voice. "What do you want?" she cried at Anil. "Haven't you people done enough?"

"Please go," Kanthi Aunty said. "You are not wanted here." There was a long silence.

Now Radha Aunty walked quickly to the bedroom door. But she was too late. Anil had left. Then I heard her breathe in deeply and realized that she was crying. She stood by the door for a moment, the tears running down her face. Then she went back towards the bed and slowly sat down on the edge of it, looking at her hands. From time to time, she breathed in loudly. I turned away from her, unable to bear the sound of her crying.

By the time we left that afternoon, a few sporadic incidents had been reported not far from where my grandparents lived. It was decided that Ammachi, Appachi, and Radha Aunty would spend a few days with us. My grandparents would stay in the spare room, Radha Aunty would have Sonali's room, and Sonali would sleep with me.

In the middle of the night Sonali woke me up to say that she had heard a noise in the hall. We sat up in bed, listening carefully. I heard someone moving around in the drawing room. I got up quietly and crept to the door. I turned the handle slowly, making sure that it didn't click as I opened the door, and I stepped out into the hall. In the dark I could make out a figure at the end of the hall, looking at the garden through the half-glass front door. Then the person moved slightly and the bandage caught the moonlight. Radha Aunty.

She had heard me. She turned and gazed in my direction for a moment, then beckoned to me. I went to her.

"What are you doing up?" she whispered sharply.

I didn't answer.

She stood looking outside again. The moon seemed to have bewitched the garden. The grass and the bushes appeared to have melted into one another, as if the moonlight had spread a fine silver netting over them. As I stood watching her in the moonlight I realized that she had changed. There was a seriousness to her face that was new, a harshness that I had never seen before. After a while she turned and, without waiting for me, she went back down the hall to her room.

Radha Aunty and Anil met each other the next Saturday at rehearsal. The week that had passed seemed to belong to another lifetime. The presence of the curfew and the sleepless nights in which every sound was a threat of danger seemed unreal. Towards the end of the week, however, the riots subsided in the rest of the country and it became clear that the trouble would never reach Colombo.

When we walked in through the gates of St. Theresa's, Anil was waiting for us. He stared at the bruises on Radha Aunty's face with a mixture of anger and tenderness.

"Does it still hurt?" he asked.

"Yes."

We began to walk towards the rehearsal hall.

"I came to see you, but you weren't there," Anil said.

Radha Aunty nodded, but she didn't give an explanation.

"Your sister seemed so angry at me that I thought it was best not to return."

Radha Aunty didn't respond. Anil glanced at her, and I wondered if he, too, had noticed that Radha Aunty had changed.

The rehearsals started late that day because the moment Radha Aunty came in, the cast and Aunty Doris crowded around her with exclamations of sympathy and horror over her wound. As Radha Aunty told her story, I noticed that Aunty Doris looked from her to Anil, a worried expression on her face. When Radha Aunty had finished, everyone was silent. Then Aunty Doris clapped her hands to indicate that it was time for the rehearsal to begin. The girl who played Tuptim was sick, and so Radha Aunty was asked to take her place for that day.

They were rehearsing one of the last scenes in the play, where Tuptim, the king's newest concubine, is captured while trying to run away with her lover. Anil played one of the guards who would bring in the slave girl. I was sitting on the steps by the stage, and from time to time I glanced at Anil and Radha Aunty in the wings. Anil was seated on a stool and he motioned to Radha Aunty to share the stool with him, but she shook her head. Anil looked at her, a little puzzled. When it was time for the guards to bring in Tuptim, Anil and the other actor took Radha Aunty by the arms. At their cue, they brought Radha Aunty in and threw her to the ground. As she fell on the floor, Radha Aunty exclaimed out loud, then sat up, rubbing her elbow.

"What's wrong?" Aunty Doris called out.

Radha Aunty glanced angrily at Anil and said to Aunty

Doris, "I was thrown too hard against the floor."

The other cast members looked at the guards and especially at Anil. Somebody said, "For God's sake be careful. The girl is bruised enough."

"Aday," another one said, "this is not Jaffna, you know."

At this remark, everyone in the cast laughed.

Anil crouched down next to Radha Aunty, concern on his face. She stood up and walked off. When they went into the wings to make their entrance again, Anil tried to touch her hand, but she moved it away.

He looked at her for a long moment and then his expression changed.

After the scene was over, we rehearsed the march of the Siamese children. I was concentrating so hard on my cue that only after I had made my entrance, bowed to the English governess, and gone to my position on the stage did I notice that Radha Aunty was no longer with the other Siamese wives. I glanced across the stage and saw that Anil had not left. He caught me watching him, and he frowned slightly as if asking where Radha Aunty had gone. I shrugged to say I didn't know.

We rehearsed the scene three or four times, and still Radha Aunty didn't return. When we were finished, I ran down off the stage and out of the rehearsal hall. An actor was seated on a bench outside the hall. I asked him if he had seen Radha Aunty, and he nodded and pointed in the direction of the toilets. I went down a passage that led from the courtyard to the toilets. Radha Aunty was not there. Then I heard a sound from behind the wall of a classroom across the way. I crept around the corner and saw Radha Aunty sitting on the edge of the classroom verandah. She was crying. When she saw me she quickly brushed her hand across her face and said angrily, "What are you doing here?"

"I was searching for you," I said meekly.

"Go away," she said and turned her head away.

I just stood there.

"Are you deaf?" she cried at me.

I turned and left. In the passageway I heard footsteps approaching. Then Anil appeared. When he saw me, he stopped. "Where is she?" he asked.

I shook my head.

He regarded me carefully and then strode past. I turned and followed him.

When Radha Aunty saw him, she rubbed her face against her sleeve and stared ahead. Anil stood in front of her for a moment. Then he sighed and rubbed his forehead. He noticed that I was looking at them and he said sternly, "Go back to the rehearsal hall."

The expression on his face was serious, and I felt suddenly frightened. I turned away and went back towards the hall.

When Radha Aunty returned later, rehearsals had already finished. Anil was no longer with her.

Aunty Doris was walking slowly around the hall, closing windows and picking up scripts. Radha Aunty began to close the windows on her side of the hall. When Aunty Doris heard her shut the first window, she turned in surprise in our direction. Then a slight frown appeared on her face. She turned back to continue closing up the room. For a while all that could be heard was the slamming of the windows and the click of the latches, the sound echoing in the empty hall. Radha Aunty and Aunty Doris worked their way around the hall, until they met at the last window.

"I want to be let out of the show," Radha Aunty said, not looking at her.

Aunty Doris nodded. "I'm sorry, child."

After a moment she closed the last window, clicking the bolts into place. It was then that the full implication of what had happened came to me. It was so clear now that I was surprised I had not seen it before, that I had not understood the moment I saw Radha Aunty with that bloody bandage around her head that her relationship with Anil was over.

Radha Aunty walked towards the door. "Come," she said to me. "It's time to go."

She left the hall and started to walk ahead of me towards the gates. I trailed after her, feeling a terrible sadness grow in me. When I reached the gate she was already halfway up the road and I had to hurry to catch up with her. At the bus stop I stood under the awning with the other passengers. Radha Aunty, however, stood at the edge of the pavement, glancing down Galle Road, her head tilted back slightly. She stood tall and straight, her hands behind her. A bus appeared and she held out her hand, commanding it to halt. It came to a stop and we got in and sat down. The bus began to move again, taking us in the direction of my grandparents' house.

Rajan Nagendra was engaged to Radha Aunty on Appachi's birthday. There was great excitement in the air that evening.

I sensed this from the way all the relatives in my grandparents' garden turned to look at us expectantly when we came in, thinking we might be the Nagendras. Radha Aunty was in her room. All the aunts and other female relatives had crowded in, and I went and stood with them. She was seated in front of her mirror while Kanthi Aunty arranged jasmines in her hair. Her hair had been pulled back and made into an elaborate coiffure on top of her head, and her face had been carefully made up so that she looked a few shades lighter. She wore a dark green Manipuri sari with a gold border. As I looked at her, I saw that she now resembled the Radha Aunty I had first imagined. But as she glanced at me and then away, I saw that her eyes had lost their warmth.

There was a whispering at the door and Mala Aunty came in a little breathless. "The Nagendras have arrived," she said. A flutter of excitement passed through the room. For a moment, there was a look of panic on Radha Aunty's face. Then her expression became impassive.

"My! He's absolutely charming," Mala Aunty whispered to one of the other aunts.

We followed Radha Aunty as she made her way down the corridor. All the relatives had come in from the garden to watch the proceedings. The cousins, too, were there. Rajan Nagendra stood up when she came into the drawing room. He had a tall, powerful physique and strong features, and I could see why Mala Aunty had described him as charming. A hush descended over the entire party.

"Hello," Rajan Nagendra said and extended his hand to her. "How are you?"

"I'm fine," she replied, and shook his hand.

He presented his parents to her, and she shook hands with

them as well. The pastor, who was seated next to Appachi, stepped forward. Then one of the aunts brought the rings on a cushion for him to bless.

As the pastor began his prayer, I gazed at Radha Aunty and Rajan Nagendra and thought of the first time I had heard about the marriage proposal, how I had looked around this drawing room and imagined it transformed by the preparations for the wedding, the buying of the sari, the making of the confetti, the wrapping of the cake, the pala harams and jasmine garlands. I knew that soon all this would come to pass, that I would find myself in the midst of that family wedding I had so longed to be a part of. But I felt no pleasure, for I knew that although everything would happen in the way I had dreamed, there would be something important missing.

The pastor now instructed Rajan Nagendra to place the ring on Radha Aunty's finger. Suddenly I couldn't bear to watch the ceremony. I turned away and walked down the corridor towards the kitchen, not quite knowing where I was going.

Ultimately I found myself in the back garden, the one in which only a few months ago I had played bride-bride. The girls had forgotten to take down the altar from the last time they had played, and it looked bedraggled now from a recent rainfall. The garlands of araliyas had come undone and lay broken and crushed on the ground. I thought of bride-bride and all those elaborate ceremonies I had invented, how I had thought that weddings could not be anything but magical occasions. How distant that time seemed, a world I had left far behind.

Inside the kitchen, Janaki was pounding something with

the mol gaha. As I listened to its rhythmic sound, I thought of her love comics and how fervently I had believed in them; believed that if two people loved each other everything was possible. Now, I knew that this was not so. I sat on the steps, resting my chin on my hands, and looked out at the garden. I stayed like that for a long time, as the mol gaha pounded away monotonously in the kitchen.

See No Evil, Hear No Evil

—◆—

I became aware of something new in our lives when my parents began to go out regularly to cocktail parties, dinner parties, and dances at the Oberoi Supper Club. They had new friends, too, Sena Uncle and Chithra Aunty, and it was with them that they went on these evenings out.

Also, every Saturday afternoon Amma and Chithra Aunty would take Diggy, Sonali, me, and Sanath, Chithra Aunty's son, to the Intercontinental Coffee Shop and treat us to such exotic food as hamburgers and strawberry cake. Then we would go shopping at Cornell's Supermarket. Cornell's had opened up recently and was the first American-style supermarket in Sri Lanka. It was a wonderful place, for there on the shelves were items like blueberry jam, kippers, and canned apricots—things I had read about when I was younger in Famous Five and Nancy Drew books but had never actually tasted. From listening to my father's conversations, I understood that this sudden availability of imported goods had to do with the new government and something called "free economy" and "the end of socialism."

One Sunday, my parents took Diggy, Sonali, and me south to spend the day by the sea. Sena Uncle, Chithra Aunty, and Sanath came along in their own car.

I was thrilled at the prospect of a day spent swimming and picnicking on the beach. When we had piled into the car, however, I noticed that there was no picnic basket in the back. I asked Amma where she had put the basket, and in response both she and my father laughed as if they had a secret. "Those picnic basket days are over," my father said, but would not say any more.

I was even more puzzled when, instead of parking by the road in our favorite spot, my father drove on till we came to a series of hotels. We had often looked at these hotels wistfully, knowing that we would never be able to afford to stay in any of them. Now, much to my amazement, my father brought the car to a stop in front of one of them. The hotel was still under construction, and above the gate a sign said PARADISE BEACH RESORT. The gatekeeper saluted us smartly as if he knew my father. Then he opened the barrier for us. Once we were inside the grounds, I saw that a section of the hotel was complete. When the cars stopped in front of this section, a man came hurrying down the steps to greet us. My father introduced him to Amma as the manager, Mr. Samar-akoon. Sonali pulled at my hand to come with her and ex-plore. Together we went up the steps, along the open hall, and out to the sea. It was the most beautiful stretch of beach I had ever seen. The sand was white and soft and the sea calm. When we had washed our feet and were making our way up the beach, Sonali said to me, "You know what? This hotel is our hotel."

I stared at her. "Who told you that?" I asked.

"I heard Amma and Appa talking about it."

I shook my head in disbelief.

"Ask Amma and see," she replied.

We were close to the hotel now, and I saw that everyone else was seated at a table on the verandah. When we reached my parents, I said to them, "Is this hotel ours?"

They looked at me, amused.

"Yes," my father said, "part of it is."

"Really?" I said. "This is really ours?"

Everyone began to laugh at my astonishment. Then Amma explained to me that my father did not work for the bank anymore. He had gone into the hotel business and Sena Uncle was his partner.

Our affluence seemed to reach a new height when my father announced that he was going to Europe to promote the hotel and also to take a holiday. He would be gone for a few months, and we were told to give him a list of five things we each wanted him to bring back for us.

Recently, I had found a yellowed copy of *Little Women*.

It belonged to Neliya Aunty, Amma's older sister. Neliya Aunty had come to live with us a year ago after Amma's mother had died. Neliya Aunty had never married and my parents felt she should not be living alone. Though she wasn't much older than Amma, she seemed to belong more to my grandparents' generation than my parents'. This was reflected in her clothes, for, unlike Amma, who wore everything from saris to dresses to pants, Neliya Aunty usually wore ankle-length housecoats at home and saris for going out. When she moved in, she had brought a large trunk that was full of photograph albums, letters, trinkets, and books, all of which smelt of camphor, and it was in this trunk that I discovered the book. I loved *Little Women* and longed to read the sequels but couldn't find them anywhere. I wondered if I dared ask my father to bring them for me. He had found me reading *Little Women* and declared it to be a book for girls, a book that boys should not be reading, especially a boy of twelve. After some hesitation, I wrote down the three sequels to *Little Women* as the fifth item.

Other than excitement about what he would bring us upon his return, we experienced little emotion at our father's departure. Even Amma did not seem overly sad. In fact, after he had left, she always seemed in a good mood. Now she began to go out every night with Chithra Aunty and her friends. The next morning she would tell Neliya Aunty about a fashion show or dance or party and how she had been introduced to different ministers and even, once, to the old prime minister, Mrs. Bandaranaike, who was looking "haggard, poor thing, now that she has been deprived of her civic rights." One day, after she had been to a particularly entertaining fashion show the previous night, Amma declared, "Everything is wonderful! Who would have thought, a few years ago, that things would turn out so well!"

Then, as if to contradict her optimism, Daryl Uncle entered our lives.

I had developed a slight fever that day and had been kept home from school. By early afternoon, however, I was feeling better. Amma had gone shopping, and Neliya Aunty allowed me to sit in an easy chair on the front verandah with my copy of *Little Women*. I was soon lost in the book. The sound of the gate opening brought me back to reality, however, and I looked up to find a white man standing inside the gate. As he walked towards me, we surveyed each other. The stranger was tall and powerfully built, and he had a beard and mustache. He came up the verandah steps and asked if my mother was in. I replied that she was not. After a moment, I stood up, went to the front door, and called out to Neliya Aunty in Sinhalese, so he wouldn't understand, that there was a white man here to see us. The man laughed and said, in perfect Sinhalese, "This is no white man you are looking at."

I stared at him, wondering how he spoke Sinhalese. He grinned back at me, enjoying my astonishment.

I was even more taken aback by Neliya Aunty's reaction when she came out onto the verandah. She stared at him in shock for a moment, then let out a cry of joy and went to him, holding out her arms, and they embraced each other, laughing. Then they noticed my surprise and laughed even harder. "Arjie," Neliya Aunty said to me, "come here. This is Daryl Uncle, one of our oldest and dearest friends."

I presented my hand, and as Daryl Uncle shook it and

leaned down to kiss me on both cheeks, I smelt the sweet odor of tobacco.

I learned that they had lived next door to each other from the time they were children. Daryl Uncle had been in Australia and was returning after fifteen years.

Neliya Aunty began to ask Daryl Uncle questions about himself. He told her that he worked as a journalist in Australia and he was here on a two-month vacation. Then they began to talk about their childhood together. As I listened to them, I realized that Daryl Uncle was not a white man but a Burgher, the same as Aunty Doris.

Neliya Aunty seemed cheerful and happy to see him, until she heard Amma's car at the gate. Then, suddenly, she became nervous as if she had done something wrong. Daryl Uncle, too, became uneasy. Our servant, Anula, ran to open the gate, and the car came in. Amma was trying to reach the garage without knocking over the flower pots that lined the driveway, and she did not even notice us on the front verandah. When she had parked the car, she came around the side of the house expectantly, since Anula had probably informed her that we had a white visitor. When she saw Daryl Uncle she stood still and stared at him, her eyes wide.

He rose from his chair slowly and said, "Nalini, how are you?"

"Daryl?" she said, as if she had just awakened from a sleep and was not sure if he was part of her dream world or her waking world.

There was a moment of silence as they looked at each other, then Amma recovered herself. She came up the steps to him, and rather than embracing him in the way Neliya

Aunty had, she pointed hospitably to the chair he had been sitting in and said, "Come, come, sit, sit." Then she excused herself and went inside to put down her parcels.

While Amma was inside, Daryl Uncle and Neliya Aunty tried to pick up their conversation again. I looked at Daryl Uncle with interest and found myself wondering why Neliya Aunty and Amma had shown such different reactions to him. I had never seen Amma so unprepared, so caught off guard.

In a few moments, Amma came out, and she was composed. She lifted her eyebrows ironically and said to Daryl Uncle, "Goodness, what a surprise."

Daryl Uncle laughed and said, "I always liked surprising you."

Amma smiled and sat down. I looked at her and was aware that I knew very little of her life before my first conscious memory of her.

A short while later, Sonali and Diggy returned from school. When they saw our visitor they stared at him, surprised as I had been to find a foreigner in our house. Amma called them to be introduced, and they approached shyly.

"This is Daryl Uncle," she said. They looked at her, a little taken aback that Amma was referring to a foreigner as "Uncle."

"He grew up next door to Neliya Aunty and me," Amma added, noticing their expressions. "He's a Sri Lankan, just like us."

That evening my fever got worse, and Amma sat on the side of my bed holding a compress of ice and eau de cologne on my forehead. I felt sorry to see the expression of concern on her face, a worry no doubt compounded by my father's absence. I closed my eyes and pretended to sleep, so that she would think I was feeling better and go to bed herself.

Not long after I closed my eyes, I heard the door to my room open and someone come in.

"How is he?" Neliya Aunty whispered.

"Better, I think," Amma replied.

They were silent for a while, then Neliya Aunty said in a low voice, "I didn't know what to do when Daryl came today. I was worried because of you-know-what."

Amma sighed, impatient with Neliya Aunty. "That was a long time ago," she replied. "It's all water under the bridge now."

Once they had gone, I lay awake thinking about their conversation. Something had happened between Amma and Daryl Uncle in the past. It sounded like they had fought at one time and this fight had created a rift between them.

When I awoke the next morning, my fever had abated, and I was no longer sure if the conversation I had heard was real or if it had been a product of my mind. Certainly Amma seemed completely herself, as if Daryl Uncle's visit had left no impression on her.

That morning Daryl Uncle came to see us again. As on the day before, I was seated on the verandah, reading. Rather than asking for Amma, he came up the steps and inquired about what I was reading. I hesitated before I held out the book to him, remembering how my father had called it a girl's book, a book that twelve-year-old boys should not be reading.

"*Little Women,*" he said warmly. "Used to be one of my favorite books."

I looked at him in surprise.

"Have you read the sequels?"

I shook my head. "I can't find them anywhere."

He thought about this for a moment and then said, "The secondhand bookshops might have them. I'm going in the direction of Maradana today, so I'll stop off and take a look."

Before I could thank him properly, Amma came out onto the verandah, having heard voices. She stopped in the doorway when she saw Daryl Uncle.

"I was just passing by and thought I'd drop in to say hello," he said.

Amma invited him to sit down. She seemed neither pleased nor displeased to see him. She placed a hand on my forehead, declared that my fever had returned, and ordered me to bed. I protested so vehemently that finally she relented and allowed me to lie on the sofa in the drawing room. I could hear them talking through the window.

After they had been on the verandah for only a few minutes, I heard them raise their voices. They were arguing about politics, and I learned that there was a war going on now in Jaffna, between the army and the Tamil Tigers, who were fighting for a separate state. War, to me, signified guns and soldiers and armored cars, and I had seen no evidence of this in Colombo. Amma, even though she was a Tamil, thought the Tigers were wrong, that they were nothing but terrorists and they were giving other Tamils a bad name. Daryl Uncle said that he understood why young men were joining the Tigers. He spoke of torture. My knowledge of torture was confined to Gothic novels in which people were stretched on racks until their limbs tore away from their bodies. The torture Daryl Uncle spoke of seemed a homegrown variety which included chilies and large red ants. Amma didn't believe him when he told her this. This government was not like the old one, she said. Besides, how could this be going on and the press remain silent about it, especially now that there was "freedom of the press"? I learned that Daryl Uncle had found out this information from a European woman who was here to study the problem. He wanted to investigate if this was true and do an article for his newspaper. Amma said he was wasting his time and he would find nothing.

They also disagreed about something called the Prevention of Terrorism Act. This, I gathered, was a new law that allowed the police and the army to arrest anybody they thought might be a terrorist without something called a warrant. Amma thought it was a good thing, but Daryl Uncle called it a "tool for state terrorism."

Neliya Aunty came into the drawing room, drawn by the sound of their voices. She saw me and asked in a whisper who was outside. When I told her, she folded her arms, and the expression on her face was the same as when somebody told a crude joke. As I looked at her, I realized that I had not imagined the conversation between her and Amma the night before. She stood for a while and listened, then she twitched the palu of her sari around her waist and returned to the kitchen. The voices outside had got even louder. Fearing now that Amma would be really rude and that Daryl Uncle would not return and I would never get my books, I called out in my best invalid voice, "Ammaaa."

She came immediately, her face flushed from the argument. Daryl Uncle put his head in through the door as well and asked if everything was all right. Amma placed her hand on my forehead and ordered me to bed in a no-nonsense voice. I wrapped my sheet around me and went off to my bedroom, since I really was beginning to feel worse. Just before I went into my room, however, I was surprised to hear Amma ask Daryl Uncle to stay for lunch. I was completely confused now about whether she liked Daryl Uncle or not.

Once Daryl Uncle had left, I heard Neliya Aunty say crossly to Amma, "I hope he stops visiting us like this. It's most improper with no man in the house."

Amma laughed. "Honestly, Neliya," she said. "How old-fashioned of you."

"I don't think it's nice. People will begin to talk."

"It's not as if he were a stranger," Amma said.

I was now puzzled by Neliya Aunty. I wondered what Daryl Uncle had said or done that had made her suddenly so against him. For my part, my feelings about Daryl Uncle were clear. I liked him, and not merely because he had offered to buy me those books.

My fever went up alarmingly that evening and my head felt so heavy that I could hardly lift it. Amma sat by my bed with the cold compress, and I could tell from the tender expression on her face that she was really worried.

"Amma," I said to her and held her hand.

"Yes," she said, stroking my hair.

"Why don't you and Neliya Aunty like Daryl Uncle?" Her hand became still.

"Why would you think that?" she asked.

I didn't answer.

"I do like him," she said. "We just have different opinions."

"Such as?"

"He thinks things are getting worse in Sri Lanka and I think things are getting better."

After a moment I said, "I like him."

"You do?" She seemed a little surprised.

That night, my sickness took a real turn for the worse and I began to have terrible bouts of vomiting. By morning, I was so feeble that I had to be helped to the bathroom. I could tell that Amma was quite concerned. She called Mala Aunty at her dispensary and asked her to come by and look at me.

I was falling asleep when I heard Daryl Uncle's voice. Presently he appeared in the doorway of my room. I opened my eyes and tried to smile at him.

He came in softly, his hands behind his back. "I have something for you," he said, and laid the books on the blanket. I cried out in delight, and one by one I picked up *Good Wives*, *Little Men*, and *Jo's Boys*. I wanted to reach out and hug him, but, feeling that this was inappropriate, I thanked him instead.

I noticed Amma standing in the doorway. She was looking at Daryl Uncle and there was an expression on her face I had never seen before.

Mala Aunty diagnosed my illness as infectious hepatitis. For the next two weeks I was very sick, and the days and nights seemed to dissolve into each other. Now and then I would

hear Daryl Uncle's voice in the hall outside, and once he sat
by my bed, holding the cold compress to my forehead.

Gradually, I became conscious of the passing of the hours
and when it was time to eat or go to the toilet. I grew more
aware of the people around me, too, and I was quick to realize
that many things had changed while I was sick. First, Daryl
Uncle had become a frequent visitor to our house. He often
spent time in my room, reading to me from one of the books
he had bought. I noticed that something had altered between
Amma and him. They spoke to each other with fewer words
and more gestures, just as Neliya Aunty and Amma did. I also
observed that on many mornings Amma dressed up in her
smartest pants suits and left the house, not returning until it
was time for Sonali and Diggy to come home from school.
She seemed very different these days, happy but strangely
nervous. Neliya Aunty, however, seemed to be in a very bad
mood, and her anger was directed mainly at Amma.

Sonali and Diggy had changed, too. Sonali had become
secretive, as if she had done something very bad, and she spent
a lot of time in her room, drawing with her felt-tip pens.
Diggy had grown morose and would spend hours in the
driveway with his air gun, shooting at an old condensed-milk
tin he set up as a target.

In the next week, both Neliya Aunty and Diggy became
increasingly sullen. Then, to my astonishment, they became
rude to Daryl Uncle, and finally he started coming less fre-
quently. Neliya Aunty never went out to greet him anymore,
and when he visited she would retire to the back verandah to
help Anula with the cooking.

Finally the situation reached a head when Diggy turned

his target practice on the neighbors' chickens. One Saturday morning, we heard the sound of his gun followed by the squawking of the hens. I went to my window and was just in time to see Amma yelling at Diggy to come down off the wall. When he did, she took him by the arm and shook him, shouting, "I've had enough! How much can I tolerate?"

It was then that Amma decided to take me away to convalesce in the hill country. I was overjoyed when I heard this. It was already May, the monsoon had not arrived, and the heat in Colombo was unbearable.

The bungalow we had rented surpassed all my expectations. It was on top of a hill, and once we had put our bags in our rooms we stood on the back verandah and looked down over the terraced garden. The garden was beautiful, with triangular and circular flower beds that contained an assortment of flowers which grew only in the hills. The garden bordered on a tea estate, and for miles below us we could see, like a green carpet, the tidy foliage of the tea bushes.

The best part was that I was going to have Amma all to myself. The only other person in the bungalow was a cook, and she left by early afternoon. It was a glorious day. After lunch and a nap, we sat in the garden and played Scrabble and ludo until the sun set. Then we went inside and ate dinner in contented silence, listening to the crickets and the call of the nightjar outside.

The next day, I was standing in the front garden in the shade of a fir tree when I saw a man walking up the hill towards the house. Even though he was quite a distance away, I knew soon enough that it was Daryl Uncle. I stared down at him, surprised, wondering what he was doing here. Then, as I watched him, I felt a sudden rush of disappointment and resentment. My bliss was to be disturbed, for I knew that the moment he entered our house I would no longer have Amma's entire attention. Daryl Uncle had seen me now, and he waved to me. I didn't wave back. When he was close enough he must have seen the expression in my eyes, because he said, "Are you all right?"

The friendly smile and the look of concern on his face reminded me of the day he had brought me those books, of how he had read to me while I was sick and had sat by my bed, holding a cold compress to my forehead. Much against my will, I felt my disappointment at seeing him begin to dwindle a little. He held out his hand to me, and I took it as we began to go up the driveway. When Amma opened the front door, she didn't seem at all surprised to see him.

Later that evening we were having tea out on the lawn when I said to him, "Why aren't there many Burghers in Sri Lanka, Uncle?"

He was sprawled out on the grass in front of Amma and me. Both he and Amma laughed.

"When the government made Sinhala the national language in the nineteen fifties many of them left because they only spoke English," he explained.

"Are they English?"

"No. Their ancestors were Dutch, but people sometimes treated them as if they were English, especially after Independence."

Daryl Uncle looked a little sad at this, and, to cheer him up and make him laugh, I said with false naiveté, "If they had married Sri Lankans, they would have been real Sri Lankans, no?"

Instead of amusing him, my remark only made him seem more sad.

"It was not that easy," he said as he studied his teacup, which sat on the grass. "Some Sri Lankan people thought Burgher people were too white to marry their children, and some Burgher people thought Sri Lankan people were too brown to marry theirs." I noticed that Amma and he were looking at each other, and for a moment, I felt as if they were no longer aware of my presence. I found myself observing his high cheekbones and the glints of gold in his brown beard, his thighs and the way they changed color at the edge of his shorts, and his gentle, courteous manner, which seemed to ease something inside Amma, softening her sharp edges. I couldn't help comparing him to my father, who, with his balding head, thin legs, slight paunch, and abrupt way of talking to Amma, cut a poor figure next to him.

Daryl Uncle was with us all the time. At night, when I went to bed, I could hear the murmur of their voices on the front verandah. Yet when I woke in the morning Daryl Uncle was never there. He would always come up to the house after breakfast. He made me laugh a lot and usually included me in his conversations with Amma. Also, Amma was happier than I ever remembered her being, and this made her even more kind and loving towards me.

Then, on the night before we left for Colombo, Daryl Uncle and Amma had an argument. When I heard their raised voices, I got out of bed and leaned out of my window, which opened onto the side garden. The cause of the argument seemed to be that Daryl Uncle was going to Jaffna for a week, the day after we got back to Colombo.

"Are you mad?" Amma shouted at him. "There is fighting going on there."

"Nothing will happen to me," Daryl Uncle said. "Neither the army nor the Tigers care about someone who looks like a foreigner."

"You're putting your life at risk for nothing," Amma insisted.

"It's not nothing," Daryl Uncle said. "People are being tortured and killed even as we sit in all this opulence."

"Rubbish," Amma said. "Absolute rubbish."

"How can you be so callous?"

"You're the one who's callous," she cried. Then her voice became tearful. "What about us? We have so little time left."

"You know I'll come back," Daryl Uncle said, his voice softening.

"If you care for me, you'll stay."

He was silent for a moment. Then he said firmly, "I love you, but I have to go. I must do it."

"You'll find nothing in Jaffna," she said quietly now, as if defeated.

"I hope to God you're right," he replied.

I shut my window, then leaned my head against the pane, feeling the world spinning around me. Moments from the time Daryl Uncle came into our lives revealed their significance to me, and I understood what he was doing here and why Amma had taken me away to convalesce. I felt a cold chill of fear as I realized that I was an unwitting accomplice in this scheme for Daryl Uncle and her to spend time together, away from the family. I thought of my father and felt my dread deepen. What would happen if he found out? Surely they would have to be divorced. I recalled Mr. and Mrs. Siriwardena down our road and what a terrible disgrace their separation had been. How the neighbors had talked about Mr. Siriwardena and his running away with the next-door servant woman; how people on our road stared at Mrs. Siriwardena when she passed them, and sometimes even laughed openly at her. Their son had been in my class, and the boys had teased him until he cried.

I shuddered at the idea of these things happening to our family. Not wanting to think about all this anymore, I went to my bed and lay down. I finally fell asleep in the early hours of the morning and dreamed that we were the little women. Amma was Jo, the tomboy, Neliya Aunty was Meg, Sonali was Amy, I was Beth, the sick one, and Daryl Uncle was Laurie, the boy next door who was in love with Jo. It was Christmas, and all us little women were longing for our father to come home.

The next day the monsoon broke. Daryl Uncle had left on the early-morning train and so he didn't come up to the house. I was glad of this.

Amma and I waited for the taxi that would take us to the station. The rain was falling in sheets of water and the living room, usually so bright and cheerful, appeared gloomy in the gray light, the colors of the upholstered chairs faded. Amma sat on a sofa and stared at the carpet. As I looked at her, I remembered my happiness on our first afternoon here, what a good time I had imagined we would have together. Now

I wondered if all she had thought about was the next day, when Daryl Uncle would arrive.

Finally the taxi came and we picked up our bags and went slowly to the door.

When we reached Colombo, Neliya Aunty, Sonali, and Diggy were waiting for us at the Fort railway station. It was peculiar to see them standing there waving cheerfully at us. Sonali and Neliya Aunty hugged me tightly. Even Diggy seemed in an exceptionally good mood, for he patted me on the back and showed me the skin of a squirrel he had shot. As I listened to them telling Amma and me about the things they had done while we were away, I felt a terrible sense of distance from them.

When we got home, there was a letter on the hall table. It was from my father. Amma glanced at it. Then, without opening it, she put it in her bag.

⸺⬖⸺

I began school the next day. After such a long period of freedom, school, with its rigid timetables, cantankerous teachers, and irritating boys, should have been unbearable, but it was a relief. Amma was to pick me up after school for the next few weeks because I was not considered well enough to cycle home with Diggy.

That afternoon Amma arrived at the school with Daryl Uncle. Seeing him made me feel a sense of dread. As I got into the car, I could tell that they had been fighting. Daryl

Uncle gave me a slight smile and Amma looked straight ahead of her. We drove in silence to Daryl Uncle's house. He lived on a street in Bambalapitiya. His house was the last one on the road, and beyond it were the railway tracks and the sea. When Amma stopped the car, Daryl Uncle tried to touch her arm, but she moved it away.

After a moment he said, "I'll be back in a week." Then he got out of the car and I climbed into the front seat. Daryl Uncle stood at his gate and waved, but neither of us waved back. Amma turned the car around, the tires squealing slightly, and drove back up the road. When we reached the top of the road, I looked back and saw that Daryl Uncle was still standing at his gate.

After a while I said to Amma, "So Daryl Uncle is going to Jaffna?"

She looked at me, shocked, and I glanced away from her quickly. When we arrived at our house, Neliya Aunty was sitting on the front verandah doing some sewing. Amma parked the car and went hurriedly past her to her room. When I came up the steps, Neliya Aunty beckoned to me furiously and asked in a whisper, "What happened?"

"What?" I said, very loud, as if I were deaf.

"Shh," she replied crossly and picked up her sewing again.

Now that Daryl Uncle was gone, Amma returned to her old routines, but without her earlier enthusiasm. She renewed her friendship with Chithra Aunty and started to go out every night to parties, fashion shows, and dances. A week passed, and Daryl Uncle didn't come to visit us. Amma pretended she had not noticed, but once, when the doorbell rang, she straightened up expectantly and sent me to see who it was.

Then one evening, while Amma was at a party, we heard on the radio that trouble had broken out in Jaffna. A policeman had been killed by the Tamil Tigers and the police had gone on a rampage. They had burned the headquarters of the opposition party, the Tamil United Liberation Front, as well as the house of a member of Parliament. As I listened to what was happening there, a frightening thought entered my mind, an idea that had not occurred to me before. Was it possible Daryl Uncle was still in Jaffna, and that was the reason he had not come to see us? The image this possibility suggested was terrifying. I longed for Amma to come home so that I could share my fears with her and have them dispelled.

I waited for her on the unlit front verandah. Finally, I heard a car pull up outside our gate and Chithra Aunty bid Amma good night. When Amma saw me, she paused and then came up the verandah steps.

"Why aren't you in bed?" she asked.

I looked at her for a moment. "There's trouble in Jaffna. A lot of people have been killed."

She drew in her breath and stared at me.

"Amma," I said, "I wonder if Daryl Uncle is still in Jaffna."

The expression on her face changed to fear.

"No," she said, "that can't be." Then, as if she doubted her own words, she said, "Oh, son, do you really think so?"

I didn't reply.

She pulled up a chair and sat down shakily, then she looked out at the garden for a long while. "I'm sure he's back," she finally said.

See No Evil, Hear No Evil

★ ★ ★

The next day, after school, Amma was waiting for me. As I got into the car, I saw the expression on her face and felt afraid. "The Jaffna library was burned by the police this morning. Ninety-five thousand books were set on fire." She started the car. "I want to go to his house and see if he's there."

We knocked on the takaran-covered gate and waited. A dog began to bark furiously from inside the house, and presently we heard the sound of footsteps coming towards us. I listened, trying to make out if they were Daryl Uncle's. Then a boyish voice asked, in Sinhalese, who we were. "It's me," Amma replied.

The servant boy seemed to recognize Amma's voice, for he opened the gate promptly. He was about sixteen years old and he wore a sarong and a shirt.

"Where is the mahataya?" Amma asked.

"He's not in," he replied.

"Did he come back from Jaffna?"

The servant boy shook his head.

"Did he . . . did he send a message for me?" Amma asked.

The servant boy looked at the ground and shook his head again.

"Maybe . . . he left a note," Amma said.

The servant boy kicked at the sand and shrugged.

Amma told me to follow her inside, and as we passed the servant boy, he looked at us quickly and I saw that he, too, was afraid.

The house was large, and all its doors and windows were closed. Rather than going to the front door, Amma hurried around the side of the house. I now saw that Daryl Uncle lived in an annex attached to the house. When we reached the door to the annex, Amma opened her bag, took out a key, and inserted it in the lock. Before she could turn the key, however, the door swung open of its own accord. We paused at the entrance, afraid to go in.

"Hello," Amma called tentatively. "Hello."

Nobody answered.

"Stay here," Amma said to me. "If I cry out, run for help."

She stepped hesitantly inside. I stood at the door, the sound of my heart thudding in my ears. I could hear Amma moving around. Then she cried out.

"Amma?" I called in a panic. "Amma?"

"Son," she called to me, in a low, urgent voice, "come quick."

I went inside and found her standing in the doorway to a room. It was Daryl Uncle's bedroom, and as I looked in, I understood why she had cried out. The room was a mess. The dresser drawers lay on the bed and the floor, their contents strewn all over. A glass had been knocked over, and there was a water mark on the night table.

"What's happened?" I asked.

"I don't know," she replied, and continued to look around the room. After a moment she said, "Come. Let's go."

As we passed the front door of the main house, she paused as if she was going to knock on the door and speak to the servant boy. Then she changed her mind and hurried down the driveway to the gate.

When we were inside the car, Amma said, "Don't tell anyone about this, you hear?"

I nodded.

She thought about what she had said for a moment and then added, "But we should tell Neliya Aunty, I guess."

We looked at each other. I was dreading it as much as she was.

When Amma had finished telling her, Neliya Aunty picked up her sewing and worked on it for a few moments. Her brows were furrowed in thought and her hands shook slightly. Finally, she put her sewing down and said to Amma, "Why don't you wait a few more days and see."

We stared at her in amazement.

"There's no proof that anything has happened," she said.

"But what about the state of the room?" Amma asked.

"You realize the consequences if you do go to the police," Neliya Aunty said. "Awkward questions might be asked."

Amma looked down at her hands.

"After all, it's possible that he stayed in Jaffna a few extra days," Neliya Aunty continued.

"Why wouldn't he have contacted me, then?"

Neliya Aunty broke off the thread and tied the end. "Be careful, Nalini," she said. "Society is not as forgiving as a sister is. You have a husband and three children to think about."

She picked up her sewing basket and went inside. In spite of her saying that nothing had happened, I could tell that she, too, was worried. I glanced at Amma inquiringly, but she was staring at her hands as if thinking over what Neliya Aunty had said. Finally, she got up and, without looking at me, she went to her room.

That evening I found it difficult to concentrate on my

homework. All I could think about was Daryl Uncle and the state in which we had found his bedroom. I recalled the conversation I had overheard the second time he visited us. I shivered slightly when I thought of the way he had described torture, how the victims were hung upside down and made to breathe chili fumes, how honey was spread over their bodies and red ants allowed to eat at them.

After school the next day, Amma was waiting for me as usual.

"I've made a decision," she said as she started up the car. "We're going to the police station."

I looked at her skeptically, thinking about the behavior of the policemen in Jaffna.

"I know," she said. "But what choice do we have? I don't know where else to go."

The police station was busier than I thought it would be. After being misdirected a few times we finally arrived at a counter. The policeman behind the counter studied us for a few moments, looking at our clothes and general demeanor to decide what treatment to give us. Fortunately, Amma's Sinhalese was good.

"I am here about a friend who's been missing for a few days," she said.

"Where does he live?" the policeman asked brusquely. He had decided to give us the more courteous treatment.

"Bambalapitiya."

"Then you must go to the Bambalapitiya station," he replied.

Amma was silent. Then she said, "Well, he doesn't really live there. He's a white man."

At the words "white man" the policeman's attitude immediately changed and he became more helpful. He took out a form and began to ask Amma questions. Amma had to re-spell Daryl Uncle's name several times before he got it right. While she was doing this, I noticed that another policeman, who was seated at a desk behind the counter, was listening. After a few moments, he got up, came to the counter, and asked the other policeman what was going on. The behavior of the policeman at the counter showed that the other policeman was his superior. The superior officer picked up the paper, looked at it, and then asked Amma, in English, if he could help her. With the relief of a traveler who discovers a fellow countryman in a strange land, Amma told him rapidly how we had been to Daryl Uncle's house and about the state in which we had found it. She told him Daryl Uncle was in Jaffna, but acted ignorant as to what he was doing there. He asked her to wait. Then he took the form and went into an office that was behind the counter. He bent down and said something in an urgent manner to the policeman in the office. The policeman looked at him sharply and then out at us. He saw that we were watching him and signaled to the other policeman to shut the door.

"What's happening?" Amma said to me in a frightened voice. "I don't like it at all."

Finally, the policeman who had spoken in English came out and motioned for us to come around the counter.

The policeman in the office rose to his feet when Amma came in and introduced himself as A.S.P. Weerasinghe. The A.S.P. was impeccably dressed, his hair well oiled, his mustache trim, and his khaki uniform well pressed. He was slightly overweight and his uniform curved over his rounded stomach. His manner was casual and friendly. "So, so," he said and smiled. "What's all this?" He indicated for Amma to be seated.

Amma repeated the story she had told the other policeman. He asked her what her relationship was to Daryl Uncle. Amma said that she had known him since they were children. He then asked her for Daryl Uncle's address. Once she had given it to him, he nodded to the other policeman, who left the room.

"I'm arranging for us to go and look at the place right now," he said.

Amma nodded gratefully.

"Don't worry, Mrs. Chelvaratnam. I'm sure it's much less serious than you think."

The A.S.P. looked the form over carefully. "I'll call some of our chaps in Jaffna and tell them to make inquiries about your friend."

Amma thanked him profusely for this.

The A.S.P. offered us a drive in the squadron car, but Amma declined, saying that she would follow in our car.

By the time we arrived at Daryl Uncle's house, the police cars were already parked outside. The servant boy opened the gate for us. He seemed frightened, and once he had shut the gate, he hurried into the house and closed the front door.

When the A.S.P. saw us, he waved cheerfully. "Where are the occupants of the main house?" he asked.

Amma told him that they were away in England for their daughter's confinement. Amma looked around the room. Then she turned to the A.S.P. and asked, "What do you think happened, Mr. Weerasinghe?"

"It's simply a case of break and enter, Mrs. Chelvaratnam," he replied.

"And what about my friend?"

"I suspect that your friend's absence and the state of the room are unrelated events."

Amma looked skeptical.

"What else could it be?" he asked.

"Well . . . you know, he is in Jaffna and everything," she said.

"But what would that have to do with the house being robbed?"

Amma said nothing.

He looked at her keenly. "Mrs. Chelvaratnam, if you are holding something back it will only impede us in finding both your friend and the culprit of this robbery."

Again she said nothing. Then she came to a decision. "I haven't told you everything," she said. "The reason he went to Jaffna was to look for evidence of torture and disappearances by . . . the police." She added quickly, "He's a journalist from Australia."

The A.S.P. smiled and lifted his eyebrows. "And you think he was killed by the police," he said, completing Amma's story.

Amma didn't answer but looked unhappy as if she realized how ridiculous her suspicions sounded.

"Mrs. Chelvaratnam," he said, "there is admittedly some misuse of power by the police, but never to the extent of torture."

Before Amma could reply, we heard the sound of a scuffle outside, followed by a shout. The dog began to bark hysterically inside the house. We turned quickly towards the door.

I could hear voices raised excitedly. The A.S.P. held up a
hand as if warning us to stay where we were.

A policeman appeared in the doorway, looking dishev-
eled. "Sir," he said. "Sir, we caught the servant boy trying to
run away. He had a suitcase with him, sir."

The A.S.P. looked nonplussed. Finally he said to the policeman, "Were there any valuables in the suitcase?"

The man shook his head.

The A.S.P. told him to bring the servant boy to him.
When the policeman had gone, the A.S.P. turned to Amma
and said, "I think we have the culprit."

The policemen brought the boy inside. They had his
hands pinned behind him in such a way that he was bent
over. He moved from side to side, struggling to escape their
grip. The A.S.P. signaled for them to release him. When the
boy straightened up and saw Amma, he threw himself down
at her feet. "Missie, missie," he cried, his voice fractured by
fear. "Help me, please! You know that I haven't done anything!"

He tried to kiss Amma's feet, but she moved back quickly.
The A.S.P. signaled to the policemen and they dragged the
boy away from Amma. They tried to bring him to his feet,
but he refused to stand. They left him kneeling on the ground,
his head bent, a lock of hair falling over his eyebrow. I glanced
at Amma to see if she was all right. She was staring at the boy
in distress.

"Boy," the A.S.P. said, "did you take anything from in
here?"

"No, sir," he replied. "I did nothing."

"Then why were you running away?"

The boy did not answer.

"I'm sure he's innocent," Amma said, pleading his case. "My friend always spoke highly of his honesty."

The A.S.P. smiled and said, "Now don't you fret yourself about him, Mrs. Chelvaratnam." He looked ruefully at the boy. "Unfortunately, dishonesty is instinctive for this class."

"He is different," Amma said. "In fact my friend told me that he would often leave money and valuables lying around and the boy never touched them."

"Then why was he trying to run away, madam?" he asked.

The boy was looking from Amma to the A.S.P., trying to understand their conversation from the expression on their faces. Now the A.S.P. waved his hand in the direction of the door. "Take him to the station," he said to the policemen. "We'll carry on our inquiry there."

The policemen gripped the boy's arms. He cried out and dug his heels into the ground. He called to Amma, begging her to save him. She took a step towards him but the A.S.P. put out his hand to stop her. He signaled angrily to the policemen to remove the boy. They tried to make him stand up. In the process his sarong came undone and fell to the floor, entangling his feet. The policemen lifted him above the sarong and dragged him, naked, around the side of the house.

Amma covered her face with her hands and shuddered. I felt my legs become weak and sat down quickly on the side of the bed. "Madam," the A.S.P. started to say, gently, but she turned away from him. He bowed slightly and left. Amma went to the window and stood there looking out at the sea. We could hear the dog crying forlornly inside the house. After

a while she turned to me and said, "I feel that boy is innocent." I looked at her, surprised by how sure she seemed
about this.

"I don't know how I know, but I just do." She waved
her hand to encompass all that had just happened. "This
whole thing seems wrong."

In the silence we could hear the sound of the police cars
starting up outside. I thought about the A.S.P. and how I had
immediately trusted him. He seemed like someone with
whom we would associate, like the kind of man with whom
my father would be friends. Now I wondered if Amma's in-
stinct was right and we had been mistaken to trust him.

That evening, my father called us from Europe. I was the
one who picked up the phone. The sound of his voice asking
how I was brought back all the dread I had felt on the night
I had heard Amma and Daryl Uncle arguing. At first I was
tongue-tied, too troubled to be able to answer his questions.
When I finally forced myself to speak, my voiced sounded
stilted, and I was glad to pass the receiver to Amma. I watched
her as she spoke to my father. Her face was impassive and her
voice normal, as if nothing unusual had happened in our lives.

The next day, when I got into the car after school, Amma
told me the A.S.P. had called her that morning. He wanted
to see us.

When we arrived at the police station, we were ushered
into his office immediately. He rose courteously and smiled,
gesturing at some chairs in front of his desk. He rang the bell
on his table and the tea boy arrived with two cups of tea.

The A.S.P. waved his hand and the tea boy served us.

"You know, madam," the A.S.P. said, still smiling, "I

have discovered a happy coincidence. I actually play squash with your husband from time to time."

Amma's teacup rattled slightly.

"I have always known him as Chelva, but never thought to connect him with your name. Then I saw your address on the form."

He looked at us merrily. "Small world, no?"

Amma gave him a faint smile. She put her cup down on the edge of his desk. "What about our friend?" she asked. "Have you been able to locate him?"

The A.S.P. sighed. "Unfortunately not. But we are working on it."

"Surely it can't take that long to trace a man who looks like a foreigner."

The A.S.P. wiped his forehead as if he was tired. "You know how it is, Mrs. Chelvaratnam. What with the terrorist bombings and bank robberies, our forces in Jaffna have their hands full." He leaned towards us. "They're trying their best. I have personally asked them to hurry it up a little."

Amma sighed, and her lips became thin with impatience.

The A.S.P. picked up a file from his desk and opened it. "We have questioned the servant boy and I'm afraid to say he did take certain things from your friend's room."

"What?" Amma said.

"Evidently," he continued, "he was right in the middle of ransacking the room when you arrived two days ago. That is why you found it in disarray."

"What exactly did he steal?" she asked.

"Let's see," he said, and rummaged through the file until he found a piece of paper. He began to read from it. "A clock radio, a watch, a camera, some Australian money, a Parker pen."

Amma shook her head, as if she could hardly believe what he was saying.

When we got up to leave, the A.S.P. walked us to the door. "By the way," he said, "that servant boy was a real jobless character. He knew all the comings and goings of your friend."

Amma straightened up slightly.

He looked at her and smiled. "I will look into your friend's absence and get back to you." He opened the door gallantly. "My regards to your husband," he said. "I'm sure he'll be fascinated by all that's happened in his absence."

When we left the building, Amma was furious.

"The bloody cheek of the man," she cried. "The bloody cheek!"

She pushed the strap of her handbag over her shoulder. "Who does he think I am? Some schoolgirl?"

I looked at Amma, worried about what would happen if the A.S.P. did indeed tell my father.

That evening, both Amma and I were very quiet. We joined Neliya Aunty, Sonali, and Diggy in the garden. A monsoon sultriness had settled inside our house, and not even the fans could dispel it. So we sat in the garden, hoping for a slight breeze to cool us down. But there was none. Everything around us, the trees, the bushes, was immobile. The whole world seemed to be braced for some oncoming cataclysm.

When I went to bed, I tried to read *Little Men*, but the

book reminded me of the time Daryl Uncle had sat by my bed reading to me. Finally, I put the book down. Only ten days had passed since I'd last seen him, yet my memory of Daryl Uncle had already blurred.

Then, in the early hours of the morning, the telephone rang. Its shrill sound entered my dream and only after a few moments did I realize its clamor was real. I sat up in bed. In the room next to mine, I could hear Neliya Aunty stirring. Amma went down the hall to the phone. She picked up the receiver and I heard the murmur of her voice. I got out of bed, retied my sarong, and went to my door. Sonali, Diggy, and Neliya Aunty had also come out into the hall. Amma stood by the phone in the darkness, the receiver hanging uselessly in her hand. "Neliya," she said softly. "Neliya."

"I'm here," Neliya Aunty said.

"Oh God, Neliya. They've found Daryl's body."

In the first light of morning, we waited on the front verandah for the police. Amma and Neliya Aunty had to go and identify the body. I looked around me, at the coffee cups in the tray on the floor, at the sky, a dull silver awning in which streaks of pink and orange were beginning to appear, and was reminded of the times we went on holidays and would awaken before dawn so we could leave before the sun became too fierce. As I drank my coffee, tasting its bittersweet flavor, I tried to tell myself that I was awake this early because Daryl Uncle was dead. I thought of what Amma had told us, how some fishermen had found his body, how it had been washed ashore on the beach of a fishing village. Yet, even while I thought about these realities my heart skipped madly as if joyful at the prospect of a holiday.

The police finally came and took Amma and Neliya Aunty to the morgue. I stood at the front gate and watched the car disappear down the road. The routines of everyday life were beginning to take place around me. Neighbors came onto their verandahs and picked up their papers, servants opened gates and waited for the bread man and the milkman to arrive; in the distance there was the sound of cars on the main road.

As I looked around me, I felt an odd sensation. Our daily routine had been cast away, while the rest of the world was going on as usual. A man I had known, a man who was my mother's lover, was now dead. I was aware that it was a significant thing, a momentous event in my life even, but, like a newspaper report on an earthquake or a volcanic eruption, it seemed something that happened outside my reality, my world.

After a while, I walked back to the house. Diggy and Sonali were still on the verandah. They looked at me carefully as if hoping I could tell them more about Daryl Uncle's death. I avoided their gaze and went inside.

When Amma and Neliya Aunty came back from the morgue some time later, the fact of Daryl Uncle's death finally began to seep into my consciousness. Neliya Aunty's eyes were swollen and she was crying into her handkerchief. Amma was not crying. Her head was tilted at an angle and there was almost a look of defiance on her face. She kissed each of us on the cheek, greeting us by name. She informed us that Daryl Uncle's body was to be cremated and the ashes sent back to Australia, where they would be buried with his parents'. She spoke in a neutral tone, as if she was relaying a piece of unimportant information. Then she went into her room to change her clothes. Neliya Aunty and I followed her. Amma was taking off her sari when we came in, and she looked up. "I still can't believe he's dead," she said after a moment. "I'm sure it'll hit me later."

Neliya Aunty nodded.

"He didn't die by drowning. You know that. He was killed, then thrown into the sea."

I winced at the directness of her words. Neliya Aunty looked uncomfortable too.

"Of course they have witnesses who saw him go swimming," she said sarcastically. "They have witnesses for everything these days." Her sari lay on the floor around her feet. She stepped over it and picked up one end. Then she looked at both of us. "We have to do something. We can't let this go by."

"Nalini," Neliya Aunty said.

"What?" Amma demanded. "You think we shouldn't do anything?"

Neliya Aunty looked down at the floor. "There's no point now," she said. "Nothing you do will bring him back."

"But something must be done," Amma cried angrily. She began to fold her sari. "People can't get away with these things. This is a democracy, for God's sake."

Neliya Aunty didn't reply.

That evening Amma developed such a severe headache

that it made her dizzy and she had to lie down. I went into her room to see how she was. The curtains were drawn and she was lying in bed, her arm over her forehead. Her eyes followed me as I came in. I sat down by her side and we were silent for a moment. Then she said suddenly, "It was horrible. I could hardly recognize him. If they had not found his wallet on him, I would have sworn it was someone else." She turned towards me. "You don't think he drowned, do you, son?"

I shook my head.

"I should have done something. I should have found a way to stop him from going. I am to blame."

"Oh, no, Amma," I said in protest. "You did what you could."

"No, no. I should have stopped him *somehow*."

She propped herself up on her elbows. "Why didn't I believe him about what was going on there? How could I have thought this government was any better than the last?"

She lay back again. "Things were going so well, I didn't want to know what was really happening."

I looked at her. The excited tone of her voice and the bright look in her eyes bothered me. I wished that she had cried. It would have seemed more natural.

"We must do something," she said, breaking the silence. "We can't just sit by and act as if nothing happened." She looked at me. "But where does one turn when the police and the government are the offenders?"

I didn't answer.

For most of the night I lay awake, thinking about all that had happened. Finally, I fell asleep and dreamt of *Little Women*. This time I was Jo and I was nursing Amma, who was Beth. Then Beth died and I awoke to find myself crying as, for the first time, the understanding that Daryl Uncle was dead came to me.

The next day, when Amma picked me up from school, she had come up with a plan.

"Do you remember Q.C. Appadurai?" she asked, as I got into the car.

I nodded. Q.C. Appadurai, or Q.C. Uncle, as we called him, was a friend of Amma's late father. He visited our house for our birthdays and we visited him on his birthday and at Christmas. All I knew about Q.C. Uncle was that there was a hint of scandal surrounding him and the servant boy who, since Q.C. Uncle had become feeble, supported him by the arm when he came to our parties.

Amma started up the car. "I made an appointment to see him today."

As we drove to his house, she explained to me that Q.C. Uncle was a civil rights lawyer and what this meant. Amma felt sure that he would be able to help us find Daryl Uncle's killers.

Q.C. Uncle lived in a big house near Kynsey Road. When we rang the bell, the servant boy opened the door and ushered us into the drawing room. After a short while, Q.C. Uncle came out of his room, the servant boy helping him. He was a small, dark-skinned man, and he wore a sarong and shirt. On his face was a pair of large, square, black-framed glasses. Amma stood up as he came in. He peered at us but didn't offer any greeting until he was seated and had stopped panting. Then he smiled at Amma and said, his voice a little hoarse and wheezy, "Nalini. How wonderful to see you."

"It's wonderful to see you, too, Uncle," Amma replied.

Q.C. Uncle nodded his head and smiled. All his movements were extremely slow and his jaw moved in a chewing motion, despite the fact that he was not eating anything.

"My dear," he said to Amma, "what can I do for you?"

"I need some advice, Uncle," Amma said. "It's about a friend of mine. He went to Jaffna a few weeks ago and . . ."

"Jaffna," he exclaimed. Then he indicated for her to continue.

Amma started to tell him what had happened, but when she mentioned Daryl Uncle's name, Q.C. Uncle interrupted her, saying, "Daryl? Wasn't that the boy you wanted to marry at one time?"

Amma looked at him and frowned. He didn't seem to have noticed her look, because he continued with a chuckle of remembrance, "I recall that well. Your parents sent you to holiday with me on my old Kerala estate. Three months you were there."

"Uncle," Amma said warningly and looked towards me.

"Yes, yes," he said, realizing his indiscretion. He waved his hand for Amma to continue. She proceeded with her story, leaving out the details of her relationship with Daryl Uncle. I noticed that Q.C. Uncle watched her with a strange expression.

When Amma finished her story, Q.C. Uncle nodded slowly, his jaws making their usual chewing motion. His eyes were half closed, and I wondered if he was beginning to fall asleep. Finally, he opened his eyes fully, looked at her, and said, "I'm sorry for you, child."

From the way he said it, I knew that he had discerned all the things Amma had omitted to tell him. Amma's hands were clenched into tight fists. "You were a famous civil rights lawyer," she said. "What would you do if you were still practicing?"

He heaved a great sigh. "If I were still practicing," he said, "I wouldn't be doing civil rights."

Amma looked at him in surprise.

"Too dangerous, my dear," he said. "In my day, politicians were rascals, but never like these ones."

"So what must we do?"

"Nothing, my dear," he said sadly.

Amma looked at him, shocked. "Nothing?" she said.

"These days one must be like the three wise monkeys. See no evil, hear no evil, speak no evil."

Amma was angry now. She put her fingertips together and contemplated them for a moment. "So," she said, "a close and dear friend dies and I must do nothing about it?"

"Exactly, my dear," he replied.

"But how can one live with oneself, knowing one has done nothing?"

"You must remind yourself that you have a family and they could be at risk."

When we stood up to leave, the servant boy helped Q.C. Uncle to his feet. Amma had an obstinate expression on her face. Q.C. Uncle placed his hand on her arm and said, "Let it rest, child."

"I can't," Amma said.

He nodded and bowed his head, as if to fate.

Just before we left him, he said to us, "When you go home, call somebody. If you hear a click when that person answers, your phone is being tapped."

We stared at him in astonishment.

On the way home, Amma drove fast, honking at any pedestrian who contemplated crossing the street in front of our car. "What has this country come to, where a man can be murdered and nothing must be done?" she cried. "The problem is that no one cares anymore. People only look out for themselves."

When we turned onto Dharmapala Mawatha, Amma had to slow down because of the increase in traffic. I glanced at her. She was chewing on her lower lip, lost in thought. We had almost reached Galle Road when she straightened up slightly and made a noise as if she had just realized something. She turned to me. "You know, there is the servant boy. I'm sure he saw something." I looked at her carefully. Q.C. Uncle's proverb about the three wise monkeys had stayed with me. He was an important lawyer, and we would be foolish not to listen to him.

Amma hadn't noticed my disquiet. "Let's go and see if the police have sent him back to the house."

I looked at the set expression on her face and I knew that it was useless to argue.

We knocked on the gate and waited. The dog started to bark. It came running down the front path and threw itself at the gate, forcing us to step back. Presently, we heard the sound of footsteps.

"Who is it?" a woman asked suspiciously in Sinhalese.

Amma and I looked at each other, surprised to hear a strange voice.

"Is your missie in?" Amma asked.

"No. She's gone to England for her daughter's confinement."

"Really?" Amma said in feigned delight. "Suriya baba is going to have a baby?"

I looked at Amma, wondering how she knew the name of the owner's daughter.

The peephole in the gate slid back and the woman stared at us, then opened the gate. The dog ran out, wagging its tail. The woman called to the dog, but it ignored her and went sniffing down the road.

"Are you new here?" Amma asked.

The woman nodded and then said, "But I used to work here until five years ago."

"What happened to the servant boy?" Amma asked.

She regarded us for a moment. "Somaratne went back to his village," she said.

"I wonder how his mother is," Amma said. "She was quite sick. Had a heart problem."

The woman looked at Amma in surprise. She became less suspicious.

"I used to give him money from time to time for her medicine. I wonder how he'll manage now."

The woman nodded in commiseration with Somaratne and his mother's plight.

"He lives in Belihul Oya, doesn't he?"

The woman shook her head. Somaratne lived *near* Belihul Oya, she corrected Amma. In doing so, she mentioned the name of the village.

Before we left, Amma slipped a ten-rupee note into the woman's hand. She held her palms together and bowed. As we got into the car, I turned and saw that the woman was watching us carefully.

When we got home, Amma phoned Mala Aunty and, as Q.C. Uncle had predicted, she heard the click. I phoned a classmate just to make doubly sure that we were being tapped. It was strange and frightening to hear that click. I was reminded of the time a family of large rats lived in our house and we were never sure where they were hiding, from which cupboard or drawer they would jump out at us, behind which door or toilet commode we would find them. In addition to fear of those rats, I remembered feeling helpless because, for a long time, nothing we did made them go away.

That evening, I was doing my homework on the back verandah when Amma came out and sat down next to me.

"I've made up my mind," she said. ""m going to Somaratne's village. The day after tomorrow is Meena's birthday. All of you will be at her house for the day, and Neliya Aunty will be visiting a friend."

I looked at her and felt afraid. "Amma, should you? Q.C. Uncle's told you that this whole thing is too dangerous."

"Rubbish," Amma said, and I could tell by the look in her eyes that there was no stopping her. She would not accept that going to look for the servant boy might not be safe.

Suddenly the thought of Amma being alone and in danger

was too much, and I said quickly, "Amma, I am coming with you."

She looked at me for a minute and then shook her head.

"We're only going to visit him," I said, my own words not calming my fear.

Amma looked doubtful.

"His family and he will be happy that a lady came all the way from Colombo to see them," I persisted.

"But everyone will wonder why you didn't go to Meena's birthday," Amma said. Yet I could tell she was softening.

"I can pretend not to feel well and stay back."

"I don't know," Amma said. "I don't like it."

"Please, Amma. It will be so good for me to be out there in the mountain air again."

Amma smiled at the lameness of my reasoning. She sighed and got up. "Let me think about it," she said, but I could tell that she had already decided to take me.

Our plans went well, and we set off for Belihul Oya by midmorning. As we began the gradual climb into the hill country, the road became winding. The tropical vegetation gave way to an increasing number of fir and eucalyptus trees, and eventually these gave way to tea bushes. I rolled down the window and let the crisp air play on my face. The road had been cut into the side of the mountain, so that on Amma's side there was the red earth of the mountain and on my side a sharp drop. I looked down into the valley below, most of which was covered with jungle.

After a while, I noticed a blue car was at our rear. I could

see it in the side-view mirror. From time to time we lost the
car as another one cut in front of it, but inevitably it would
turn up again. Finally, I drew Amma's attention to it. She
nodded and I saw that she, too, had noticed the car. "Let's
stop and see if it continues," she said.

She pulled over to the side of the road. We watched as
the car drew closer, and much to our relief it went right past
us. Amma glanced at me and we both laughed at how suspicious we had become.

After being misdirected a few times, we finally arrived at Somaratne's village. It was set among green terraced paddy
fields. A crowd of village children heard the sound of our car
and came running down the slopes and across the path that
led through the paddy fields. They approached us with smiling faces.

"We are looking for Mahagodagé Somaratne," Amma
said.

The children now became nervous. One of them, an
older girl, shoved at a little boy and he ran back up the hill.
Then she gestured to us to follow her. Amma and I looked
at each other uneasily.

The girl led us up some steps cut into the side of the hill
to Somaratne's hut. A woman was sitting in front of it. Between her knees she held a cleaver, against which she deftly
sliced vegetables. The child who had gone ahead of us sat
near her, and some women had come out of the neighboring
huts and stood watching us. As I looked at their faces, my
uneasiness increased. When we reached her, the woman

glanced up at us quickly and then continued slicing her vegetables.

"We are looking for Somaratne," Amma said to her.

"I am Somaratne's mother," she replied.

"We would like to speak to Somaratne."

"He is not here."

"Where can we find him?"

"I don't know."

Amma looked at me. The woman was lying.

"Listen," Amma finally said, "a friend of ours lived where Somaratne used to work. He died and we are concerned . . ."

"And what about my son?" the woman said. "Are you not concerned about him?" She had raised her voice slightly. The other women began to come towards her hut. "What do you care?" she continued bitterly. "You rich folk from Colombo, what do you know about our suffering?"

The women had now gathered around us and they nodded and looked at us with anger in their faces.

"Come," I said softly to Amma. "It's dangerous."

She ignored me.

"Look," Amma said, "I think our friend was murdered and Somaratne knows who did it."

The woman laughed harshly. "So you want Somaratne to identify the murderer?" she said. "And what will happen to Somaratne then? Have you thought of that?"

Amma was silent.

"No," she said, "why should you? To people like you, we are not even human beings."

The other women murmured in agreement.

"You Colombo people lead such a protected life," one

of the women said. "You don't know what goes on in the rest of the country."

"Yes," another woman cried, "why don't you go back to Colombo and leave us alone."

"I had two sons," Somaratne's mother said. "The first was killed by the army during the 1971 insurrection. Now my second son comes home with his right arm paralyzed. Do you want to paralyze his other arm, too, or make him lose an eye?"

I looked around at the women and saw that they were becoming increasingly hostile. I touched Amma's arm and said, trying to keep my voice steady, "Come, Amma, before anything happens."

She looked at me for a long moment, then nodded her head.

As we walked down the hill, a stone came hurtling past us. Without looking back, we hurried. Then more stones were thrown and we began to run. We had just reached the bottom of the hill when I felt a sharp pain in my back as a stone hit me. I cried out and stumbled, nearly falling over.

"Arjie," Amma called out and came to me. She put her hand on my back, but I broke away from her and continued to run towards the car.

By the time we got into the car I was crying out of fright.

"Son," Amma said. She put her hand on my shoulder.

I tried to shake it off. "It's so stupid! We should never have come on this trip," I shouted at her. "You're so selfish. All you think about is yourself. Thanks to you, we nearly got killed."

She looked at me as if I had hit her. Her hand fell from my shoulder.

"You were told this whole thing was too dangerous, but you never listen."

She sat motionless, frowning slightly.

She started up the car and we began to drive away from the village. I felt terrible now that I had yelled at her so. She was staring straight ahead of her. She reached up and quickly rubbed her hand across her cheek.

"Amma—" I started to say, but she waved impatiently for me to be quiet.

After a while she pulled the car up by the side of the road, then she got out and slammed the door. I watched her stand there, her back to me, and even though I was sorry to see her cry I was also glad of it. I hoped with all my heart it meant that she finally realized that things had gone too far. I leaned back in my seat and looked at the view in front of me, the clear blue sky, the mist-capped mountains, and thought how out of place their beauty and serenity seemed with all that had happened to us.

When Amma got back into the car, we continued our journey in silence.

By the time we arrived home, it was starting to get dark. Neliya Aunty, Sonali, and Diggy were waiting for us on the front verandah. Our trip had taken much longer than we had anticipated, and they had all returned from their day out.

"Where on earth . . ." Neliya Aunty started to say, but before she could finish her question, we went quickly into the house. She followed us. When we were far enough from Diggy and Sonali, she said to Amma in a low voice, "A man came to see you today."

We stared at her.

She gave Amma a card. "He said he was with the *Sydney Morning Star.*"

Amma took the card and looked at it.

"Isn't that the paper Daryl worked for?" Neliya Aunty asked.

Amma didn't respond for a moment. Then she shrugged and put the card in her bag.

"What does he want?" Neliya Aunty asked anxiously.

Amma started to walk towards her room. Neliya Aunty followed her. "Nalini, I'm warning you. Don't get involved. It's too dangerous."

Amma went into her room without answering. Neliya Aunty looked at me helplessly and shook her head. "She's going too far," she said. "Where will all this end?"

I looked at her and, for once, I was on her side.

That night, after finally falling asleep, I dreamed that we were on the beach in front of my father's hotel. The sea receded for miles, building into enormous waves that then rushed towards the shore. Amma was on the beach and she beckoned to me. I took her hand and we ran after the sea. A wave now towered in the distance. It reached its full height and began to come towards us. Instead of turning back, Amma insisted that we sit on the sand and wait for the wave to break around us. Before the wave could reach us, however, I woke up. Through my window I could see the first streaks of pink in the sky. I lay in bed, looking out and wondering what this day would bring.

It was a Sunday morning, and so we had breakfast a little later than usual. Amma looked weary and took only one piece of toast, which she didn't even finish. Neliya Aunty was watching her carefully, and Diggy and Sonali, too, sensed that something was wrong. In the middle of the meal, the phone rang and I answered it, surprised not to hear the click. It was a friend of Diggy's, and I handed the phone to him.

After breakfast, Sonali went for a piano lesson and Diggy cycled off to visit a friend. I settled on the verandah with a book. I was unable to concentrate, though, and after a while I put the book down. A knock at the gate made me turn my head. The gate was ajar and presently a white man came inside. He was short and balding and he wore round glasses. My hands suddenly became cold and sweaty.

"Is your mother in?" he asked.

I nodded and went to get Amma. When I told her who was here, she looked alarmed; then her features became impassive. She followed me out onto the front verandah.

"Mrs. Chelvaratnam?" he said.

"Yes?"

"I'm with the *Sydney Morning Star*. I came to see you yesterday."

She nodded and pointed to a chair. She sat down as well.

"I believe you are a friend of Daryl Brohier."

Amma did not answer at first. Then she said, "Not a very good friend."

I gave her a quick glance, but she didn't look at me.

"Yes," the man said, and from the way he smiled slightly, I could tell that he didn't believe her.

"Mr. Brohier was a colleague of mine. Were you familiar with any of the work he was doing in Sri Lanka?"

"I thought he was here on holiday," Amma replied.

The man crossed his legs impatiently.

"We are suspicious about the circumstances of his death. Do you share similar suspicions?"

Again, Amma paused before responding. Then she shook her head.

"You saw the body, didn't you?"

"Yes."

"Was there anything odd about it?"

"No."

"I see." He leaned back in his chair and studied Amma for a moment. She looked at her hands, then glanced at him and smiled.

"Will that be all?" she asked.

He sighed and stood up. "Thank you for your time," he said.

Amma bowed slightly, acknowledging his thanks. She accompanied him to the gate. After he had gone, she stood there and stared down the road for a long time. Then she stepped back inside, placed the latch on the gate, and slowly came up the steps of the verandah. Without looking at me, she went inside the house.

I should have felt relieved that Amma had lied to the man, that she had decided not to pursue the matter anymore, but all I felt was a terrible sadness. After a while I got up and went to my room. I realized now that we had come to the end of our quest. Daryl Uncle's killer would never be brought to justice. In the bookcase in front of me, I noticed the Little Women books that Daryl Uncle had bought me. I took them down and laid them out on my bed. The pictures on their covers brought back the memory of that day Daryl Uncle had brought them into my room and put them out on my blanket. I picked up *Little Women* and opened it. It was the chapter called "Pleasant Meadows," where the father of the family comes home and the little women sit at his feet, all their troubles at an end. It was one of my favorite passages, yet reading it now brought me no pleasure. The world the characters lived in, where good was rewarded and evil punished, seemed suddenly false to me. My father would soon be coming back too, but our troubles were not over. I thought of how strange it would be to have him back here, sitting at the table every morning reading the newspaper, his loud voice announcing the news of the day to Amma and forcing the entire household into a premature awakening. I thought of Amma and wondered how she would be able to fit into this old life again. We would return to a regular routine, yet nothing could take us back to where we had been before the day I looked up from my book and saw Daryl Uncle at the gate.

My father arrived the following week, on his birthday. He had phoned Amma from England to request that she have a big party to celebrate the event. It was to be a grand affair, bigger than anything we had ever had at our house. Over seventy-five people had been invited and the whole dinner was catered.

The night of the party, I stood on the verandah and watched as the guests came in. I glanced from time to time to where Amma stood at the bottom of the front steps, greeting them as they arrived. She wore a royal-blue silk sari, sprinkled with tiny crescent moons. She had been to the hairdresser's in the afternoon and her hair was up, a crescent-moon clasp holding it in place. Outwardly, she seemed happy, almost gay. Yet once, when there was a lull in the flow of guests, I saw her raise her hand to her temple, a sudden tired expression on her face.

Amma had placed little clay lamps along the border of the garden. They provided the only light, and in their flickering illumination, the guests, the waiters, the tables of food, and indeed the whole garden, seemed insubstantial.

Small Choices

One day, my father received a letter from the widow
of an old friend. The letter was from Jaffna.

"Listen to this," he said to Amma and Neliya Aunty, and
he began to read the letter.

"Dear Mr. Chelvaratnam, I am writing to request a favor
in memory of my late husband. My son, Jegan, is a qualified
accountant. He's twenty-five years old and has spent the last
year as a relief worker for the Gandhiyam movement, but,
due to recent problems, I removed him from the organization. He is currently unemployed. Would you be able to find
him a post in your business? I am sure his skills will be useful

to you. Yours truly, Grace Parameswaran. P.S. I found the attached document among my husband's belongings, and I am sending it to you as a souvenir of your friendship with him."

My father held out a yellowing piece of paper to Amma. We crowded around her so that we could read it as well. The paper was torn from an exercise book, and the writing on it was badly formed and with spelling errors. "We, Robert Chelvaratnam and Buddy Parameswaran make the following declarashon: We will always protect each other and each oth-ers' familys until death does us part. Signed with our mingld blood . . ." At the bottom of the page were two rust-colored thumbprints.

We stared at my father, finding it hard to imagine he had been capable of such a spontaneous act, that he had felt so strongly about someone he had slit his thumb and mixed his blood with his.

My father must have read our thoughts, because he frowned in embarrassment and took the paper back from Amma. "If I had known that this would be used to blackmail me one day, I would never have done it."

"But who is this Buddy Parameswaran?" Amma asked.

"A school friend."

"I've never heard of him."

"By the time I met you, I had lost touch with him."

"Why?"

My father shrugged. "Just happened that way. We were very close, but then I went to university in England and he stayed here to do Oriental Studies." He smiled ironically. "He became a great orientalist and I became a great banker."

"Are you going to hire the boy?"

My father picked up the letter and glanced at it again. "I don't know," he said. "It says that the boy worked with the Gandhiyam movement."

"But that's good, no? These Gandhiyam people are helping Tamils who were affected by the communal riots."

"People say that they are in league with the Tigers. A little while back, the police arrested Gandhiyam workers—don't you remember? It was in the papers and everything."

My father picked up the yellowed piece of paper and looked at it for a moment. He scowled and then put it down. "I suppose I should at least see the boy."

He got up from his chair and, as if the boy were right in front of him, said sternly, "But first I'm going to quiz him carefully about his politics. Any Tiger nonsense and he will be out on his ear."

I watched my father as he walked away down the hall. Unlike Amma, he was a distant figure who had very little effect on our everyday reality. We dealt with him mainly through avoidance. The family squabbles that took place, the secrets, were kept from him by an unspoken understanding. He was a figure we held in awe, and his presence represented an authority my sister and brother and I would seldom defy.

A few evenings later, Sonali, Neliya Aunty, and I were in the garden, searching for snails among the rosebushes, when we noticed a young man standing inside the gate, looking at us.

Neliya Aunty straightened up and said, "Yes? Can I help you?"

"Is Mr. Chelvaratnam in, madam?"

"He's having a shower. You are . . . ?"

"Jegan Parameswaran."

"Oh," Neliya Aunty said in recognition. "Come, have a seat."

She ushered Jegan to a chair and then hurried inside to get my father.

Sonali and I stayed in the garden, looking at our visitor. He was clean-shaven and had straight hair that fell over his forehead and was short at the back. His skin was very dark and had a healthy glow to it. He saw me watching him and smiled. His teeth, like his eyes, were brilliant against his dark skin. I returned his smile shyly.

"What are you doing?" he asked, noticing the pail in my hand.

"It's for snails. We're getting rid of them before they ruin the roses."

He nodded.

At that moment my father came out onto the verandah. From the serious expression on his face I could tell that he planned to make the meeting as short as possible. When he saw Jegan, however, he stood still and stared at him as if he had seen a ghost. Jegan rose to his feet, alarmed.

"My God," my father said finally in an awestruck tone, "I feel as if I have stepped back in time."

Jegan smiled, relieved. "Yes, sir, I resemble Appa a little."

"Resemble!" my father cried. "You are him! All your gestures, your voice."

He ran his eyes over Jegan and then, seeing that Jegan looked embarrassed, he pointed to the chair he had been seated in and said, "Come, come, sit, sit."

My father sat down as well, still staring at Jegan. He sighed and shook his head. "I'm sorry. I am thinking about your father and our youth together."

"Yes," Jegan said, "he often spoke of it."

"Did he?"

Jegan nodded. "Especially in those last months . . ." Jegan looked at his hands for a moment. "He was very proud of your achievements."

My father stared at Jegan. He suddenly looked ashamed.

"Sir," Jegan began to say, but my father held up his hand.

"No 'sir' with me," my father said, and his voice was filled with emotion. "You must call me 'Uncle.' "

"Uncle," Jegan continued, "my mother wrote to you—"

"Don't worry," my father said. "I'm sure we can arrange something."

"Do you want to know a little about my background?" Jegan asked.

"What do I need to know? You are Buddy's son. That's good enough for me."

Now Sonali and I looked at my father with unconcealed astonishment, recollecting the way he had threatened to quiz Jegan about his Tiger connections. He must have seen the expression on our faces, because he said to us crossly, "Where are your manners? Go and get a drink for our guest."

We went inside to the kitchen.

When we came out onto the verandah again with Jegan's drink, Amma and Neliya Aunty were seated with my father. From the bemused expression on Amma's face, I could tell that she, too, had noticed how quickly my father had retracted his earlier threats.

She glanced teasingly at my father and said to Jegan, "So, tell us about this Gandhiyam movement you were in."

My father looked at her and frowned slightly.

"It's an organization to assist Tamil refugees who were affected by the nineteen seventy-seven or eighty-one riots. We help them settle in Tamil areas."

Amma continued: "Are you Gandhiyam people connected with the Tigers?"

Before Jegan could answer, my father cried out, "Chi, chi, chi! No politics." He gestured to me to offer Jegan the drink, and I did so.

"There may be those who are sympathetic, but it's not the policy of the organization," Jegan said, answering Amma's question.

"And you?" she asked. "Are you 'sympathetic'?"

"What are you saying?" my father cried. "Don't insult the boy. Why, if the Tigers had such fine chaps in it, I would be the first to support it."

"Oh, I'm just curious, you know," Amma said, and gave my father a sidelong glance.

I noticed that Jegan was looking at his hands, a small smile on his face.

Sonali was seated near Amma, but instead of joining her, I went to sit down in a corner of the verandah where I could observe Jegan without his being aware of it. When I had served him the drink, I had got a closer look at him. What had struck me was the strength of his body. The muscles of his arms and neck, which would have been visible on a fairer person, were hidden by the darkness of his skin. It was only when I was close to him that I had noticed them. Now I admired how well built he was, the way his thighs pressed against his trousers.

Jegan had noticed that I was looking at him, but he didn't seem disturbed by it. In fact he glanced at me from time to time and smiled, as if to say that it was all right. His smile made me feel shy but also happy.

Lately, I had found that I looked at men, at the way they were built, the grace with which they carried themselves, the strength of their gestures and movements. Sometimes these men were present in my dreams. I felt the reason for this sudden admiration of men had to do with my distress over the recent changes in my own body, changes I had witnessed in Diggy a few years ago when he, too, was thirteen. I had grown long and awkward and my voice sometimes slid embarrassingly into a high pitch. Also, I had started to notice a wetness on my sarong in the morning. I had once heard my father explaining to Diggy what this was, so I was not unduly worried about it. But I longed to pass this awkward phase, to become as physically attractive and graceful as the men I saw around me.

My father had invited Jegan to stay for dinner, and once Amma and Neliya Aunty had gone in to see about the food, my father was silent, lost in thought. Then he turned to Jegan and said, "You know, I can't help but feel bad that I never came to your father's funeral."

"It's all right, Uncle," Jegan replied.

"No, no," my father said. "I should have come."

"The funeral was in Jaffna and you must have been busy."

"I'm trying to remember why I didn't come, but I can't think of the reason," my father continued as if he had not heard Jegan. "The only word that comes to mind is 'time.' My grandfather used to say that you could miss a man's wedding but never his funeral."

He looked down at his drink for a moment and then up at Jegan. "I loved your father, you know," he said.

Jegan nodded.

"When I left for England, I was more sorry to leave him than I was my own family." My father paused and stared out at the garden. "While I was in England, we grew apart."

After Jegan had left that evening, my father sat on the front verandah, sucking contemplatively on a toothpick. Amma and Neliya Aunty came out and sat with him. "You know," my father said, and he took the toothpick out of his mouth, "there's that storeroom above the garage? It's doing nothing, no?"

Amma sat back in her chair and looked at him skeptically. "You think so?" she said.

"Why not? We're always talking about letting it out. Better to someone we know. Besides, I would like to do it. For Buddy's sake."

Amma shrugged. "I don't mind."

I felt a thrill of excitement go through me. The thought of Jegan moving into our home, of my being in constant contact with him, filled me with an unaccountable joy. I felt that his presence would invest this commonplace, familiar environment with something extraordinary.

★ ★ ★

A few days later, Jegan came to live with us. We returned from school to find Amma on her way to the room above the garage, a pile of linen in her hand.

"Jegan is here," Amma called to us. "Come and say hello."

We followed her down the driveway. As we climbed up the stairs, I could hear Jegan moving around inside his room. Diggy, I noticed, walked ahead of us, impatient to be the first one to enter the room. He had not been around when Jegan had visited, and he was anxious to meet the new addition to our home. I admired his lack of reticence in knocking briefly on the door before entering.

Jegan was unpacking when we came in, and he greeted us with a wave of his hand. Diggy shook hands with him as if he were his age, and then looked around the room with frank curiosity. The room had been transformed from a cluttered storage space into a very comfortable apartment. Amma and Neliya Aunty had taken a lot of trouble to make it look good. Some of the old furniture that Amma had put away with the intention of selling had been brought in. The place seemed to have become sacred by his presence, and I did not dare venture too far into it.

⸺◆⸺

Jegan started work in my father's office. Soon he and my father seemed inseparable. Every morning they would leave for work together and often return in the evening at the same time. Jegan would go for a jog then, and later in the evening he would join my father for a drink in the garden. These evening drinks became a ritual, and if for some reason Jegan was late coming home, my father would wait for him before having his drink. I would often sit on the verandah listening to their conversations, usually out of sight behind one of the reed mats we hung from the eaves of the verandah to keep out the sun. I always had a book with me in case somebody caught me listening.

At first my father talked to Jegan only about his friendship with Jegan's father, but gradually he started to tell him other stories about his childhood. I was intrigued by these conversations, for they were my first real intimation that my father was more than just a figure of paternal authority. I began now to see him as a man who had been a boy like myself.

Once my father told Jegan about an affair he'd had with an English girl when he was studying in England. She had worked in the university cafeteria, and she had really wanted to marry him. He had been keen on the idea, too, until he returned to Sri Lanka for a holiday and came to his senses. An English girl, he had realized, would never fit in with his family. Also, she was from a working-class family, and "low class was low class whether it was English or Sri Lankan." This story, more than any of the others, truly amazed me. A love affair with a white person, with all the taboos that surrounded it, took a certain spirit and nerve, a certain thumbing of one's nose in the face of society. True, my father had finally ended it, but I could not even imagine him beginning the relationship. It did not fit with the strict, proper man I knew.

One evening, not long after Jegan had started working for my father, I was surprised to hear them talking about antagonism in the office towards Jegan.

"The trick is not to take it seriously," my father said. "They'll soon get used to you."

"But what if they don't, Uncle?" Jegan asked.

My father clicked his tongue against his teeth dismissively. "I'm the boss. If they don't like it they can leave."

Jegan was silent.

"The truth is that you are very good," my father said. "Both my partner, Sena, and I know that. The old adage 'You can't keep a good man down' is very true. Especially now. With this free economy, any man who has a talent and works hard can get ahead."

He leaned over and patted Jegan on the knee. "You have a bright future. You mustn't let these petty things stop you."

Jegan seemed fonder of me than he was of Diggy or Sonali. Whenever he saw me sitting on the verandah he would stop by and talk to me. He had a nice way of talking which didn't include any boasting or coarseness. He often told me about his work with the Gandhiyam organization and about Dr. Rajasundaram, the founder. The life he had led while working in the movement seemed very different from the life I knew—so much more purposeful. From the way he talked I realized that this had been a particularly happy time in his life.

My father seemed very pleased with this growing connection between Jegan and myself, and once I heard him talk to Jegan about it in the garden.

"I'm glad you take an interest in him," he said. "That boy worries me."

I leaned forward, wondering what it was that worried him.

"Why, Uncle?" Jegan asked.

My father was silent for a moment. "From the time he was small he has shown certain tendencies."

"What do you mean, tendencies?" Jegan asked.

"You know . . . he used to play with dolls, always reading."

My face suddenly became hot at the realization that he was discussing this with Jegan, for whom I had such high regard. I thought to get up, go into the garden, and thus interrupt this mortifying conversation. Fortunately my father was embarrassed as well, for he said, "Anyway, the main point is that I'm glad you're taking an interest in him. Maybe you'll help him outgrow this phase."

"I don't think there's anything wrong with him," Jegan said.

For as long as I could remember, my father had alluded to this "tendency" in me without ever giving it a name. Jegan was the first one ever to defend me, and for this I grew even more devoted to him.

A few weeks later, an incident took place that showed a new side of Jegan.

It happened one morning. Sonali, Diggy, and I went out of the gate on our way to school to find a man pasting a large poster on our wall that had a picture of a lamp on it. I had seen many of these posters around Colombo recently and would not have paid much attention to them had Amma not pointed them out every time we passed one, saying angrily, "Is this what they call democracy?"

I had asked Amma once why she was angry, and she explained what was happening in Sri Lanka. This was the year of elections, but the government wanted to stay in power for another six years, so they were holding a "referendum" to extend their term, without an election. If you thought the government should continue to rule, you put a tick next to the lamp sign on your ballot. Otherwise, you put a tick next to the pot sign. Amma said that it was wrong not to have an election, but, worse, government supporters were putting posters everywhere to "influence people's minds," and this was illegal.

Sonali went back in the house to fetch my parents, and by now a few neighbors were watching from their gates. My parents and Neliya Aunty came out. Jegan was with them. They stared at the man in astonishment.

My father walked up to him. "Who gave you permission to do this?" he asked in Sinhalese.

The man acted as though he had not heard my father. Jegan now moved to my father's side.

"This is a private wall," Jegan said. "If you don't stop that now, we're going to call the police."

The man smiled at Jegan, challenging him to do so.

"I'm telling you to stop it now," my father said, his voice rising.

In response, the man picked up a poster and slapped it against the wall.

Then, before anyone could react, Jegan stepped forward, caught the man by his arm, and, with a quick twist, threw him to the ground. We stared at both of them in shock. Jegan now stood with his legs on either side of the man. "Get up and take that poster off the wall," he said. He spoke quietly, but there was a terrible anger in his voice.

The man glared at him and refused to move.

Jegan went to the wall and ripped the poster off.

"Ey," the man cried out, and scrambled to his feet. "That's government property."

"Government property, is it?" Jegan said grimly, and he tore the poster in two.

"You pariah, wait and see what'll happen to you," he said.

Jegan took a step towards him. The man hurriedly picked up his pail of glue and backed away. When he was a safe distance from Jegan, he spat on the ground and shouted, "You don't know who you're dealing with."

Then, fearing that Jegan might come at him again, he turned and hurried up the road.

Once he had gone, there was an audible sigh of relief from all of us. "Good work," Perera Aunty, our next-door neighbor called out. "Taught the bugger a lesson."

"It seems that they're doing this everywhere," Mrs. Bandara, the neighbor who lived across the road from us, said. "They put a lamp banner in some woman's garden, and when she protested they assaulted her."

I stared at Jegan, feeling admiration but also uneasiness. How effortlessly he had grasped the man by the arm and flung him to the ground. Where had he learned to do that? I noticed that my parents, too, were looking at him speculatively.

My father turned to Jegan. "You shouldn't have done that."

Jegan looked at him in surprise. "Why, Uncle?" he said. He sounded hurt.

"These days it is necessary to be discreet. We could have let him put up the poster and torn it down later."

"But he had no business to put up the poster in the first place. This postering is illegal," Jegan said.

Amma and Neliya Aunty nodded in agreement.

"That's not the point," my father said. "One must be careful not to antagonize the wrong people."

Jegan looked at the poster in his hand. He was clearly disappointed by my father's reproof.

＝◆＝

In the weeks that followed, Jegan was doing so well at my father's office that my father and Sena Uncle decided to promote him to a senior supervisory position. He would be in charge of doing the hotel inspections so that Sena Uncle and my father could be free to begin plans for a new hotel in Trincomele. The next time my father went down to do inspections, Jegan came along with us. Our hotel was about a three-hour drive south of Colombo and was one of many in the area. The people in the town near it were poor and lived in very small houses. Some of them made their living by selling trinkets to tourists. Others worked in the hotels. The only rich person in the town was the Banduratne Mudalali, who owned most of the hotels. He lived in a big house on top of a hill, and we would often see him being chauffeured around in his Pajero jeep.

Jegan had not been to our hotel before, and he was impressed by how beautiful it was. He especially liked the dining room because it had a rock garden in the middle of it and a small waterfall which cascaded down the rocks.

On our first evening there, my father invited Jegan to join him for their customary evening drink. He didn't object when I came along with them to the table the waiter had placed on the beach. The sun was setting, and the beach was quite crowded with foreigners and local villagers. We sat in silence, watching the sky change color at the horizon. Then Jegan leaned forward in his chair and looked keenly at something on the beach. My father regarded him, curious. Jegan turned to him and said, "Is what is happening what I think is happening?"

I turned to look down the beach now, wondering what Jegan had seen. There was nothing out of the ordinary. As was usual at this time, there were many foreign men around. A lot of them were talking to young boys from the village.

"Yes," my father said.

"And they come back to the hotel?"

My father shrugged. "Sometimes."

"You don't mind?"

"What am I to do? They have paid for the rooms. Besides, if I tried to stop it, they'd simply go to another hotel on the front."

"But isn't it illegal?"

My father chuckled. "I don't see any police out there, do you?" He poured himself another drink. "It's not just our luscious beaches that keep the tourist industry going, you know. We have other natural resources as well."

He held his glass up to Jegan. "Cheers."

Jegan didn't respond. Instead, he stared down the beach again, a stern expression on his face.

On the afternoon of the second day, I was reading in the hammock in front of my parents' room when I saw Jegan striding across the garden towards our rooms, the manager hurrying behind him. From the grim expression on Jegan's face and the harassed look on the face of the manager, I could tell something was wrong. "Aiyo, sir, don't," the manager said. "The boss is sleeping."

Jegan ignored his plea, stepped onto the patio outside my parents' room, and knocked on the glass door. After a moment, my father came to the door and parted the curtain. When he saw the look on their faces, he opened the door and came out, closing it softly behind him.

"What's wrong?" he asked.

Before Jegan could answer, the manager said, "Aiyo, sir, small problem, sir."

"Small!" Jegan said to him angrily. He turned to my father. "This man tells me that I am not supposed to correct the staff myself. I must give him all my criticism and he will convey it to them."

The manager now seemed very distressed. My father indicated to him that he was excused and he hurried off.

My father looked at Jegan for a moment. Then he stepped off the porch and pointed to some chairs that were near my hammock. As they walked towards me, I became very still. He invited Jegan to sit down.

"Yes," he said, "those were my orders."

Jegan looked at him in surprise.

"Why, Uncle?" he asked.

"That's the way we do things here," my father replied, brushing something from his sleeve.

Jegan regarded him for a moment and then said, "It's a Tamil-Sinhala thing, isn't it?"

My father was silent.

"That . . . it's ridiculous," Jegan cried.

"Look," my father said, "you don't understand."

"Why don't I understand, Uncle?"

"The political climate is very volatile. With the Tigers killing Sinhala policemen and the Tamil party calling for separation, the Sinhalese are very anti-Tamil right now."

"What about the Sinhalese massacring innocent Tamils during the riots last year?"

My father gestured with his hand to show that he didn't disagree with Jegan. "The fact is one must be careful these days. Things are very unstable in this area. During the riots, the mob came here calling out my name. If it wasn't for my manager and other senior staff, this hotel would have been destroyed."

Jegan looked at him, surprised.

My father nodded. "Yes," he said. "I never talk about it because I don't want to upset my family. They don't know how it was in this area. The Banduratne Mudalali, who owns a lot of the hotels around here, is very anti-Tamil. His thugs did terrible things. Tamil families were dragged out of their houses and hacked to death. They poured kerosene on them and set them on fire."

Jegan was silent.

"Look, son," my father said, "I didn't think there would be a need to explain this to you. But the truth is I have given you a high position and there's bound to be some resentment in part because you're Tamil."

"You gave me the position because I was good, Uncle, not because I was Tamil."

"They don't see it that way. You know how we Tamils are always accused of favoring each other."

"Yes, yes. And the Sinhalese, they never do that?"

"But we are a minority, and that's a fact of life," my father said placatingly. "As a Tamil you have to learn how to play the game. Play it right and you can do very well for yourself. The trick is not to make yourself conspicuous. Go around quietly, make your money, and don't step on anyone's toes."

Jegan sighed impatiently.

"Look at me," my father said. "I've done well for myself, haven't I? I'm happy, aren't I?"

Jegan didn't answer.

My father leaned forward and patted him indulgently on the knee.

"It's good to have ideals, but now you're a man, son. Soon you will become a husband and a father, and you must think about what that means. You have a bright future ahead of you. Don't spoil it." He stood up. "Our manager here is a fine man. Listen to him and he'll teach you a lot."

My father put his hand on Jegan's shoulder for a moment

and then he went back to his room. As he opened the door to go inside, I heard Amma ask sleepily if everything was all right.

"Yes," my father replied. "Everything is fine."

The conversation I had heard between them had disturbed the tranquillity of the afternoon. The recent riots, which had seemed so removed from my life, now took on an immediate and frightening dimension. I thought about what might have happened if we had been here at the time the riots broke out. I remembered the day they had started. Slowly, the news about what was happening in other parts of the country had begun to come into Colombo. The things we heard were so terrible that everyone had been sure there would be a forty-eight-hour curfew, and people had rushed to the shops to stock up on provisions. But there had only been night curfew, and, in Colombo at least, things had gone back to normal in a few days. What seemed disturbing, now that I thought about those 1981 riots, was that there had been no warning, no hint that they were going to happen. I looked all around me at the deserted beach, so calm in the hot sun. What was to prevent a riot from happening right now? I thought. Even as I lay in this hammock, was it not possible that a mob was getting ready to come to our hotel? I shuddered.

A slight noise made me look up. Jegan had risen from his chair. He started to walk away, and suddenly I didn't want to be alone with my thoughts. I called out to him.

He came over. "How long have you been here?"

I looked at him to show that I had heard their conversation.

He began to push my hammock back and forth as if it were a swing.

"Do you think those riots will happen again?" I asked.

He didn't answer. Instead he said, "Come, let's go for a walk on the beach."

I got out of my hammock.

"You know," Jegan said, after we had walked in silence for a while, "this reminds me of Jaffna and the time I used to go for sea baths with my classmates."

"I've never been to Jaffna."

"Well," he said, "this is not a very good time to go." Then he added, "The police and the army are very cruel in Jaffna. They do terrible things to the Tamils there."

"Torture?"

He looked at me in surprise. "How did you know that?"

"I know," I replied, not wanting to tell him about Daryl Uncle.

"Were you ever tortured?" I asked.

He glanced at me quickly and then away. "No," he said. "But I knew somebody who was."

Now I watched him closely.

"A friend. We worked together in the Gandhiyam movement." He looked at me. "In fact, you remind me of him, when he was your age. We were . . . we were very good friends."

We had reached a rock now and he motioned for us to sit down on it.

"So what happened?" I asked.

"He left for Canada as a refugee, and I went off and joined the Tigers."

I stared at him in shock.

"Don't tell anybody, okay?"

I nodded, still staring at him. "Are you a Tiger?" I asked in a hushed voice.

He smiled. "Not anymore." He saw that I was waiting for him to continue. "If you become a Tiger you cannot question anything they do. Recently they killed a social worker because he disagreed with their opinions." He looked at the sea moodily. "On the other hand, what is the alternative? We cannot live like this under constant threat from the Sinhalese, always second-class citizens in our own country. As my father used to say, 'It's small choices of rotten apples.' Here you can be killed by the Sinhalese and there you can be killed by the police or the Tigers."

We sat on the rock for a long time, talking. He told me about the Tiger training camp in South India. He also spoke about his friend in the Gandhiyam movement. I could tell that he had loved him very much; his having been tortured had affected him deeply.

⊏⧓⊐

The bond between Jegan and me grew stronger after that conversation on the beach. When we were back in Colombo, he invited me to go jogging with him. Every evening, after Jegan came back from work, he would change into a pair of shorts and a T-shirt, and together we would set off for the Ministry of Sports grounds. We would take the bus down Bullers Road and get off near Radio Ceylon. From there we would walk to the grounds, which were next to Independence Square. Diggy was furious with envy when he found out about these outings. He wanted to come as well, but couldn't swallow his pride and ask Jegan. For his part, Jegan never invited him, and I was glad of this. I had been excluded and humiliated by Diggy plenty of times, and it felt good to get my own back.

One evening, we were warming up before our run when I noticed that Jegan was looking at two men who were warming up near us. They noticed him now, and he raised his hand tentatively in greeting. They nodded, but they had a warning look in their eyes, as if telling him not to approach them. When we started to jog, however, they caught up with us. Gradually, Jegan picked up his speed and left me far behind. The two men kept up with him, and I noticed that they drew closer and talked to him. Once we had finished jogging and were seated on the grass, they came and sat somewhere behind us. Without turning around, Jegan said something to them in Tamil which I didn't understand. They replied, and I noticed that Jegan turned slightly to his left to watch as three men jogged by. One of them, the older one, had on an expensive brand-name track suit, unlike the simple shorts and T-shirts we wore. After a while the men sitting behind us got up and began to jog again.

"Who were those men, the ones you talked to before?" I asked him.

"Oh, just old school friends," he said casually, but he had a troubled expression on his face.

He stood up and said it was time to go. As we left the grounds, I noticed he was looking at an expensive car that was parked nearby. It had a small Sri Lankan flag attached to its antenna, and there were two men in uniform leaning against the side of it.

That evening, I was looking for the cinema page in the

newspaper when I came across a picture of the man we had seen at the sports grounds in the expensive track suit. He was distributing awards at a school prize-giving event. I read the caption under the photograph and discovered that he was a Tamil minister in the government.

The next evening, instead of walking to Bullers Road to catch the bus, Jegan turned right and set off in the other direction. "Where are you going?" I asked.

"Oh," he said, "didn't I tell you? I've decided to use Police Park instead. It's much closer than the Ministry of Sports and we'll save on the bus fare."

Although his reasons made sense, I didn't entirely accept his explanation. Something was troubling him, but what it was I couldn't tell.

Then a few days later I found out.

We came home from school one day to find Amma and Neliya Aunty sitting on the verandah, looking alarmed.

"What happened?" Diggy asked.

"The police were here," Amma said.

"The police!" I said. Amma and I looked at each other, remembering our last encounter with the police.

"What did they want?" Diggy asked.

"They wanted to speak to Jegan," Neliya Aunty said.

"Why?" I asked, feeling suddenly afraid.

They both shrugged.

"Anyway," Amma said, "I called the office. Jegan and your Appa should be here soon."

We went to put away our schoolbags. As we walked

down the hall, Sonali took my arm and asked what I thought
was happening. I shook my head. I couldn't help remembering that conversation Jegan and I had had on the beach. I
wondered if the police visit was connected to his having been
a Tiger.

When my father and Jegan arrived home, I was surprised
to discover that my father was thinking along the same lines
I was. Once Amma told them what had happened, my father
turned to Jegan and said, "I've never asked you this, son, but
I need to know. Were you or are you connected with the
Tigers?"

Jegan was silent for a moment. Then he nodded. My parents looked at him, appalled. "But not anymore," Jegan said
hurriedly, trying to reassure them.

"Are you sure, son?" my father said gravely. "This is not
the time to hide anything from us."

"I'm sure, Uncle," Jegan replied.

"But what do the police want, then?" Amma asked anxiously.

My father telephoned a friend of his who was high up in
the police and explained the situation to him. Then he just
listened and nodded for what seemed like a long time. When
he put down the phone, Amma asked what the man had said.

"He'll look into it," my father said.

"Meanwhile, what do we do?" she asked.

"He advised us to go to the police station without waiting
for them to come to us. That way they'll know we're innocent."

"Is that the best thing to do?" Amma asked.

"I'm afraid so."

Amma and I looked at each other doubtfully.

My father stood up. "Better put on a fresh shirt and tie," he said to Jegan. "Things like that are always important."

Jegan nodded but didn't get up. He looked very frightened.

My father patted him on the back. "Don't worry, son," he said. "You are innocent, so what can they do?" As an afterthought he added, "Anyway, it's best not to mention this Tiger business."

That evening, we sat around on the front verandah and waited for my father and Jegan to return. Even though the next day was a school day, neither Amma nor Neliya Aunty forced us to go inside and do our homework. I glanced at Neliya Aunty and Amma, and I was reminded of that terrible morning when we had sat on the verandah waiting for the police to come and take them to identify Daryl Uncle's body. As the hours passed, Amma and Neliya Aunty got up from time to time to do little tasks, but they always returned to the verandah. Gradually the darkness obliterated the red glow of the sky.

Finally, we heard my father's car outside, and Amma sent me to open the gate. The glare of the headlights prevented me from seeing into the car; it was only when it had passed me on the way to the garage that I saw that Jegan was not inside.

I closed the gates and went up the driveway. Amma had come down the verandah steps, and she saw the expression on my face.

"Only Appa came back," I said.

She drew in her breath. My father had closed the garage door and was walking towards us.

"What happened?" Amma called out to him. "Where is he?"

"Oh, they just kept him for the night," my father said. He was trying hard to sound casual.

"What?" Amma cried.

"Just routine stuff."

"How can it be routine to keep someone in jail overnight?"

By now Neliya Aunty, Sonali, and Diggy had joined us. My father looked at Amma, irritated. "They just wanted to ask him a few questions, that's all."

"Couldn't he have gone back tomorrow morning?"

My father shrugged.

"You didn't say anything?"

"I did, but under the Prevention of Terrorism Act they have the right to keep him."

"But he's not a terrorist!"

My father was silent for a moment. His face looked suddenly tired. "Don't be so sure about that," he said. We stared at him.

"Evidently they spotted him at the Ministry of Sports grounds chatting with two men whom they later arrested. The men were planning to assassinate a prominent Tamil politician because he is considered a traitor by the Tigers." I gasped involuntarily. Everyone turned to look at me.

"Wait a minute. You go jogging with him, no?" Amma said to me.

"Did you see him talk to these men?" Neliya Aunty asked.

I nodded.

"Son," my father said gravely, "tell us exactly what you saw."

I told them all that I had seen. How Jegan had recognized the men and how they had chatted briefly while they were jogging and later as well when we sat on the grass. I also told them about Jegan's decision afterwards to change sports grounds, a decision which now made sense to me.

"He's innocent," Amma said, once I was finished. "How could he have been involved in the assassination plan?"

"How do you know he's innocent?" my father asked. "We can't be a hundred percent sure."

"You mean you honestly think he's guilty?" Amma asked, astonished.

My father was silent. We all stared at him, angry and hurt that he would really believe this.

"Look," my father eventually said, "the best thing is to get as little involved as possible. If they find out that Jegan is connected to the assassination attempt, we could be accused of harboring a terrorist."

"Nonsense," Amma said. "Why would they accuse us?"

"These days, every Tamil is a Tiger until proven otherwise."

"So you're just going to leave Jegan there?"

My father turned to her, impatient now. "You forget, Nalini, that I have a business to maintain. There are many Sinhalese in this city who would love to see me go under. I have to be very careful."

★ ★ ★

The next morning, I was awakened by the sound of my father calling to Amma. Just from the tone of his voice I could tell something had happened. I hurriedly knotted my sarong and went out into the hall. Amma and my father were leaning over the newspaper on the dining table. I came up to them and looked at the column they were reading. The heading read KEY SUSPECT IN ASSISSINATION PLOT DISCOVERED.

"See that!" my father said to Amma, jabbing his finger at a line in the article. " 'The suspect, Jegan Parameswaran, resides with a well-known Tamil hotelier.' "

He groaned and pushed his hair back from his forehead. He and Amma regarded each other for a long moment.

The phone rang then, and Amma went to pick it up. "Oh, hello, Mala," she said.

I could hear Mala Aunty's excited voice on the other end of the line. "Yes, we saw the article," Amma said wearily.

For the rest of the morning the phone rang constantly.

My father came home very late for lunch that day. We had already returned from school when he arrived. He looked grim as he sat down at the table. We waited for him to speak, but he didn't say anything until he had dished out some food onto his plate.

"The office staff have read Jegan's name in the paper," my father said to Amma. "Some were sympathetic, but others said nothing. It's only a matter of time before the hotel staff finds out." He took a mouthful of food. "You won't believe what I found on my desk this morning."

We waited for him to continue.

"A hate note," he said bitterly. "Accusing me of being a Tiger."

"But how did the note get on your desk?" Amma asked.

"How do you think? A staff member put it there."

We stared at him, shocked. I had been in my father's office many times and I knew all his employees. It was impossible to think that any of them was capable of such maliciousness.

My father pushed his plate away. "And the filthy phone calls, both for Sena and me. Poor Mrs. Wickramasinghe, our receptionist, was in tears by lunchtime."

He shook his head and sighed. "I don't know if I'll ever be able to live this down."

That evening, the police released Jegan. There were no charges laid. My father went to pick him up, and we waited on the front verandah for them to return. When we heard the car outside, Diggy and I went and opened the gate. Jegan was seated in the front with my father. My father stopped the car in the driveway and they got out. By now Amma and Neliya Aunty and Sonali had come to the edge of the verandah, and we all looked at Jegan, not knowing how to react.

He sensed our discomfort, for he smiled and held out his hands, saying, "See, I'm all in one piece."

This broke the tension, and we all began to ask him questions at the same time.

"Are you really okay?"

"How was it in prison?"

"They didn't ill-treat you, did they?"

"We were so worried, you can't imagine."

"It must have been such a nightmare."

My father held up his hand and said jovially, "Please, please, the boy has had enough interrogation."

We became quiet. My father had acted very shabbily in the whole affair, we all felt.

"Why don't you go and have a bath," Amma said to Jegan. "You must be dying for one."

Once Jegan had gone to his room, Amma sent me after him with a fresh towel. As I went up the steps to his apartment, I could not hear him moving around inside. I knocked on the door and waited, but there was no response. "Jegan," I called out softly, and after a while he said, "Yes."

I opened the door. He was lying across his bed and he quickly sat up. He turned his head away, but not before I saw that he was crying. I stood in the doorway, not knowing what to do. "Amma told me to give this to you," I finally said, and held out the towel.

He didn't move.

I placed the towel on the table and turned to go, but he beckoned to me to come and sit by him on the bed. He rubbed his hand across his cheeks and then went to the bathroom. After a while, he came out, and, apart from the slight redness of his eyes, there was no sign that he had been crying.

"Don't tell anyone about this," he said.

I nodded.

Later, Jegan joined my father for a drink on the front lawn. I watched them from the verandah, where they couldn't see me. For some time they didn't talk, then my father said, "I've been thinking."

Jegan studied him carefully.

"Would you like to take a few days and go to Jaffna?"

Jegan sat back in his chair.

"I mean, it would be good for you to take a small holiday after all this." My father shifted uncomfortably in his chair.

"Why, Uncle?" Jegan asked.

"I just think you need the holiday. A chance to get yourself together."

"I'm fine," Jegan said.

My father looked at him and said irritably, "How can you be fine? You just spent the night in jail."

"The best thing for me is hard work," Jegan replied. "I need to get back into my routine."

My father was silent for a moment. Then he picked up the newspaper that was beside him on the grass and gave it to Jegan. "I was hoping I wouldn't have to show you this, but I guess there's no help for it."

Jegan placed the newspaper on his lap and leaned over to read it. When he was finished, he sat back slowly in his chair. He picked up the paper and glanced at it again. He turned to regard my father. "The office staff read it?"

My father nodded. "It was in the Sinhala papers too."

"What did they say?"

"Most of the Tamil and Muslim staff came by my office to say they didn't believe it. But the Sinhalese staff, with the exception of Mrs. Wickramasinghe, were silent."

"So they believe that I am a Tiger."

My father sighed. "There is a lot of jealousy because I gave you such a high position."

"What about the hotel staff?"

"They know as well. Mr. Samarakoon called to express his regret over the whole thing."

Jegan looked at the paper; then he grabbed it and threw it on the lawn.

"It's unfair," he cried. "I'm innocent." He turned to my father, agitated. "Can't we sue the papers for defamation?"

My father looked down at his drink.

Jegan sighed and rested his forehead on his hand. After a while he straightened up. "So what are you telling me, Uncle?" he asked in a dull voice. "Does this mean that I'm fired?"

My father glanced at him quickly, a hurt expression on his face.

"Of course not. What kind of a man do you think I am?"

Jegan lifted his hand in apology.

"I just want you to take a small holiday, that's all."

Jegan shook his head. "Going away won't solve anything," he said. "The best thing is to face the problem."

My father shrugged to say that it was Jegan's decision.

Jegan went to work the next morning. Before I left for school, I saw him coming out of his room in his tie and short-sleeved shirt. As I looked at him, I wondered if he was wrong to ignore my father's advice. The hate note and the general attitude of the staff had made me realize the gravity of the situation. I was surprised that he couldn't see it, too, that he didn't feel a few days away would help ease the tension in the office.

That afternoon, I was lying on my bed when I heard Jegan outside, calling my name. I got up, surprised that he was home early, and went to the window. He was dressed in his shorts and T-shirt.

He looked at me and said, "Why aren't you ready?"

"I didn't know you were home."

"Hurry up, hurry up," he said.

I was stunned; he had never spoken to me like that before. I put my book down hastily and started to get dressed.

As soon as I came out the front door, he began to walk briskly down the verandah steps towards the gate. I hurried after him. All the way to the park he was very quiet. I glanced at him from time to time, but he looked so forbidding that I didn't dare say a word. There was a slight sadness in his face, too, and this melancholy expression made me realize that something had indeed happened at the office.

When we reached the park, he didn't jog at my speed, as he usually did. Instead, he ran very fast.

After I finished my few laps I sat on the grass, watching him.

Eventually he slowed down to a brisk walk. As he passed me, I saw that he was no longer angry. Finally, he stopped altogether, walked over, and sat down next to me. He tried to smile. "That was a good run," he said.

I nodded.

We sat in silence for a little while. I could see that his face was still sad.

"How's work?" I asked hesitantly.

He made an exasperated sound. "Awful," he said.

Then he told me what had happened. The office peon had delivered a parcel to the wrong address and Jegan had reprimanded him for his carelessness. He had been insolent,

and Jegan had threatened to dismiss him. The peon had
stalked out of his office, close to tears. The secretarial staff
had taken the man's side. What made Jegan really angry was
that my father had also sided with the man. I, too, was angry
when I heard this.

"He's an idiot," I said, referring to my father. "Just ignore
him."

"I wish I could," he said. "Who knows? Maybe everything will go back to normal in a few days."

Later that evening, I was helping Sonali with her homework
when we heard my parents in their bedroom. They were
talking about what had happened. We looked at each other
and we stopped talking and listened.

When my father had finished relating the incident, Amma
said, "You should have taken Jegan's side. After all, he is more
important than the peon."

"As Tamils we must tread carefully," my father replied.
"Jegan has to learn that. Even I have to be circumspect when
I'm talking to the staff. If I was Sinhalese, like Sena, I could
say and do whatever I liked."

Amma sighed. "It's so ridiculous," she said.

"What to do? One has to be realistic."

"I know. I've stopped talking to our Kolpetty Market
butcher in Tamil," Amma said. "Poor man is quite relieved.
One doesn't feel safe speaking Tamil these days."

"It's just a bad time," my father said. "Once the government destroys these damn Tigers, everything will go back to
normal."

"Maybe these Tigers and their separate state are not such a stupid idea after all."

"Are you mad?!" my father said, incredulous that she should say such a thing.

"I know," Amma said, "I should have my head examined. But seriously, what do we have to offer our children when they grow up? I don't want them to live as we do. Always having to watch what they say and do."

Sonali and I glanced at each other. It was so odd to hear Amma speak in favor of the Tigers. I wondered what had brought about this change of feeling, then remembered Daryl Uncle's death.

Then, a week later, inspection time came around. My father didn't have to go, because Mr. Samarakoon could supervise Jegan, but he and Sena Uncle decided to accompany him.

"It's better this way," my father explained to Jegan. "Sena's and my being there will show that we support you and will discourage any dissension among the staff."

Jegan nodded and, probably because of the incident with the peon, he seemed rather relieved.

Chithra Aunty was going, too, this time, and my father wanted Amma to come with them. Since Neliya Aunty was also going away for the weekend, Amma took us along as well.

From the moment we entered the hotel premises, I found myself watching the staff carefully to see how they reacted to Jegan. Mr. Samarakoon came hurrying down the front steps to greet us. He shook Jegan's hand warmly, as if nothing had happened. The reception staff and our guest-relations officer also made a point of coming to the front steps to greet him. I was grateful to them for their kindness, and I felt sure that this visit was going to be un-eventful after all.

Then later that evening, Chithra Aunty, Amma, Diggy, Sonali, and I went for a walk along the beach. Jegan came along too. We walked past the entire row of hotels and came to a fishing village. We noticed a van parked on the beach ahead of us and some young men dancing in front of it. Even from a distance, we could hear the sound of singing and laughter. As we drew near, we saw that they were passing a bottle from one to the other.

Amma stopped and said, "Let's turn back."

"Nonsense," Chithra Aunty said. "It's just some students having a little fun."

Amma looked at Jegan.

"Best to avoid them, Aunty," he said. "Since they're drinking, you never know."

"Don't be silly," Chithra Aunty said. "Come, come." She grabbed Amma's hand.

As we drew nearer to the van, the men became silent. They regarded us closely, but once we had passed they went back to their singing.

"See," Chithra Aunty said, "it was nothing."

We reached our destination, which was a big rock that jutted out into the water. While Sonali ran around gathering shells, Amma and Chithra Aunty sat on a ledge in the rock and chatted. Jegan, Diggy, and I climbed to the top of the rock and looked out at the sea.

When the sun had almost set, we began to walk back to the hotel. The van was still there, but now the singing had subsided. When we drew near, I saw that the back was open and the men were sitting there with their legs hanging down. They looked at us silently as we passed, and this time I felt more uncomfortable than I had earlier. We had only gone a few yards beyond the van when one of the men called out, "Ado, Tiger."

We turned involuntarily.

Jegan took a step towards them.

"Don't," Amma said, and she put her hand on his arm. He stood looking at the men for a long moment and then turned around.

"Let's go," Chithra Aunty said.

We began to walk rapidly away from them. Amma kept her hand on Jegan's arm, as if she feared that he would go back.

Just then a bottle flew past us and landed in the sand with a dull thud. "Run!" Amma cried. "Run!"

We hurried across the beach towards the hotel. Amma kept her hand around Jegan's arm, making sure he stayed with us. Only when we were a safe distance from them did she let go of him.

"Who are those men?" said Chithra Aunty. "How did they know about the Tiger thing?"

Jegan was gazing back at the van. The look in his eyes disturbed me.

"Jegan," Amma said, and she touched his arm. "Let's go."

He shook her hand off roughly.

She motioned to us and we continued towards the hotel. After a while Jegan turned and followed us.

As we drew near our hotel, we saw my father and Sena Uncle having their drink at a table near the beach. They waved to us gaily. When we were a little closer, however, a look of concern crossed their faces.

Sena Uncle got up from his seat. "What's wrong?" he called out to us as we approached. Amma held up her hand to say that she would explain.

When we reached them, Amma said, "We had such a close shave just now."

We sat down and she began to explain what had happened.

I noticed that while she talked, Jegan seemed lost in thought. When she finished, both my father and Sena Uncle were silent. After a moment, my father sent a waiter to fetch Mr. Samarakoon. When he arrived, my father asked Diggy to get up from his chair and said to Mr. Samarakoon, "Come, come, sit, Mr. Samarakoon."

"Tell him what happened," my father said to Amma.

She repeated her story. When she was done, Mr. Samarakoon shook his head and sighed.

"Do you know these characters, Mr. Samarakoon?" my father asked.

"They're the Banduratne Mudalali's sons and their friends, sir."

"Oh," my father said. "Those are the ones who . . ." He stopped himself. Mr. Samarakoon glanced quickly at Amma.

"The ones who what?" Amma asked.

Nobody answered her.

"Do you think that there'll be more trouble?" my father asked Mr. Samarakoon.

"Hard to say, sir," he replied.

My father nodded thoughtfully. "Tell the night watchman to be especially alert tonight."

Mr. Samarakoon nodded. My father indicated that he could go.

Once Mr. Samarakoon had left, Amma turned to Chithra Aunty and said, "Chithra, what's going on?"

"Nothing, darling," Chithra Aunty said brightly.

"Sena?"

"Nalini . . . please."

Amma looked sternly at my father. Sena Uncle and Chithra Aunty sensed that there was going to be a fight and so they got up and excused themselves.

When they had left, Amma continued to stare at my father as if ordering him to speak. Finally, he shrugged and said, "I guess you might as well know."

Then he told her about what had happened during the 1981 riots, and how the Banduratne Mudalali and his sons were responsible for all the killings and burnings in this area. They wanted this town to be completely free of Tamils, and they were backed by a cabinet minister who was a well-known racist.

When my father was finished, Amma didn't say anything. She looked out at the sea, and there was a tired expression on her face. Then she shifted in her chair and sighed. "You know," she said, "I've been thinking about emigration."

My father looked at her in shock.

"Canada and Australia are opening their doors. It would be a good time to apply. For the sake of the children."

My father shook his head emphatically. "I'll never emigrate. I've seen the way our people live in foreign countries."

"It's better than living in this terrible uncertainty."

He turned to Amma angrily. "How can you want to emigrate? You saw the way our friends lived when we went to America. They come here and flash their dollars around, but over there they're nothing."

"It's not a question of wanting or not wanting to go. We have to think about the children."

"Don't worry," my father said. "Things will work out."

And then after a while, "Besides, what would I do there? The only job I'd be fit for would be a taxi driver or a petrol station man."

That evening, Diggy, Sonali, and I sat on the patio outside our bedrooms, waiting for our parents so we could go for dinner. Diggy had a gloomy look on his face, and he began to walk back and forth. Sonali sat close to me, as she often did when she was scared.

"Do you think that anything will happen tonight?" Sonali asked me.

Diggy stopped walking and glared at her.

"No," I said soothingly.

Diggy clicked his tongue against his teeth impatiently and continued his pacing.

"You know," Sonali said, "sometimes I wish I was a Sinhalese or a foreigner."

"I don't," Diggy said. He glared at us again. "I'm proud to be Tamil. If those damn buggers come here, I'll . . ."

He began to pace again, more rapidly than before.

Amma came out onto her patio and called us. We got up and went to her. Even though she was dressed for dinner, she looked very tired.

At dinner that evening, we were all silent. When we had finished, my parents decided to have coffee served on their patio. We walked across the sand towards their room. The lamps along our path were only a few feet high, and with their rounded shades they looked like illuminated mushrooms. They provided only enough light for us to see directly in front of us. Thus, we were close to my parents' room before we noticed a group of people gathered in front of one of the patios.

"What on earth!" my father exclaimed.

We quickly walked over to them.

As we drew near, we saw that they were standing in front of Jegan's patio. They were all guests, and they were talking agitatedly in various languages. When we reached them, we saw the cause of their excitement. Across the window someone had written in Sinhalese, "Death to all Tamil pariahs." By now a few of the housekeeping boys had come up to the group as well.

"Sir," one of the guests said to my father, "what do the words mean?"

My father didn't reply. He and Sena Uncle pushed through the crowd and stepped up onto the patio.

"Please, everything is all right," my father said very slowly and loudly so that they could understand him. "Everything is under control. You can go back to your rooms."

Whether they understood him or not, people continued

to stand there. Since the crowd was attracting more guests, my father called to one of the housekeeping boys to fetch Mr. Samarakoon and our guest-relations officer, Miss De Silva. He stood on the patio until they arrived. My father told Miss De Silva, in Sinhalese, to inform the guests that everything was fine. She spoke to them in two or three languages.

One of the guests said something to her. She turned to my father and said, in Sinhalese, "Sir, they want to know what happened."

"Tell them that it's just a prank," my father replied.

She told them this, but some of them shook their heads skeptically. One of them pointed to the writing on the window and asked a question. She shrugged and said something that I didn't understand, and now the guests looked even more doubtful. By now my father, Sena Uncle, Mr. Samarakoon, and Jegan had gone into the room, leaving Miss De Silva alone with the crowd. After a while, some of the guests began to disperse.

We went onto the patio and into the room. Jegan's suitcase was open and his clothes were strewn all over the bed. Apart from that the room was untouched. Jegan sat on the edge of his bed, staring at the contents of his suitcase. When we came in, he glanced at us quickly and then looked down at the bed again. My father, Sena Uncle, and Mr. Samarakoon were examining the lock of the front bedroom door. Now Miss De Silva came in to tell my father and Sena Uncle that the guests had gone back to their rooms. My father thanked her.

She looked at Jegan and said, "Sorry."

He nodded.

Once she had gone, my father sat down on the dressing-table stool.

"What do you think, Mr. Samarakoon?"

"Inside job, sir."

"Yes," Sena Uncle said. "Obviously, the person who did this had a key."

"You mean, one of the housekeeping staff?" Amma asked, incredulous.

They didn't reply.

We were silent, letting the implications of this sink in.

Chithra Aunty was the first one to speak. "Who would have thought?" she said. "They all seem so nice."

"So what are you going to do?" Amma asked.

My father shrugged.

"What can we do?" Sena Uncle said. "The staff member who did it is obviously in league with the Banduratne Mudalali. If we call the police, they will come, harass the innocent housekeeping staff, and then leave without arresting the culprit."

There was a knock at the door.

"Come in," my father called.

Miss De Silva entered the room. She looked very upset.

"Aiyo, sir," she said to my father and Sena Uncle. "Big mess, sir. Tourists are checking out left, right, and center."

My father rose to his feet in alarm. "But we explained to them that everything was okay," he said.

She pointed to the writing on the window. "Someone has spread a rumor about the writing, sir. The guests think it says the hotel is going to be bombed tonight."

"Honestly," my father said, "how ignorant can these foreigners be?" He signaled to Sena Uncle and Mr. Samarakoon. "Let's go and see if we can salvage the situation."

At the doorway, my father turned. "Jegan, pack your things and move them to another room," he said. He looked at Miss De Silva. "Get one of the housekeeping staff to rub off the writing."

Amma nudged us and we followed them out. I looked back and saw that Jegan was still sitting on his bed. He had not started to pack the contents of his suitcase.

None of us felt like going to bed, so we went to sit on the patio outside my parents' room. We had not been there very long before the head housekeeper came looking for my father. Amma told him that my father was at Reception. Instead of going to find him, however, he remained where he was, staring into space.

"What's wrong?" Amma asked.

"Aiyo, madam," he said, and then he was silent.

"Tell, will you? What's wrong?" Chithra Aunty said.

He sighed deeply. "All of us are scared to clean the window. If we do it, we might be in trouble next."

Amma stood up. "I'll wash it off, then." She looked at us and said, "One of you come with me."

I immediately volunteered, and Sonali came along as well.

Jegan was still sitting on the bed, his bag unpacked. Amma looked at him for a long moment and then she went to the window. She examined the writing and turned to the head housekeeper. "Bring me some turpentine and a rag," she said. He nodded and left.

Once he had gone, Amma turned to Jegan. "It's not good for the staff to see you like this. They'll lose respect."

Jegan made a sound of contempt. "What respect?" he said. "Anyway, it's only a matter of time before Uncle will have to do the inevitable."

"What are you talking about?" Amma cried. "We are all upset. This is not the time to babble on about nothing."

At that moment the head housekeeper knocked. Amma got the rags and turpentine from him and closed the door.

She glanced at Jegan, a troubled look on her face, and went out onto the patio. She poured some turpentine onto the rag and began to clean the writing. After a moment she called to Sonali and me, "Don't just sit there catching flies. Come and help me."

That night Sonali was too afraid to sleep alone, so I offered to sleep in her room. We lay awake for a long time, listening to the sound of the waves hurling themselves against the beach.

"What did Jegan mean when he said it was only a matter of time?" Sonali asked.

"I'm not sure," I said.

After Sonali had fallen asleep, I lay thinking that something was about to happen, but what it was I couldn't tell. Tomorrow we would be returning to Colombo after lunch, and for once I was not depressed that our holiday had ended.

My sense of foreboding, that something significant was about to take place, proved to be correct the next morning. We knew something was wrong when we came to breakfast and found our father not there.

"Where is Appa?" Sonali asked.

Amma didn't answer her. She indicated for us to be seated. She looked very tired, as if she had hardly slept last night. Soon Chithra Aunty, Sena Uncle, and Jegan joined us. They were all very quiet. I looked at Jegan, trying to catch his eye, but he refused to look at any of us. He finished his breakfast quickly, then excused himself and went to continue his inspection with Mr. Samarakoon. Once he had left, the atmosphere became less tense.

"Why don't we go for a sea bath after breakfast," Chithra Aunty suggested. "We can all do with some cheering up."

Amma nodded.

After breakfast, when we went across to our rooms to get changed, we saw our father. He was seated on his patio, and when he saw us he didn't even acknowledge our presence. As I drew near, I could see that he had a glass of whiskey in his hand. I looked at Amma, but she looked down at the sand. Neither she nor Chithra Aunty seemed surprised that he was drinking at this time.

Amma said to me irritably, "Hurry up and get changed."

When I had changed and come outside, Sonali was waiting for me. "You know what?" she whispered. "I went to Amma and Appa's room to get my swimsuit and I think Amma was crying."

Before I could say anything, Amma came out onto the patio in her bathing suit, smiling, but I could tell by the redness of her eyes that Sonali had been right.

The sea was beautiful that morning, the sun shimmering off the waves, yet I felt no joy. Amma and Chithra Aunty swam away from us and spent a long time talking to each other. After we had been in the sea a little while, I had to use the toilet, and so I made my way back to the beach.

As I approached my room, which was next to my parents', I noticed that my father was still sitting where we'd left him, the glass of whiskey in his hand.

When I had finished using the toilet and come out into my room, I saw Sena Uncle crossing the sand towards my parents' patio. My window was open, so I could hear their conversation.

"He's finished the inspection," Sena Uncle said. "It's time to tell him."

My father was silent.

"Chelva," Sena Uncle said, "it's best to get it over with."

My father sighed deeply. "I can't."

"I understand how hard this is for you . . ."

"No you don't," my father cried. "Buddy Parameswaran was my best friend, we made a promise to each other . . ."

"What's to be done?" Sena Uncle said gently. "Things can't continue this way. If they do, the whole business will fall apart."

"I can't do it. You do it."

"No, no, Chelva. You have to do it. He must hear it from you."

"Please," my father said. "Please do it for me."

"We are offering him an alternative," Sena Uncle said. "What he makes in the Middle East will be twice what we are paying him."

"Oh God, oh God," my father said. He put his drink down and I could hear the scraping of the chair as he stood up.

After a few moments, they went across the sand towards the main part of the hotel.

I sat down on my bed. My father and Sena Uncle were going to fire Jegan. Now I understood what he had meant last night about my father having to do the inevitable. Jegan had known since yesterday that this was going to happen. I couldn't stand to be in the room anymore, so I got up and went outside.

I crossed to the edge of the beach, where the green goatsfoot ended and the sand began. Instead of walking on the sand, I made my way through the goatsfoot, feeling the thick leaves crunch under my feet. I could see my family still in the water, but, wanting to be alone, I set off in the opposite direction. I was angry by now, but at whom I didn't know. I thought about my father, but I couldn't feel angry at him, because, when I remembered that yellowed piece of paper and the promise he had made to Jegan's father, I actually felt sorry for him. I thought of the number of times he had abandoned his promise, how he had left Jegan in jail overnight, how he had taken the side of the office peon against him, and I wondered if he had actually had a choice in any of these matters. I thought, too, of how Jegan had said that his father was so proud of my father's achievements, and I wondered what his father would think if he were alive now and could see what a mess everything had come to.

I stopped walking and stared out at the sea. How could Jegan and I go on being friends after this? Would he become for me what his father had become to my father? A distant memory, so forgotten that even his death would not touch me? No, I would not accept that. The sound of the waves crashing on the beach reminded me of that afternoon Jegan and I had gone for a walk together, how we had sat on a rock and talked for hours. I had never talked to anybody like that before, nor had anybody spoken to me with such frankness. I turned around and started to walk towards the hotel.

When I got there, I found Jegan out in front. He was putting the luggage onto the roof rack of the car. He saw me but didn't greet me. I watched him as he began to pass a rope through his side of the rack. He told me to stand on the other side of the car and help him. I did so.

"How are things?" I finally said.

" 'Things' are fine," he said.

I threaded the rope through my side of the rack and gave it to him. As he took it, our eyes met for a moment.

"I guess you heard," he said.

I nodded.

"Well, it's not the end of the world." He shrugged.

"Appa was talking about a job in the Middle East . . ."

"There are other alternatives," he said.

I looked at him and felt suddenly afraid. "What do you mean?" I asked.

He didn't answer. He pulled at the rope firmly to hold it in place and then passed it to me.

"You can make a lot of money in the Middle East, you know. Twice what you'd make here," I said.

"What do you know about it?" he said. "You're just a boy."

His words struck me like a physical blow. I looked at him, but he refused to meet my eye. Then I threw the rope at his face. It struck him on the cheek, but he didn't react. He simply picked it up, passed it one last time through his side of the roof rack, and tied it. Without even glancing at me, he turned and walked back to the hotel.

As I watched him go up the steps, I thought bitterly of how wrong I had been to think that friendship was possible between us. I hated Jegan now with a hot, tearful anger.

When we arrived at our house that evening, Jegan went straight to his room. Neliya Aunty had come down the verandah steps to greet us, and she looked after him in surprise. She glanced at Amma inquiringly, but Amma closed her eyes slowly to warn Neliya Aunty not to say anything, that she would tell her later.

The next day, when we came back from school, Amma was at the end of the driveway. She was supervising the gardener and his assistant as they moved the old storeroom things back into Jegan's room. I stared in dismay as the two men heaved an old almariah up the stairs.

"Jegan has left?" I asked Amma, hardly able to believe that he had.

"What does it look like?" she replied abruptly.

"He's gone back to Jaffna?"

"Go inside and change out of your uniform," she said a little more kindly.

"Did he . . . did he say anything before he left?"

She shook her head.

I watched for a few more minutes as the two men took the almariah through the door into Jegan's room. Then I turned and went back towards the house, feeling a tightness rise into my throat. Jegan had left without even saying good-bye. I could hardly believe he had done that. Before I went up the verandah steps, I looked down the driveway again at the gardener and his assistant taking furniture up into the room that had belonged to Jegan.

I did not know it at the time, but we would never see Jegan again.

The referendum took place a few weeks after Jegan's departure. It was a disturbing day. My parents went to the polling booth near us, but they never got a chance to vote. A member of Parliament arrived with his thugs, held the voting officials at gunpoint, and then proceeded to stuff the ballot boxes with false ballots.

That evening, we watched the results begin to come in on television, and it was soon clear that the government had won. They would remain in power for another six years.

My father got up and went out into the garden, where Anula had set up his usual cocktail. Only Amma and I followed.

"Chelva . . ." Amma began. "We need to open our eyes. We need to think about our future."

My father shook his head. "Never. I will never leave this country," he said.

Amma tried to persuade him to change his mind and apply to Canada or Australia, but he would not hear of it. Angry and frustrated, she stood up and went back into the house. I stayed behind to keep my father company, and sat on the swing, sharing his silence. The sun was declining and a dark blot seeped across the sky, obliterating shades of red and yellow. I looked at the expression on his face, and I felt I understood what was in his heart.

My father did not come inside for dinner that evening. Instead, he sat on the lawn and drank until long after the sun had set.

The Best
School of All

Towards the end of the Christmas holiday, we were at dinner one evening when my father put his fork down emphatically on his plate.

"I've come to a decision," he said. Then he looked at me. "I'm transferring you to the Victoria Academy in the new year."

I stared at him, my fork held in midair. The Queen Victoria Academy was the school Diggy attended. Why was I being taken out of St. Gabriel's and sent there?

Nobody else at the table seemed surprised by the news, and I realized that I had been the last to hear of his decision.

"But *why?*" I asked.

"Because it's good for you."

I didn't like the sound of this.

"What's wrong with St. Gabriel's?"

"Nothing. It's just that the Victoria Academy is better for you."

My father was being evasive, and this made me even more suspicious.

"Why is it better?"

My father picked up his fork to indicate that the subject was closed. "The Academy will force you to become a man," he said. Sonali, Amma, and Neliya Aunty smiled at me sympathetically before they continued with their meal. Diggy had a look on his face that told me he understood all the things my father had not said. I decided to corner him that evening and see what I could get out of him.

I found him in the garage, fixing the chain on his bicycle. When I came in, he looked up for a moment, then went on working. I stood by his bicycle and watched him.

"Why am I being transferred to the Victoria Academy?" I asked.

He continued to fiddle with the chain for a moment, then he looked up at me. "Because Appa is worried about you."

He said this as if I were in some kind of danger.

"Appa is worried about me? What for?"

He didn't answer. He tested the pedals to see if the chain now worked. Then he straightened up. "He doesn't want you turning out funny or anything like that."

I felt a flush rise into my face.

Diggy was looking at me, his eyes slightly narrowed. "You're not, are you?"

"Not what?" I asked, not meeting his gaze.

He picked up a piece of rag and wiped his greasy fingers.

"Listen," he said, after a moment, "since you're coming to the Victoria Academy, I want to warn you about Black Tie."

"Black Tie?"

"The principal. His real name is Mr. Abeysinghe, but we call him Black Tie because he always wears one. You'd better watch out for him," Diggy continued. "Once you get on his bad side, that's it." Then he began to detail the punishments one received for getting on his bad side. "Once, he slapped a boy and broke some of his teeth. Another boy in my class got caned so severely his trousers tore. Then he made the boy kneel in the sun until he fainted."

I was appalled. "What did they do?"

"One of the boys had hair that was too long and he wore his top two shirt buttons open. The other blinked too hard and Black Tie thought he was winking at him." He leaned towards me. "Never blink too hard in front of him, and most of all, don't lick your lips. If you do that, for sure he'll think you're trying to mock him."

This was so preposterous that I wondered if he was exaggerating. I found it difficult to believe that anyone would punish boys so severely for such negligible wrongs. At St. Gabriel's, the most the fathers would do was give the wrongdoer a smack on the palm with a ruler. Diggy had seen the doubt in my eyes, for he said, "You better believe me. If you don't, you'll be sorry."

"Why doesn't someone do something about it?" I asked.

He laughed. "Like what?"

"Like complain to their parents."

His eyes grew wide. "Never complain," he said. "Once you come to the Queen Victoria Academy you are a man. Either you take it like a man or the other boys will look down on you."

If I had not been pleased with the idea of transferring to the Victoria Academy, I now hated and feared it. I thought of approaching my father, but I knew this would be useless. From the way he had spoken at the dinner table, it was clear that his decision was final. The school was two streets away from St. Gabriel's, on the sea side of Galle Road. I had never actually seen the building; the school hours of both St. Gabriel's and the Victoria Academy were from 7:30 to 1:30, but I had always been dropped off before Diggy. After school, the car always picked us up in front of St. Gabriel's gates. All I knew of the Victoria Academy was the older boys. I would watch them from my classroom window as they swaggered along the railway lines or on the beach, their arms around one another. They seemed so grown-up in their long pants, and the way they laughed and called to each other, their voices loud and strident, made me a little frightened. Now, their loud confidence seemed a symbol of all the horror that awaited me in the new year.

The remainder of the Christmas holidays was completely ruined for me. I could think only of what lay ahead when school began. Diggy held out one ray of hope, however. Black Tie, he told me, might not be with the school much longer. He had heard this news from one of the prefects.

I learned from my brother that there was a dispute going on between Black Tie and Mr. Lokubandara, the vice principal. Diggy wouldn't tell me what the conflict was about, but he did inform me that Mr. Lokubandara was a "political appointee," his cousin being a minister in the cabinet. This meant that, in fact, he had a lot more power than Black Tie, and so Black Tie might well lose the struggle and have to resign.

I was surprised to see that as Diggy related all this he looked worried.

"Does the vice principal give worse punishments than Black Tie?" I asked.

"He's a snake in the grass," Diggy replied, but he would not say any more than that.

The Christmas holidays ended all too soon, and one morning I woke with a sense of foreboding, a feeling that something terrible awaited me that day. Then I saw my new school uniform over the chair.

The uniform at St. Gabriel's was shorts and a shirt, and this would be the first time I'd be wearing long trousers to school. Amma and Neliya Aunty oohed and aahed when they saw me in them, saying how quickly time had passed and that it seemed like yesterday they were changing my nappies. I remained untouched by their sentimentality and admiration. All I could think of was the boys in shorts at St. Gabriel's. I longed to be with them.

When the car came to a stop in front of the Victoria Academy, I got out and stood for a moment, looking at the building in front of me. It was a grand structure, about a hundred years old, a long rectangular block with sloping roofs and tall windows that extended from midway up the building to the top. The bottom half was covered with ivy. The building had three domes, one at each end and one in the center. Under the central dome was a small balcony. On the balcony stood a figure dressed all in white. "Black Tie," Diggy said to me, and the awe in his voice seemed to match the image of this figure in white, highlighted against the old building. I stared at Black Tie in surprise, for Diggy had failed to mention a very significant detail of his attire: a sola topee, that white domed hat I had only seen in photographs from the time the British ruled Sri Lanka.

When I was closer to the balcony, I got a better look at Black Tie. Though he was a fat man, his posture was upright. He wore a carefully pressed white suit that also belonged to another era, a white shirt, and, of course, the black tie.

Diggy took me in through the main entrance and led me towards a door at the other end of the building. This door opened out onto a quadrangle where a game of rugger was in progress. I paused in the doorway, reluctant to descend into the quadrangle. Most of the boys were much older and bigger than I was, and they were playing rugger with a brutality I had never seen at St. Gabriel's. Diggy signaled impatiently to me, and I had no choice but to follow him. I crossed the quadrangle watchfully, afraid that one of the players would run into me and knock me over, but I made it safely to the other side.

Diggy led me up a set of stairs to a row of classrooms. The open corridor outside the classrooms was filled with boys

about my size, yet they seemed much older. The bravado
with which they walked and the crude words they used reminded me of the boys I had seen playing on the railway lines
and beaches. I would have taken this bravura to be their true
nature had I not noticed that they stood aside respectfully to
let us pass. Diggy, being an older boy, hardly deigned to notice them.

We finally arrived at my classroom. There was a group of
boys standing in the doorway, and they glanced our way with
curiosity. One boy in particular was examining us. I noticed
that Diggy avoided meeting his gaze.

"This is your class," Diggy said to me.

"This is 9C, Chelvaratnam," the boy said.

I was surprised that he knew Diggy's surname. Diggy
looked at him for a moment and then he said pityingly, "I
know it's 9C, Salgado."

"This is a Sinhalese class, not a Tamil class. You want 9F,
Chelvaratnam."

"No, I don't, Salgado," Diggy replied. "I want 9C."
They stood looking at each other like two dogs who had met
on the edge of their territories. Then, much to my surprise,
Diggy backed down. He turned to me and said gloomily,
"This is your class," and began to walk away. I looked after
him in alarm, not wanting to be left alone with Salgado. He
soon disappeared into the crowded corridor.

"How come you're in a Sinhala class?" Salgado asked me.

"My parents put me in a Sinhala class from grade one
because they wanted me to learn Sinhalese," I said. My voice
sounded anxious, and I wondered if they had noticed it.

"We don't want you here," Salgado said, and he stood

in front of the doorway. "Go to the Tamil class."

I stared at him. I couldn't very well go down the corridor to 9F. I didn't even speak Tamil.

Then a voice behind me said, "But Salgado, aren't you always saying that Tamils should learn Sinhalese?"

I turned to look at the speaker. A boy was standing at the open window of the classroom, his elbows on the windowsill, hands cupping his chin. He had a small, musing smile on his face.

"Aday, Soyza, you better watch out or I'll give you something," Salgado replied, but his threat had an empty ring to it.

The boy named Soyza smiled indolently, thus dismissing Salgado's threat. "What's your name?" he said to me.

"It's Arjun."

"We only use surnames here," he said, kindly.

"It's Chelvaratnam," I said.

"Well, come in, come in, Chelvaratnam," he said and waved his hand theatrically. "Don't be shy."

Now Salgado moved aside and let me in. Soyza came away from the window. He beckoned to me to take the desk next to his. At that moment the bell rang and the boys hurried to their seats.

As I started to sit down, Soyza said, "Be careful, there's a nail in the corner of that chair."

I glanced at the chair and then nodded my thanks. Our eyes met for a brief instant, then Soyza looked away as if he was embarrassed.

When the teacher came in and began the roll call, I wrote the word "thanks" on a piece of paper and passed it to Soyza.

I watched out of the corner of my eye as he opened the note. I was surprised that instead of seeming pleased, he frowned as if I had committed an impropriety. He folded the paper and put it inside his desk. I stared at him, wondering what I had done wrong. Although he was aware that I was looking at him, he refused to meet my gaze. Later on, however, he relented, offering me the use of his protractor in geometry class.

I found myself looking at Soyza often during the classes that morning. Though delicately built, his body was well-proportioned and lacked the awkwardness of most other boys his age. His face was full of contrasts. His upper lip was thin, his lower lip full; his forehead was fine and well-shaped, his eyebrows thick and unruly. Yet the overall effect was attractive.

In the days that followed, it became evident to me that Soyza had a certain power which gave him immunity from bullies like Salgado. Where this came from I didn't understand. It was certainly not his physical strength. His long eyelashes and prominent cheekbones gave his face a fragility that looked like it could be easily shattered. Yet there was a confidence about him, an understanding of his own power. He was also daring, for, unlike any of the other boys, he wore his hair long. It fell almost to his shoulders. I noticed that whenever he went out into the corridor between classes or to the toilet, he always reached into his desk for black hair clips and pinned his hair up so deftly it looked like he had short hair.

★　★　★

After I had been at the Queen Victoria Academy a few weeks, an incident occurred which only increased my curiosity about Soyza.

Our physical training teacher had resigned and gone to work in the Middle East, and a prefect had been appointed to supervise the class until a new teacher was found. Not long after the prefect arrived, Soyza asked his permission to use the toilet. It was granted and he left the room. As he did so, I noticed that the other boys watched him, a few of them smirking at one another. About fifteen minutes passed and Soyza still had not come back. I was surprised that the prefect seemed oblivious to his absence.

Soyza only returned at the end of the interval. There was something different about him, and it took me a moment to realize what it was. His clothes, which had been immaculately ironed that morning, now looked rumpled.

A week later, during the interval, I was in the toilet, washing my hands at the sink, when Salgado and some of his friends walked in. The toilet was almost deserted. I noticed that they were looking at a boy who was using the urinal. Now the boy became conscious of them. He hurriedly zipped up his trousers and stood there, not knowing what to do. He turned away from the urinal to face us, and I saw that he was afraid. He began to walk towards the door, but Salgado and his friends were blocking the way.

"I say, Cheliah," Salgado said. "Don't you know better than to come to the toilet unaccompanied?"

Cheliah didn't answer. Now the other boys moved in

around him. Salgado gave a signal and the boys grabbed Cheliah from behind. He cried out, but one of the boys swiftly put his hand over Cheliah's mouth, silencing his cries. Now Salgado kicked open a cubicle and the boys crowded inside, dragging Cheliah with them. I turned and fled from the toilet.

I walked quickly down the passageway to the stairs that led to my classroom. When I reached them, I saw Soyza coming in the opposite direction. He noticed the expression on my face and signaled for me to wait for him.

"What's wrong?" he said when he reached me.

I shook my head, unable to speak.

He took my arm and said, "Come with me."

He led me down another corridor to the playground. There was a garden roller under a tree, and he suggested we sit on it. He carefully laid out his handkerchief before he sat down. Then he looked at me, waiting for me to begin my story.

When I was finished, he stared ahead for a while, his elbow on his knee, his hand cupped under his chin. Then he turned to me and said, "Cheliah is the leader of the Grade 9 Tamil class. He and Salgado are sworn enemies."

"So, it's a Sinhala-Tamil thing," I said, more a statement than a question.

He nodded.

"Why doesn't anybody stop it?" I asked.

He smiled. "Salgado and others like him are in high favor with Lokubandara. They can do whatever they like."

Now I remembered how Diggy had referred to the new vice principal as a "snake in the grass."

"What is he like, this Lokubandara?" I asked.

Soyza looked at me, considering whether to answer. "I'm going to tell you something," he said finally. "But you must never repeat this to anybody."

Then he began to tell me about the conflict between Black Tie and Lokubandara, which my brother had only mentioned. I never imagined the struggle to be so complex and bitter. Soyza told me that the teachers, clerks, prefects, a few older students who were in the know, and even the canteen aunties were divided into two factions: supporters of Black Tie and supporters of Lokubandara. Mr. Lokubandara wanted to change the name of the school, which he felt was too British. The name he had in mind was that of a Buddhist priest who had done much to preserve traditional, vernacular education. Further, he wanted to make the Victoria Academy a Buddhist school. Here, Soyza paused and glanced at me. "Since all Sinhalese are Buddhists, that means the school would be a Sinhala school, and there would be no place for Tamils in it."

I nodded slowly, understanding the seriousness of Lokubandara's plans.

Black Tie, Soyza continued, was a Buddhist, but he was opposed to Lokubandara's ideas. He wanted the school to be for all races and religions.

I felt a bit overwhelmed by the complexities of Soyza's story, and wondered how it was that he seemed to know so much about the politics of the school.

That day, Lokubandara visited our class. When Salgado and some of his friends saw him in the doorway, they cried out to him in Sinhalese, "Sir, sir. Come in, sir." When he walked in, Soyza glanced at me significantly to indicate that this was Mr. Lokubandara. A thin, short man, he wore thick glasses with black frames.

He smiled and walked to the front of the class. "What?" he said, also in Sinhalese. "No teacher?"

"Don't know, sir," Salgado replied, eager to be helpful. "Maybe she'll come soon."

Mr. Lokubandara glanced around the class and smiled benignly. "Good, good," he said as if blessing us. "Continue with your studies." Then he turned and left.

He was not what I had expected at all. It was impossible to imagine that this man had anything to do with the fight I had witnessed that morning in the toilet.

I had been at the Victoria Academy for almost two months before I actually saw Black Tie close up. A rubber-band-and-paper-pellet fight was raging in our classroom that day when suddenly someone cried out, "Black Tie, Black Tie!"

There was a mad scramble as the boys ran for their seats. They took out their books, and I, too, reached into my bag and brought out a book. Then I heard an exclamation from Soyza and turned to see him searching frantically in his desk. "My hair clips," he said. "I can only find one."

By now a silence had descended over all the classrooms, and the only sound that could be heard was the brisk tapping of Black Tie's footsteps as he drew near. "Never mind," I hissed at Soyza. "Just use one clip, then."

He nodded and quickly put his hair up. I was relieved to see that it stayed in place. I checked my shirt buttons and sleeves and smoothed down my hair. My hands were damp, and I rubbed them against the sides of my pants. As Black Tie drew nearer, I prayed that he would walk right past us. My prayers were not to be answered, however, for the footsteps came to a halt outside our door.

Black Tie pushed the door open and walked into the classroom. We rose quickly to our feet. "Good morning, sir," we chorused. He didn't respond as he stood by the teacher's desk, scrutinizing the class. This was the first time I had seen him this close. His face, under the sola topee, was round and might have been jolly but for his aquiline nose and the severe, downward turn of his mouth.

Now Black Tie stepped forward, his eyes widening as if he had seen something astonishing.

"You," he suddenly said, and I thought he was pointing at me. "Come here."

I started to go towards him, but he waved me back and said, "Not you, hooligan." He pointed a little to my right. "You," he said.

I turned quickly and I saw the cause of Black Tie's amazement. A lock of Soyza's hair had come undone and was hanging down the side of his neck. His face had become rigid.

"Come here, come here," Black Tie said, and Soyza went to him.

Black Tie reached out and pulled the clip from his hair. Soyza winced slightly as his hair fell around his shoulders. Black Tie stared at him as if he could hardly comprehend what he saw. "What's this?" he finally said. Soyza didn't answer. "How did you get away with this?"

Still Soyza didn't answer. Black Tie grabbed him by the

ear and pulled his head to one side. Soyza's features became contorted with pain. "Answer me, hooligan."

"Sir," Soyza finally gasped, "I used hair clips, sir."

"And the teachers and prefects have permitted this?" Black Tie looked hurt, as if he had been betrayed by them. "This is precisely what's wrong with this school," he said, pulling Soyza's ear harder. "This is what the school is coming to." Now Black Tie let go of Soyza's ear and grabbed his hair. He pulled his head back so that his face was turned up towards him. Soyza's eyes were open wide with fright. Then Black Tie raised his hand and slapped him. From the force of the blow, Soyza stumbled back against the teacher's desk. Black Tie pulled him forward again. "Scallywag," he said, "don't ever think you can get away with this in my school. As long as I am principal, we will have discipline in this school." He slapped Soyza a second time, his blow ringing out in the silence. He grabbed him roughly by the arm and pushed him out of the classroom. Before he shut the door, he turned to look at us warningly. Then we heard their footsteps getting fainter as they moved down the corridor.

A sigh of relief ran through the class and everyone took their seats. I had never seen anyone slapped like that before, and my cheeks felt hot, as if I had been the one who had received those blows. Some of the boys began to titter now and comment on the look of shock on Soyza's face. They said that he would now become one of the "ills and burdens." In front of Black Tie's office, one of the boys explained to me, there was a row of benches and tables where he kept what he called "the future ills and burdens of Sri Lanka." Once you became an "ills and burdens," you remained one for a long time. Every morning you had to report to the principal's office and stay there, usually for the whole day.

"Hooligan!" Salgado cried in a perfect imitation of Black Tie's slightly nasal voice. He strode to the front of the class and gazed at us with his brows furrowed. Now all the boys began to giggle. Salgado dragged a boy out of the front row. "What's this?" he said, pointing to his hair. Then he pretended to slap him, and the boy reeled across the room. Now the boys began to laugh loudly. I stared at them in disbelief, wondering how they could make fun of what had happened to Soyza.

Soyza wasn't released until school was over for the day. I stayed behind in the classroom, waiting for him. When he came in I was shocked by his appearance. His hair had been cut short and hung in jagged layers close to his head. He smiled and imitated the look of horror on my face. "Don't you like it?" he asked, touching the edges of his hair. "It's the latest thing in town. The Black Tie bob cut."

"How could he do that?" I said. "He had no right to."

"Of course he had the right to," he said. "He's Black Tie."

"It's not fair. He can't get away with this."

Soyza studied me with mock pity. "You poor thing," he said, "you really are fresh meat, aren't you."

"Stop joking," I cried at him. "It's not funny."

"Why not? I think it's extremely funny."

"You should do something, Soyza."

"Ohhh," he said. "And what should I do?"

"You should tell your parents," I said, not caring what Diggy had told me about the price of complaining to one's family.

He didn't reply. He turned away and began to pack up his schoolbag.

"If I were you I would—"

"Well, you're not me," he snapped back. "You don't know anything about it. . . ."

Angrily he pushed at his books, forcing them deeper inside the bag. I wondered if I had accidentally struck something, some unhealed wound of his.

Now Soyza seemed exhausted. I stood watching him, and then, without quite realizing what I was doing, I reached out and touched his head. He moved away, as if my hand had stung him, and I quickly lowered it, embarrassed by my involuntary gesture. Soyza was frowning now in the same way he had done when I had passed him that note in class. Without a word, he picked up his bag and went out of the room. I followed him.

He, too, had cycled to school, and we went together to the now deserted bicycle shed.

I was unlocking my bicycle when Soyza suddenly said, "What do you know about me?"

"What?" I said, taken aback by the question.

"Never mind," he replied, and bent down to fiddle with the lock on his bicycle.

Yet I had heard the question clearly and was left wondering what he had meant by it.

Our first period the next day was physical training, so once again a prefect came to supervise us. A short while later, a teacher came into the room. He was a frail-looking man with stooped shoulders. We rose to our feet and he gestured to us vaguely to take our seats. The prefect must have been expecting him, for he didn't seem surprised by his arrival. He got up from the teacher's chair and sat at one of the desks in the front row. Still without addressing a word to us, the teacher began to write on the board. When he had finished he stepped back and looked at his writing. Now we, too, got a clear view of what he had written.

> We'll honor yet the School we knew,
> The best School of all:
> We'll honor yet the rule we knew,
> Till the last bell call.
> For, working days or holidays,
> And glad or melancholy days,
> They were great days and jolly days,
> At the best School of all.

I stared at the lines, wondering what they meant and why he had written them on the board. Now the teacher turned to us. He indicated to a boy in the first row to stand. Then he pointed to the board to show that the boy was to recite the lines. As the boy read them aloud, the teacher leaned his head to one side, listening intently. After the boy had finished, the teacher gestured to him to sit down and motioned for the next boy to read aloud from the board. When it was my turn, the teacher listened to me with a slight frown. This made me think I had not read as well as the other boys. I was surprised therefore when, after everybody in the class had read aloud, he asked me to stand up and read the lines again. This time, as I recited, he nodded slowly to himself, and I could tell that he was actually pleased. When I was finished, he peered at me as if he were shortsighted and said, "What is your name?"

"Chelvaratnam, sir."

He took out a piece of paper from the file he carried and gave it to me. "Read this, Chelvaratnam," he said.

I looked at the piece of paper. Photocopied on it was a poem called "The Best School of All," by a Sir Henry Newbolt. I saw that the words on the board had come from this poem. I read the whole poem aloud. When I was finished, the teacher nodded and held out his hand for the piece of paper. Then, without a word, he picked up his file and left the room.

"Who's *that*?" Salgado asked the prefect.

"That was Mr. Sunderalingam, the English and drama teacher," the prefect replied. He looked at me. "I think he's going to rope you into some play or other."

Later that morning, during Social Studies class, Black Tie's personal prefect, a thin, hook-nosed senior student called Kulasekara, came to our room. He was well known throughout the school, and because he always brought bad news with him, he was nicknamed the Angel of Death. Since Soyza had already left for Black Tie's office, we looked fearfully at the prefect, wondering why he was here. The teacher stopped her lecture and waited for the prefect to state his business. "The principal wants to see Chelvaratnam," he said to the teacher.

I jumped, nearly knocking my books onto the floor. Now the teacher turned to look at me. "Chelvaratnam," she said, and indicated that I was free to go.

I remained where I was.

The other boys began to look at me and titter in anticipation of having another "ills and burdens" student in their class.

"Are you Chelvaratnam?" the prefect asked.

I nodded.

He crooked his finger at me.

After a moment, I got up. In my nervousness I bumped against a desk on my way to the front of the class.

When we were outside the classroom, I said to the prefect, "Are you sure it's me he wants?" He didn't answer. "What have I done?" I whispered, my voice cracking with fear.

He smiled. "Whatever it is, you're going to get it."

As we walked down the corridor, I tried to think why Black Tie would want me, how he even knew my name. Try as I might, I couldn't think of a single reason for my being taken to see him. As we passed a window, I glanced at my reflection to make sure that I looked neat and clean. The prefect noticed this and smiled again.

Black Tie's office was on the second floor, and we had to go up a flight of concrete stairs. When we reached the top step, I saw that there were two rows of benches and tables in front of the office. Soyza was sitting in the first row, and his eyes widened when he saw me. He raised his eyebrows questioningly and I shook my head to say that I didn't know why I had been summoned.

Outside Black Tie's office hung portraits of all the old

principals of the Victoria Academy. Above the arched, heavy
wooden door was the crest of the school. The prefect went
into the office, closing the door behind him. After a moment,
he came out and called me inside.

When I entered the office, I stopped for a moment in
astonishment. Mr. Sunderalingam was seated next to Black
Tie. He smiled, as if to reassure me, and motioned to me
to come nearer. Black Tie studied me as I came forward.
He seemed very different from when I had seen him in
our class, for he had a small smile on his face and was
leaning back in his chair in a relaxed fashion. He was not
wearing his topee and I now saw that he was almost completely bald.

Black Tie raised his hand for me to stop, and I stood at
attention. He held out two pieces of paper, which the prefect
then handed to me. I took them and continued to stand at
attention.

Black Tie regarded me quizzically. "Chelvaratnam, look
at those papers," he said.

I quickly glanced at the papers. There were two poems
photocopied on them. The first I recognized as "The Best
School of All," and the second was called "Vitae Lampada."

I looked at Mr. Sunderalingam, puzzled.

"I want a perfect recitation," Black Tie said. "Tomorrow,
last period, here in my office."

Stunned, I said nothing.

"Do you understand me, Chelvaratnam?"

"Yes, sir," I replied smartly.

He waved his hand and the prefect led me to the door.
When I walked out, Soyza raised his eyebrows again and

I shrugged my shoulders to show that I still didn't know what was going on. I began to walk down the stairs, clutching the poems. When I got to the bottom, I heard someone call my name. I turned to see Mr. Sunderalingam signaling for me to wait for him.

"I say, Chelvaratnam," he said when he reached me. "You must be wondering what all this is about."

"Yes, sir," I said.

He took out a handkerchief and mopped his forehead. "Our beloved principal is a man of too few words, no?" He waved his handkerchief at the poems. "Those poems. You are to recite them at the upcoming prize-giving."

I looked at him in amazement.

"Yes," he said. "I told our beloved principal how impressed I was with your reading."

"That . . . that's wonderful, sir," I couldn't stop myself from saying.

"It is an honor, Chelvaratnam," he replied.

When Mr. Sunderalingam had walked away, I glanced at the two pieces of paper in my hand and nearly laughed out loud. I had expected to receive some terrible punishment when all along Black Tie wished only to confer this honor upon me.

After school that day, Soyza caught up with me as I was wheeling my bicycle down to the gate. He asked me what had happened in Black Tie's office. I told him and he, too, seemed impressed by the distinction I had been given. We had reached the gate by now, and he rode away on his bicycle. Diggy was standing under a tree with his bicycle, waiting for me.

"Are you friends with Soyza?" he asked, as I came up to him.

"Yes," I said, surprised that he knew his name.

He frowned. "You better watch out for him," he said. "You don't want to become associated with Soyza."

"Why?"

"Never mind why. Just listen to what I say."

"But I like him."

Now Diggy shifted uncomfortably.

"He's an extremely nice person," I said, trying to goad Diggy into giving me more information.

"You better be careful. . . . Listen," he said after a minute, "I'm going to tell you something about Soyza, because I don't want you to become like him."

I waited.

"Have you noticed that Soyza sometimes goes out during free periods?"

"Maybe I have."

"Do you know where he goes?"

"How would I know?"

"To the head prefect's room."

"So what? He's always getting into trouble."

"But do you know what he does there?" He leaned towards me. "Sex," he said. "He has sex with the head prefect. He lets the head prefect do all kinds of things to him."

I stared at him, astounded.

Diggy smirked. "Don't say I didn't warn you. If you remain Soyza's friend, people will think you're like him and you'll become the laughingstock of the whole school."

It suddenly occurred to me that Diggy was making all this up. What he had said was too preposterous to be true.

"Liar," I said to him. "You're a liar."

Diggy didn't reply. He got on his bicycle and began to ride away.

"I don't believe a word you say!" I called after him. Without turning around, he held up his finger at me.

Then something Soyza had said the previous day came back to me—that moment in the bicycle shed when he had asked, "What do you know about me?" An awful doubt began to form in my mind. Could he have been referring to what Diggy claimed he did with the head prefect?

And yet, sex? It didn't make any sense. The more I thought about it, the more sure I was that Diggy had invented the whole story to shock me and insult someone I liked.

That evening, I eagerly began to study the poems. I found them hard to memorize, however, and even harder to recite with any conviction. There were many expressions and words I wasn't familiar with, and the precise meaning of the poems eluded me. They spoke of a reality I didn't understand. "Vitae Lampada" was about cricket, but not cricket the way I understood it. It said that through playing cricket one learned to be honest and brave and patriotic. This was not true at the Victoria Academy. Cricket, here, consisted of trying to make it on the first-eleven team by any means, often by cheating or by fawning over the cricket master. Cricket was anything but honest. "The Best School of All" was no better. In this poem, the poet looked back on his school days as the best days of his life. I found it puzzling that one would be nostalgic for something one had longed to escape.

It took me a long time, but finally I was able to commit those poems to memory.

Later, as I lay in bed, what Diggy had said came back to me. I tried again to imagine Soyza and the head prefect together. At fourteen, I was aware of what the sex act between a man and a woman entailed. But between two boys? I thought about the head prefect. I had seen him once in the corridor. He was short and stocky, his nose wide and flat, his lips too full, their pinkness contrasting oddly with his dark skin. Soyza, on the other hand, was so delicately built. The difference between them only heightened my curiosity. But try as I might I couldn't figure the whole thing out, and eventually I put Diggy's silly story out of my head and fell asleep.

The next day I set out for Black Tie's office in the last period.

I got to the top of the stairs and I saw Soyza, sitting on one of the benches among the other "ills and burdens." He called me over and informed me that Black Tie had gone on one of his rounds of the school. I would have to wait for him. The neatness of Soyza's uniform and the way he sat, hands clasped primly on the table in front of him, made me certain that what Diggy had said about him the day before was nonsense.

I asked Soyza to listen to my recitation and correct me if

I made any errors. He took the poems from me and waited for me to start, but, alarmingly, I couldn't remember the lines. "That's strange," I whispered to him. "My mind is a blank."

"Think only of the first line," he said. "After that everything will come naturally."

Much to my relief, this worked. He gave me the first line and the rest came to me easily.

I was halfway through the second poem when one of the other "ills and burdens" nudged me. I turned around and saw that Black Tie was at the top of the stairs, listening to me. I became silent. Soyza hurriedly gave the poems back to me.

All the "ills and burdens" rose to their feet.

"Chelvaratnam, come," Black Tie said. Then, as an afterthought, he added, "And you too, Soyza."

Soyza and I looked at each other as we followed him into his office.

Black Tie took his seat. He pointed for Soyza to stand in a corner and he told me to give the poems to him. My hand shook slightly as I passed the pieces of paper to Soyza. He saw this and smiled encouragingly. His smile reminded me that I should start by thinking of the first line, and I began to feel more confident.

Then Black Tie did a surprising thing. He reached behind him, took out a cane from his umbrella stand, and placed it on the desk. "If he makes a mistake, stop him," Black Tie said to Soyza. His words carried a threat, enforced by the cane on his table.

I gazed at that cane and the poems fragmented in my mind, like a shattered reflection on a pond. I could capture only a word or a phrase and sometimes even a complete stanza, but where and how they fitted together I couldn't remember.

"Chelvaratnam," I heard Black Tie say, as if from a distance, "I'm waiting."

I willed my mind to be calm, but to no effect.

I heard Soyza's voice. " 'It's good to see the School we knew, the land of youth and dream.' "

It was as if he were speaking to me in a foreign tongue. Somewhere in my mind it registered that he was prompting me. I tried to recall what he had just said. It was the first line of the poem, and surely, if I could concentrate on it, the rest would follow as it had done a short while back. " 'It's good to see the School we knew,' " he repeated, " 'the land of youth and dream.' "

His words echoed over and over in my mind but they yielded nothing. They were like the prayers we had learned as children, senseless incantations that we repeated to ourselves each night.

" 'There's a breathless hush in the close tonight,' " Soyza read. The line was familiar, but I couldn't tell if it was the second line of the same poem or the first line of the other poem. I looked at him as if I hoped to find the answer to my dilemma on his face.

"Chelvaratnam," I heard Black Tie say. "You haven't learned the poems, have you?"

Again his voice seemed to come from a distant place. Before I could formulate an answer, he raised the cane from the desk. My mind stopped rippling and became clear. Not with the words of the poems, but with the understanding of imminent danger. The sense of distance I felt disappeared.

"Sir," I said quickly. "Yes, sir, I have learned the poems."

He shook his head regretfully, as if my answer had come too late. He beckoned to me. I remained where I was and said again, "I do know those poems, sir. I studied them the whole of last night."

He shook his head again. "Come here, Chelvaratnam," he said, almost gently.

"Please, sir," I said, my voice cracking, "give me another chance sir."

He tapped the cane on the desk. Then he lifted his hand for me to give it another try.

I glanced at Soyza for the first line again.

" 'It's good to see the School we knew, the land of youth and dream,' " he said.

I ran the last phrase of the line through my mind, trying to remember what followed it. Then suddenly a line came to me, and with the joy of a traveler who has reached his destination, I blurted out, "It's good to see the School we knew, the land of youth and dream, / This is the word that year by year, while in her place the School is set, / Every one of her sons must hear and none that hears it dare forget . . ." My voice trailed off as I noticed Soyza's eyes widen in alarm. I had moved from "The Best School of All" into "Vitae Lampada."

"Chelvaratnam," Black Tie said after a moment, a pained expression on his face, "of all the vices, falsehood is the most terrible."

"Please, sir," I said. "Sorry, sir."

"Chelvaratnam, come here."

I remained where I was.

"If you had come to me today and told me the truth, I would have been angry that you hadn't learned the poems, but I would not have been"—he lifted his finger for emphasis—"sad."

He called to his prefect, who came and pushed me towards Black Tie. When I was close enough to him, Black Tie reached out and grasped me by the ear. He pulled me down so that I was leaning across his desk. "You see, Chelvaratnam, if I do not punish you now, you will go into life thinking you can get away with lies." He moved his chair back so as to position himself better. "Falsehood is the biggest malaise in this country, the cause of all its problems. If most of the politicians today had received a good thrashing, we would not be having the problems we currently have." He lifted the cane and then paused. "One day, Chelvaratnam, you will thank me for this."

With that he hit the back of my legs. I cried out as I felt the sting of it spread up my thighs. Black Tie kept his hand firmly on my shoulder as he brought the cane down again on the same spot. After that I lost count of how many times he struck me. The school bell rang, signaling the end of school, but that did not stop him. He continued to cane me until he felt the vice of falsehood had been banished from my being. When he was done, he turned and put the cane away in a businesslike fashion. "Tomorrow," he said to me, "come before the interval, and this time have those poems memorized." With that, he dismissed us.

When we got outside the office, I was trembling. Soyza gave me the poems, and I took them quickly, not wanting him to see how my hand shook.

"Where is your bag?" he asked.

"In class, where do you think?" I replied angrily, even though I was not angry with him.

"Mine too," he said.

We walked along the corridor, buffeted by the stream of boys hurrying to get out of school. My legs were smarting. By the time we reached our classroom, everyone had gone, and we packed our bags in silence. As I looked at the poems, lying on my desk, I thought about the trouble they had caused me, of the humiliation and pain of the caning I had just received. Suddenly, I grabbed the pieces of paper and ripped them in two.

"Hey!" Soyza shouted at me. "Are you mad?"

He tried to stop me, but I continued to tear the paper. I threw the pieces into the air.

"I don't care," I cried. "I hate them, I hate them."

My voice broke. I turned away and finished packing my bag, wiping my cheek with the back of my hand.

Soyza bent down and picked up the shreds of paper. He put them on the edge of my desk. "Gosh," he said, "what a drama. You should become a Sinhala film star after that performance."

I didn't reply.

"I can just see it," he said. "New sensational darling of the silver screen."

"Stop it," I yelled.

"What are you going to do now?" he asked after a moment.

"I don't care."

Yet even as I spoke, I felt the stupidity of my words.

Tomorrow I would have to present myself to Black Tie with the poems in hand. I sat down. "I don't know what to do."

Soyza thought about it for a moment, and said, "Why don't you try to find the poems?"

"Where?"

"What about the British Council library?"

"How would I get in there?"

"I have a membership," he said quickly. He turned away and closed up his schoolbag. I waited for him to offer to go to the British Council with me, but he didn't say anything. Then I saw that he was hesitant about inviting me, as if he was not sure I would want to be seen in his company.

"Can you take me?" I asked.

He nodded and seemed relieved that I had asked him.

He picked up his bag and we went out of the room. I looked at him as he walked a little ahead of me down the corridor. I was puzzled by his shyness, especially as he was usually so confident.

We had arranged to meet at the gates of the British Council that evening. When I arrived on my bicycle, Soyza was already there waiting for me. He was wearing jeans and a shirt, both of which were carefully ironed. I also noticed that he had taken a lot of trouble with his hair, for he had oiled and parted it so that the jagged ends were less noticeable. It was strange to see him out of school uniform, and as I looked at him, I thought for the first time about his life outside school, a life of which I knew nothing. What did his parents do for a living? How many brothers and sisters did he have? I wondered if he ever thought about me in this way.

When we walked in, the security guard at the gate didn't bother to ask if we were members. Soyza took me to where the microfiche machines were, and we looked up Sir Henry Newbolt.

We found his books quite easily and took them to the reading room to look for our poems.

"Gosh," Soyza said, after he had read a few of them, "this fellow really loved school."

"Must have been a teacher's favorite," I said bitterly.

"Or must have been cricket captain or something," Soyza added.

We looked at each other and smiled.

"Must have been on the rugger team," I said.

"No, no," Soyza cried. "Must have been a rugger *captain*."

"Do you think tennis captain too?"

"Of course. Triple colorsman at least."

Now we were chuckling, and it was a relief to be able to hold up for ridicule all that was considered sacred by the Queen Victoria Academy.

"I bet you anything," I said, "that he was cricket captain, rugger captain, and tennis captain all in one year."

"And don't forget leader of the debate team and chairman of the English Literary Association," Soyza added. "Otherwise, how else could he know such big words?"

He peered at the book, then held up his finger authoritatively and read in a sonorous voice, " 'Qui ante diem periit: Sed miles sed pro patria.' "

The expression on his face, as if he understood what he was saying, made me laugh.

The other people in the reading room turned to look at

us. The librarian rose from her seat, and we picked up the book and fled to the photocopier. As we stood in line for the machine, I noticed that Soyza was looking at me. He smiled tentatively, as if he was not sure that I would return his smile. I felt suddenly shy but, wanting to acknowledge his gesture of friendship, I smiled back.

When we walked to the gate afterwards, we were both strangely subdued. I kept trying to think of things to say, but nothing came to mind. We unlocked our bicycles and rode in silence to the top of Alfred House Gardens. Then we stopped.

"How does your family call you? Is it Arjun?"

"No. Arjie."

"Arjie." He said it as if he were thinking over the word. "Can I call you Arjie, then?"

"Yes. And you? What do . . ."

"Shehan."

He grinned suddenly and bowed. "Well, good night, Ar-jie."

"Well, good night, Shehan," I replied in an equally playful tone.

He waved and rode off in the direction of Cinnamon Gardens. I watched him for a while and then I set off in the opposite direction.

As I rode along Duplication Road, I said the word "Shehan" to myself, trying to get used to its newness on my tongue. Our laughter over the poems had made me feel good. The terror that awaited me tomorrow was still with me, but, for the moment, I had pushed it into the back of my mind. I was content, as I cycled home through the rapidly descending night, to think of Shehan and the relief and pleasure we had shared in holding up the Victoria Academy to ridicule. I thought for a moment about Shehan and the head prefect, and what Diggy had said. I couldn't imagine Shehan, who had such a sense of humor, who was moody and prim, even being friends with the head prefect.

That night I dreamt of Shehan. We were in the Otter's Club pool, swimming and joking around. He was in a very mischievous mood, and every time I spoke to him he answered in Tamil, knowing that I didn't understand. He swam away from me and I chased after him until finally I caught him in the deep end. I wound my legs around his so that he couldn't escape. He splashed water in my face and tickled me, but I would not let him go. I was very aware of the feel of his legs against mine and of the occasional moments when, in trying to prevent him from getting away, my chest would rub against his.

The next morning I noticed the familiar wetness on my sarong.

I went to Black Tie's office at the beginning of the second period that day. Shehan was in his usual place. We looked at each other and there was, in our silent exchange, an acknowledgment of our newly found friendship. As I sat down next to him, I thought about my dream the night before, and caught myself studying him, the way his skin became lighter below the top button of his shirt, the way sweat had gathered in little spots on his chin and his upper lip, the way his hair was damp around the edges and clung to his temples in little curls. When he leaned towards me to whisper something, I smelled the odor of sweat mixed with Lifebuoy soap.

Shehan was called in to prompt me. But it was useless. The moment Black Tie removed the cane from his umbrella stand, the words of the poems again fragmented in my mind. Black Tie's face changed color with anger. He made me lean over his desk once again and he caned me until he was breathless. Then he caught me by the ear and led me out onto the balcony. I was to kneel there until such time as I learned the poems. I felt worse when Shehan, too, was brought out and made to kneel on the balcony with me. He was to help me learn the poems. Black Tie went inside and closed the glass door, and I saw him return to his desk and continue his work.

I turned to Shehan and whispered, "It's not fair. You didn't do anything."

Shehan clicked his tongue against his teeth dismissively and shrugged, as if kneeling on the balcony, under a sun that was reaching its midday fierceness, didn't bother him at all.

"Come," he said, and picked up the poems.

"It's no use," I replied. "I know those poems. I just can't recite them with that cane on the desk."

"What are you going to do, then?" he asked.

I glanced down at the front lawn of the school, which was empty of students and peaceful. A slight breeze blew across the grass, creating a wavelike pattern as it went. Outside the school gates, the vendors sat on the pavement preparing their wares for when school would finish. One of them had a little child who was playing hopscotch on the deserted road. As I gazed at the child, a feeling of hopelessness descended on me. I heard in the distance the bells of St. Gabriel's, announcing the end of a period, and my despair increased. Their sound was a reminder of a more carefree time, when school had been looked forward to rather than dreaded. How rapidly and sadly my life had changed.

After about an hour, Black Tie's prefect came to call us in. This time, when I still couldn't recite the poems, Shehan received a punishment as well, for wasting his time on the balcony and failing to help me learn the poems. I looked on in agony at the grimace on Shehan's face as Black Tie held him by the ear and brought his cane down on him repeatedly.

We were sent out to the balcony again. I whispered to Shehan, "I'm sorry."

"It's not your fault," he replied, and from the way he tilted his head back and wrinkled his nose, I could tell that he was trying not to cry.

I realized that it was my responsibility to get us out of this situation. Then I remembered Mr. Sunderalingam and the fact that he was the one who had recommended me to Black Tie in the first place.

I waited till the interval bell rang, and I gathered up the courage to go inside and ask Black Tie if I could use the toilet. He considered my request for a moment and then assented. I hurried down the stairs and along the corridor that led to the staff room. It was a sacred place, and under usual circumstances I would have been too scared to enter it. Now, however, desperation made me brave. I knocked on the door and waited. After a moment someone called out for me to enter, and I opened the door and went in. All the teachers stopped talking and turned to stare at me. I saw Mr. Sunderalingam and said, "Please, sir. May I speak with you?"

Mr. Sunderalingam nodded and stood up. He led me to a secluded verandah outside the staff room.

"How's the poetry recital, Chelvaratnam?" he asked.

"That's what I want to talk to you about, sir," I said.

Then I told him everything that had happened.

When I finished, he said, "You must bear with our principal, Chelvaratnam. He belongs to the old school that believes you can beat knowledge into a student."

Seeing that this had no effect on me, he went on: "Did you know that he was brought up by the old principal?"

I looked at him, interested.

"Yes. He was an orphan and the old principal, Mr. Lawton, raised him and educated him. The values he was taught are the ones he still holds on to, so you must not blame him too much for what he did to you."

Mr. Sunderalingam saw that I was still not convinced by his arguments. He looked ahead for a long time, then he said, "Chelvaratnam, are you aware of the dispute that's going on between our principal and the vice principal?"

I nodded hesitantly, not sure if I should let on that I knew.

"I have reason to believe our principal is losing the battle, and if he *is* overruled, Tamils like us will suffer. Our loyalties must therefore be with him."

He paused for emphasis, then continued.

It seemed that the chief guest at the prize-giving in a little over a week's time would be a minister of the cabinet, who, it was rumored, was next in line for the presidency. This minister was an old boy of the Victoria Academy and was the principal's last hope. "Vitae Lampada" and "The Best School of All" were two poems that the minister liked and knew very well, because he had won the All Island Poetry Recital Contest with them. Black Tie would be creating his speech around those poems, and he would appeal to the minister and the other old boys to prevent the school from altering. It was hoped that the poems would remind the minister of his schooldays and he would take some action.

"So you see, Chelvaratnam," Mr. Sunderalingam concluded, "the student who recites those poems will have the honor of helping our beloved principal save the school."

I stared at him, not knowing what to say. I had come to ask Mr. Sunderalingam to get Shehan and me out of our current situation, only to be given further reason why I should be trapped in it. I realized that I'd been away too long and Black Tie would soon wonder what had happened to me.

"Sir," I said, "can you help me?"

He nodded. "I'll come by the office after school and tell him about your visit." He saw the fear in my eyes and smiled. "Don't worry, Chelvaratnam. Our principal is a strict man but he is not cruel."

He nodded, indicating that our meeting was over.

I thanked him and went back towards Black Tie's office, working over in my mind what he had said. He had told me all this about Black Tie as a way of justifying what had been done to me. Yet he had not succeeded in winning my sympathy. Mr. Sunderalingam had said Black Tie was strict but not cruel, but he was wrong. Black Tie was cruel. If not, how could he have made us kneel on that balcony for all those hours, how could he have slapped Shehan for having long hair and then cut off his hair in such a terrible way? I was not sure that, as a Tamil, my loyalties lay with Black Tie. I thought of Mr. Lokubandara and the way Salgado and his friends had assaulted that Tamil boy. I thought of the way Black Tie had beaten both Shehan and me. Was one better than the other? I didn't think so. Although I did not like what Mr. Lokubandara stood for, at the same time I felt that Black Tie was no better.

The principal looked up from his work when I came into his office.

"What took you so long?" he asked.

"There was a long line, sir," I replied.

He pointed for me to take my place on the balcony with Shehan. As I went past his desk, I glanced at him and was aware that I now saw him differently.

Mr. Sunderalingam came to Black Tie's office when school was over. He walked in and approached Black Tie's desk. Shehan noticed where I was looking and he altered his position so that he could see inside as well. Mr. Sunderalingam was gesturing towards the balcony and talking to Black Tie. Shehan looked at me, his eyes widening with the realization of what I had done during the interval. I smiled, trying to assure myself as well that the outcome would be good.

After a while Mr. Sunderalingam left. Black Tie continued to sit at his desk.

"What do you think will happen?" Shehan asked in a whisper.

Before I could reply, Black Tie pushed his chair back and stood up. He came to the balcony door and opened it.

"Chelvaratnam, Soyza, come in off the balcony," he said.

He went back to his chair, and we got up stiffly and went to stand in front of his desk.

"You are free to go."

We stared at him in surprise.

"Hooligans," he said, but there was almost an amused note in his voice. "Do you want to leave or are you too attached to my balcony?"

"To leave, sir," we replied quickly.

"Then go," he said, "before I change my mind."

We turned and hurried towards the door, afraid that indeed he would change his mind.

When we got to the bottom of the stairs, we looked at each other in amazement. "It worked!" Shehan cried. "I can't believe it!"

He laughed out loud and grabbed hold of me, spinning me around with him. Then he did a most unexpected thing. Quickly, before I was aware of what was happening, he kissed me on the lips. My mouth must have opened in surprise, because I felt his tongue against mine for a brief instant. Then it was over. "Come on," he said and grabbed my arm. "I'll race you."

Without looking at me, he began to run. I stood where I was, disoriented by what had happened.

He turned to me, saying, "Come on. Don't be such a girl."

Still dazed, I began to trail after him.

When I reached the classroom, he had already packed most of his things. Now his mood had changed and he seemed distant, almost angry. He didn't even glance at me when I entered. I began to pack my bag slowly. He slung his bag over his shoulder, and, without a word, he walked towards the classroom door.

"Wait," I called out.

He turned.

Now that I had asked him to stop, I didn't know what to say.

"What's the hurry?" I finally said. "Do you have a train to catch or something?"

He didn't reply, but stood and waited for me to gather my things.

We began to walk down the corridor together. I looked at Shehan, but he refused to meet my eye. I felt that somehow he was angry at me, that I'd let him down. In the meantime, I was still trying to recover from the impact of that kiss, trying to understand what it meant.

We had reached the bicycle shed by now, and he still hadn't said a word. He bent down and began to unlock his bicycle. I watched him, feeling that something was coming undone between us, something imperceptible. I knew that I had to act now to save it from unraveling completely.

"What shall we do this evening?" I asked abruptly.

He stopped what he was doing and looked at me carefully.

"What do you want to do?" he asked.

I shrugged. "I don't know." I was not sure of the correct response.

He shrugged too, as if he didn't care. He began to wheel his bicycle out of the shed.

"Shall I come to your house?" I said.

He turned to look at me. Then he nodded and got on his bicycle.

"Wait!" I cried. "I don't know the address."

He got off his bicycle and opened his bag. He took out a piece of paper, wrote his address on it, and handed it to me.

"About five-thirty?" I asked.

"Yes," he said, and got on his bicycle and rode away.

It was only once I had got home that my shock over Shehan's kiss wore off. Then all I could think about was the sensation of that kiss. I lay across my bed, trying to relive it, but it had happened so fast that I could not remember very much. I closed my eyes and tried to re-create it, lingering over the details, playing out the incident and extending it into the realm of imagination. First my mind's eye rested on Shehan's face, the fullness of his lower lip, the slight ridge above his upper lip, as if someone had taken a light-brown pencil and outlined it. Then I imagined him kissing me, not quickly but slowly, lingeringly, so that I could feel the full impact of the kiss. I tried to remember the instant when his tongue touched mine. It had been rough and wet, but beyond that I hadn't had a chance to experience how it felt or tasted. As I lay there, looking up at the mosquito net above me, I realized I had not only liked that kiss but I was also eager to experience it again in all its detail and sensation.

Shehan lived in a big house in the exclusive neighborhood of Cinnamon Gardens. The house had a high wall around it and a takaran-covered gate. I leaned my bicycle against the wall and knocked on the gate. He must have been sitting on the steps waiting, for he immediately appeared. When he opened the gate, he seemed nervous about something. He greeted me shortly and then led me into the house.

The inside of the house was in a poor state. The red floors had not been stained for so long that the gray of the cement showed through. The upholstery on the settees was faded, and the wooden arms of the chairs were unvarnished. As I glanced around me, I somehow knew that Shehan didn't have a mother. As if to confirm my thoughts, an old bent-over servant woman came out of a doorway behind the stairs and looked at me and then at Shehan with an inquiring air, as if she owned the house.

"A friend," Shehan said to her, embarrassed, and then hurried up the stairs, calling to me to follow.

When we were inside his room, he slammed the door shut and locked it.

"She thinks she owns the house," he said, seeming now to relax a little. He grinned at me and said, "Welcome to my humble dwelling."

The furniture in the room was old and heavy and belonged to another era. The bed was very high, almost level with my waist, and the four bedposts were carved.

"It belonged to my grandmother," Shehan said, noticing me studying the bed.

"It's nice."

He shook his head. "It's too hard," he replied, and to demonstrate he sat on the bed and bounced up and down. He indicated for me to try it as well. I did so. Now Shehan was lying back on the bed, watching me. He had suddenly become very serious and he was looking at me as if waiting for me to do something. I glanced at him and then at my hands, feeling awkward and afraid at the intensity of his expression. I felt a tightness in my stomach. He was waiting for me to act, but what was I to do? Did he want me to kiss him? I was not sure how to go about it, given that his face was too far from me. The moment was beginning to pass, and soon I knew that it would be too late. I sought desperately for something to say, and before I could stop myself, I blurted out, "Do you have a mother?"

Shehan drew in his breath. He sat up, then he got off the bed.

"I mean, where is your mother?" I said, trying to cover up.

He went to the window and stood there, looking out. The expression on his face was somber. "My parents are divorced," he said, after a moment. "My mother lives in England with her new husband." His voice was dull and heavy as he spoke, but I knew that the reason for this tone was not his mother but what had just happened between us. Shehan put his hand to his forehead as if suddenly tired. Then I knew that I had disappointed him. He had expected something from me and I had been unable to provide it.

"I better go," I said.

He nodded and turned away from the window.

When Shehan bade me goodbye at the gate that evening, he was polite, in the same way he would have been with a stranger. As I cycled home, I felt frustrated and angry at my own inadequacy. I had failed both of us in some significant way.

My family was already in the middle of dinner when I came home.

"Where have you been?" Amma cried when she saw me.

"I went to visit a friend," I said and slipped into my seat. Everyone looked at me with interest, because I had never had a friend before.

"That's good," my father said. "I'm pleased you're making friends at the Victoria Academy."

"Who is this friend?" Amma asked.

"Shehan Soyza," I replied abruptly, not wanting to talk about him. I noticed that Diggy was watching me closely. I ignored him and began to help myself to some stringhoppers and curry.

"Where does he live?" my father asked.

"Cinnamon Gardens."

Both my parents seemed pleased at this, for it meant that Shehan was from a good family.

"Why don't you invite him to lunch on Sunday?" Amma said.

Diggy frowned at me and shook his head, telling me to decline Amma's offer. I felt suddenly irritated with him, an irritation compounded by my feeling of failure at Shehan's house.

"Yes," I said to Amma, "I would like that." I smiled mockingly at Diggy. "I'll phone him right after dinner."

Later, Diggy came to my room while I was writing in my new 1983 diary, a present from Neliya Aunty, who wanted me to have something to "contain all my scribblings." From the look on his face, I knew that he had come to chastise me for inviting Shehan. I closed the diary and raised my eyebrows

to show that he was disturbing me. He sat down on the corner
of my bed.

"You're going to be sorry," he said to me.

"What?" I replied in a rude tone of voice.

"You're going to be sorry for being friends with this
Soyza or Shehan or whatever his name is."

"And why is that?"

He was annoyed that I was pretending not to understand
what he meant. After a moment he smiled and said, "I can't
wait for Appa to meet Soyza. Then he'll definitely know that
you're . . ." He stopped himself, but I knew that he was talking about what my father seemed to fear was wrong with me.
I straightened up in my chair and watched him carefully. I
knew that if I was to get anything further out of him, I would
have to push him into revealing it.

"You're talking through your hat," I said in a dismissive
tone. "Amma and Appa will like Shehan. Everybody likes
Shehan. You know I do. Very much."

The statement had the desired effect on Diggy. He looked
at me intently. "What do you mean you like Shehan very
much?"

I was not sure how to answer this. "I just like him," I
said, trying to make it sound like the most obvious thing in
the world.

"How?"

"What do you mean, 'how'?"

"*How* do you like him?"

I fiddled with the lock on my diary, disconcerted.

Diggy smiled. "You don't know what you're talking
about," he said.

"Of course I do."

He shook his head and stood up. "You don't." He crossed to the door, but before he went out he said, "You just be careful. That Soyza could easily lead you down the wrong path." He left, closing the door behind him.

Then the meaning of what Diggy had said hit me, and a realization began to take shape in my mind. A fact so startling that it made my head spin just to think about it. The difference within me that I sometimes felt I had, that had brought me so much confusion, whatever this difference, it was shared by Shehan. I felt amazed that a normal thing—like my friendship with Shehan—could have such powerful and hidden possibilities. I found myself thinking about that moment Shehan had kissed me and also of how he had lain on his bed, waiting for me to carry something through. I now knew that the kiss was somehow connected to what we had in common, and Shehan had known this all along.

<hr>

Sunday arrived and I was as excited as I had been during the spend-the-day mornings of my childhood. Before getting up, I lay listening to the sound of the birds in the guava tree outside my window. The moment I had waited for since Friday night was finally here. Soon Shehan would arrive, and after that anything was possible. I was excited but also scared. I worried about being inadequate to do what was expected of me. I feared that, once again, I would blunder into saying or doing something stupid, and Shehan would want nothing more to do with me; that he would think me stupid and naive and turn away from me with disdain.

When Shehan finally arrived, I couldn't help studying him, as if I hoped to find my discovery physically manifested in his person. I led him to the back to show where he could park his bicycle, feeling shy and tongue-tied in his presence. I searched my mind for things to say, but nothing came. He must have sensed my uneasiness, for he, too, was quiet.

As we came back towards the front of the house, we saw that Sonali and some of the girls from our neighborhood were playing hide-and-seek. They invited us to play with them, and even though we were both too old for such a childish game, I agreed. The silence between us had now grown embarrassing, and I was afraid of what would happen if we were alone with nothing to do. Sonali was the catcher, and while she stood by the front verandah, counting to one hundred, we all ran to hide. I motioned to Shehan and he followed me. I led him down the driveway and into the garage, leaving the door a little ajar so that Sonali wouldn't think this was where we were hiding.

The garage was dark, except for the light that came in through the doorway. There was an old chest of drawers at the back, and we huddled up against the side of it. I was standing behind Shehan, and he turned to me. We grinned at each other delightedly, our earlier uneasiness forgotten in the fun of hide-and-seek. We looked towards the door and waited for Sonali to come and find us.

In the silence of the garage, all I could hear was the sound of our breathing. Then the rhythm of Shehan's breath changed slightly. I glanced at the back of his head. He was staring at the door, but I knew that he was no longer looking at it. I felt a dread begin to build inside me as I recognized what was happening. Shehan was giving me another chance to make up for my inability to act the last time we had been alone together. I knew I had to do something this time. It was my very last chance. Not fully understanding what my gesture meant, I reached out and put my hand on his hip. His breath caught for a second, then it escaped. He moved back against me. We were still. My heart was so loud in my chest that I felt it drowned out the sound of our combined breathing. Tentatively, like a bird approaching an out-stretched palm, I began to inch my fingers towards his stom-ach, ready to remove my hand at the slightest indication of displeasure. Soon my hand was on his stomach, and now I could feel through his cotton shirt the rhythm of his breathing. I paused, not knowing how to proceed from here. As if he had read my thoughts, he covered my hand with his and squeezed it. Then he turned towards me and his eyes were bright in the dark. I waited. He leaned forward and placed his mouth on mine. He closed his eyes but I kept mine open, fascinated by the muscles of his face, the way they tight-ened and loosened with the movement of his lips. Now I could feel his tongue against my teeth, a silent language that urged me to open my mouth. Before I quite knew it, I was responding to the prompting of his tongue. My eyes closed then and my mouth opened. As in a dream, I felt myself slipping into a blackness where all my thoughts disintegrated. The entire world became the sensation in my mouth and Shehan's tongue probing, retreating, intertwining with mine.

Then Sonali's voice called out, "Ready or not, I'm com-ing." Shehan pulled away from me with the sigh of someone who has been awakened from a pleasant sleep. I opened my eyes, unsure if the world around me was a part of my dream or reality.

Sonali's footsteps were coming up the driveway towards the garage door. Shehan lightly placed his hand on the side of my face. Then he turned to the door. Sonali now appeared, standing in the doorway.

"I'm here," she said tentatively, peering into the garage. "I'm coming to catch you."

We didn't respond or move.

She stood there for a few moments longer and then, either because she was afraid of the dark or because she thought she was mistaken and we were not in there, she walked away.

The moment she had left, I drew Shehan back against me. He sighed and tilted his head up to me. Now I kissed him. I was aware of my mouth in a way I had never been before, aware of its power to give and receive pleasure. My hands, of their own will, began to circle his stomach and chest. I could feel the contours of his ribs and the indentation of his navel. He took one of my hands and moved it down to his trousers. After a few moments, he turned around towards me, and I felt his hands pulling at the buttons of my trousers, the elastic of my underwear. I began to fumble with his buttons, unable to open them. He had to undo them himself. Then he kissed me again and I was aware of the heat of his body against mine as he pressed me against the wall. Once again, I felt myself slipping into darkness, as if I were sinking to the bottom of a pool where only smell, taste, and sensation existed.

It was soon over for me, however, and I felt myself being pulled back to reality, like a swimmer to the surface. I now became conscious of my naked backside pressed hard against the rough wall, bruising every time Shehan pushed up against me, of the squelching sound of Shehan's body against my now wet stomach, his breath loud in the stillness of the garage, his hands on my hips in a painful grip. I looked at his face, his expression one almost of pain, and suddenly it was too much for me. I wanted him to stop what he was doing, but before I could say anything, his hold on my hips tightened and he began to thrust even harder against me. I struggled, trying to push him away from me, but he was oblivious. All at once he sighed deeply and became still, and I felt a wetness against my thighs. I stood motionless, helplessly angry, the wetness a violation. Shehan breathed in sharply, straightened up, and moved away from me.

His expression now belonged to the Shehan I knew, for he smiled and winked at me conspiratorially. I wanted more than anything to be out of that garage, and I bent down and began to pull up my underwear and trousers. As I buttoned myself up, I could feel the wetness soak into my clothing. I began to walk quickly towards the garage door. Shehan was getting dressed, and he called out to me to wait for him. I stood impatiently while he tucked in his shirt and buttoned his trousers. He walked towards me, and when he was right by me, he leaned over and kissed me. I drew away from him. His tongue felt like a damp towel.

When I stepped outside, I was momentarily blinded by the glare of the sun. I squinted and looked down the deserted driveway. Sonali and her friends must have given up on us and gone to play another game. Shehan and I made our way to the front of the house. I felt suddenly afraid at the thought of meeting anyone. I looked down at my trousers to see if the wetness had seeped through. Except for a small spot, it was not visible. Shehan's clothes were wrinkled, and I glanced anxiously at mine, wondering if they, too, bore signs of what I had just done in the garage.

Shehan noticed that I was looking myself over, and he smiled. "Don't worry," he said, teasingly. "You look fine." I ignored him and continued to inspect my clothes.

The front verandah, too, was deserted. As we went up the steps, I heard the clatter of cutlery and plates in the dining room and the murmur of voices. We had been in the garage so long that my family had started lunch. Now Shehan seemed a little alarmed too.

When we entered the dining room, the family looked up at us.

"Oh, there you are," Amma called out jovially. "I was wondering where you had gone."

"We went for a walk," I said.

"At this time?" Neliya Aunty said. "You could have caught sunstroke, child."

My parents and Neliya Aunty were looking at Shehan, waiting to be introduced. Diggy was glowering at him.

"This is Shehan," I said.

My parents and Neliya Aunty bowed their heads slightly.

I indicated to Shehan to sit down in a chair across from me. As I pulled my chair out, I saw my father glance at Amma, and in that instant, I knew that he disapproved of Shehan. Had he sensed his difference? I felt a sudden dread at what had taken place in the garage, and I shuddered inwardly at the thought of what would have happened if my father had discovered us there. Diggy had become conscious of my father's disapproval, and he smirked at me triumphantly. All of a sudden his story about the head prefect came back to me. I stared at Shehan and realized, too late, the truth. Diggy's story had not been a lie, and, worse, I had let Shehan do to me what the head prefect had done to him.

I looked around at my family and I saw that I had committed a terrible crime against them, against the trust and love they had given me. I glanced at Amma and imagined what her reaction would have been had she discovered us, the profound expression of hurt that would have come over her face. She noticed that I was studying her, and she smiled. I looked down at my plate, feeling my heart clench painfully at the contrast between the innocence of her smile and the dreadful act I had just committed. I wanted to cry out what I had done, beg to be absolved of my crime, but the deed was already done and it couldn't be taken back. Now I understood my father's concern, why there had been such worry in his voice whenever he talked about me. He had been right to try to protect me from what he feared was inside me, but he had failed. What I had done in the garage had moved me beyond his hand.

Amma began to ask Shehan polite questions, as if to make up for the disapproving look on my father's face. As Shehan answered, I watched him, feeling resentful, angry at myself that I had done such awful things with him. I thought of the expression on his face as he had pushed against me, and I felt a sudden contempt and loathing for him. It seemed hard to believe that I had longed for his kiss the whole weekend, had waited with such expectancy to discover more. Now I wished I had never invited him, never set eyes on him.

★ ★ ★

Once lunch was over, Shehan and I left the dining room as soon as it was politely possible to do so. I took him to my room and shut the door behind us.

"Was something wrong in there?" Shehan said, and motioned with his head towards the dining room.

"Nothing," I replied curtly.

"Your father doesn't like me," he said.

"Rubbish."

Shehan was looking closely at me, and I turned away and studied my bookshelf. "Do you want to play a game?" I asked.

In reply, he came up behind me and tried to encircle me with his arms. I broke away from him. "Are you mad?" I hissed at him. "What would happen if someone came in and found us?"

He lifted his hand in apology. Then he sat down on the edge of the bed.

"I have Scrabble, Chinese checkers, and ludo. Which one do you want to play?"

He didn't answer. He was looking down at his hand, sulkily. I felt irritated with him.

"I have Scrabble, Chinese checkers—"

"I heard you," he snapped back.

"Which one will it be, then?"

"I don't know. Scrabble. It doesn't matter."

I took down the Scrabble box and began to set it up on the bed.

"Shall we play with a dictionary or not?"

"Not," he said mockingly.

I put my hand into the Scrabble bag and took out seven

letters. Then I passed the bag to him. He looked at the bag, but didn't take any letters.

"Aren't you going to play?" I asked.

He didn't reply.

"Fine. We don't have to play."

I began to empty all my letters back into the bag.

"You're feeling guilty," he suddenly said. "You're feeling guilty about what we did."

"Why should I feel guilty?"

"Because you think it's bad."

"And what do you think? What does your head prefect think?"

He looked up at me, startled. I stared directly at him, refusing to apologize.

"I don't know what you're talking about," he said, as if I were behaving irrationally.

"Yes you do, yes you do," I cried at him, my anger spilling out of me now. "Don't think I don't know about you."

He stared at me and then said, "You're jealous."

"What?" I said.

He smiled jeeringly. "I believe you're jealous."

"Why should I be jealous of such a disgusting thing? The whole school knows about you. You're the laughingstock of the entire school."

"At least I know what I want and I'm not ashamed of it."

"You should be. It's revolting."

"You didn't find it revolting in the garage. In fact you were the one who touched me first."

"I wish to God I had never done that," I said. "I'll never do it again."

He laughed. "That's what you say now. Tomorrow you'll come begging."

He leaned over to me. "I know your type. You and the head prefect and others like you. Pretend that you're normal or that you're doing it because you can't get a girl. But in the end you're no different from me."

Then I hit him. One moment he was sitting on the bed, the next moment he was on the floor. We stared at each other, both of us shocked by my swift, violent reaction. Then he got up, and, without a word, he crossed to the door and opened it. He stood for a moment, as if waiting for me to ask him to stay, but I didn't. He shut the door and went down the hall and I began to put the Scrabble game away.

That night I dreamt of Shehan. I was walking down a corridor in school, and when I reached a door, I knocked and went inside. Even though it was bright daylight outside, the room was so dark I couldn't see in front of me. I felt a presence before me and I knew that it was Shehan. His hands were on my hips now, moving slowly towards my stomach. They seemed bigger than I would have expected them to be. Then he pressed me against the wall and I realized that, though it was Shehan, he had the size and strength of the head prefect. I began to panic. I tried to escape from him, but he held me tightly against the wall. Now he placed his lips over mine and I couldn't breathe. Purple spots appeared before my eyes and my lungs began to hurt so much I felt they would tear apart.

I awoke gasping for breath. I sat up in the darkness, breathing deeply and thankfully. After a while I lay back on my pillow. I looked up at the patterns the moonlight made on the ceiling, and I thought of the tender look on Shehan's face before he had kissed me, the feel of his body against mine after he had opened the buttons of his trousers. Then, to my horror, I felt the stirring of desire within me. I looked away from the ceiling, reminding myself about the loathing I had felt, the way my backside had hurt as he pushed me against the wall. But these memories only served to increase my desire.

For the remainder of the night, I tossed and turned restlessly in my bed, torn between my desire for Shehan and disgust at that desire.

The next day, as I walked across the quadrangle to my class, I thought about my dream and also about my conflicting feelings. I dreaded that moment when I would actually see Shehan and be confronted anew with all that had happened. He was already at his desk when I arrived in class. He was reading a book, and he glanced at me quickly before returning to it. I walked to my seat and put my bag down. Now that I was closer, I saw that something had changed in him. The careless bravado that he always used to mask his feelings was gone. Instead, his emotions were as clearly visible as the veins below the surface of his skin. During the physical training period, he didn't ask permission to leave the class. Instead he remained at his desk, reading. The other boys were quick to notice this too, especially Salgado. When the bell rang, he purposely brushed against Shehan on his way to his desk and then watched for his reaction. Shehan continued to read his book as if he had not noticed Salgado.

Later in the day, Black Tie came to our class. It was between periods, and so the boys had grown unruly. There was a game of touch football in progress, the blackboard duster being used as the ball. Suddenly the lookout at the door called out "Black Tie!" and everyone ran to their seats. In the silence we heard Black Tie approaching, and I was reminded of the poems. His footsteps came to a stop in front of our class.

He strode in as if he had come for a particular reason. We all stood up and chorused, "Good morning, sir." He ignored our greeting and surveyed the class. I looked at him, wondering if it was me he wanted, but his eyes rested on Shehan. Then he said, "Soyza. There you are."

I stared at Black Tie, wondering what this meant.

He beckoned to him. "Come here, scallywag."

Shehan was looking at Black Tie, dismay evident in his face. After a moment, he walked reluctantly towards him.

"Soyza, where have you been?" he said.

"Sir?" Shehan said in surprise.

"Why haven't you reported to my office, Soyza?"

"But, sir," Shehan said. "You said that I could go . . ."

"I never said anything of the kind," he replied.

"Yes, you did, sir," Shehan said insistently.

Black Tie's face filled with anger at Shehan's tone. He grabbed him by the ear.

"Hooligan. Don't tell me what I said and didn't say. I told you that you were free for the day, that's all."

Still holding Shehan by the ear, he pulled him towards the door.

Even though Shehan's head was pulled to one side, his eyes met mine for an instant before he was dragged out of class.

In that moment my conflicting feelings for Shehan disappeared and all my anger at him dissolved in the face of this new horror that had descended upon him. The only thing I was concerned about now was Shehan's welfare. I listened to their footsteps getting fainter. When Black Tie had dismissed us, I, too, had thought it was for good. But we had forgotten that once you became an "ills and burdens," you remained one for a long time.

For the rest of that day, all I could think about was Shehan, and a profound sense of misery began to seep through me. I was so lost in thought that the science teacher had to call to me three times before I heard her. As a punishment for not paying attention, I was sent outside the classroom. I stood in the corridor, looking down at the deserted quadrangle. I thought of Shehan and wondered if he was being punished again, if Black Tie had caned him and made him kneel on the balcony. I leaned against the wall, feeling as if I was going to cry. The more I thought about Shehan and the way I had treated him, the worse I felt. With the terrible regret of a realization come too late, I saw that I had misjudged what we had done in the garage. Shehan had not debased me or degraded me, but rather had offered me his love. And I had scorned it.

Once school was over, I sat waiting for him. Finally he arrived, and when he saw me, he paused for a moment and then went to his desk without looking at me. I watched him pack his bag. The expression on his face was forbidding, but beneath the sternness I could tell he was close to tears. I was not used to seeing Shehan like this, with all his self-possession gone and the despair so visible on his face. He was the leader in our friendship, the one who had guided me, who had comforted me on Black Tie's balcony.

"Shehan," I said, "I'm sorry."

He looked at me. "Why? Why should you be sorry?" he said, and now the angry words were spilling out of him. "Everything has worked out for you. You're no longer an 'ills and burdens.'" He pushed the books into his bag. "And as for what happened between us, nobody knows about it, so you can pretend it never happened."

"That's not fair," I cried.

He made a dismissive sound and picked up his bag. Without a word he left the classroom and I heard him go down the corridor.

All that afternoon, I sat on our front verandah, waiting for something. I didn't know what I was expecting, but I couldn't make myself do anything but sit there and wait. Then the phone rang and I stood up involuntarily. I heard Amma pick up the receiver and call out to Sonali that the call was for her. As I heard Sonali come down the hall to the phone, I realized that I had been hoping Shehan would call me or come to me to say everything was forgiven. Now I saw the absurdity of my expectation. If I wanted to make up with Shehan, I would have to go to his house and do it myself.

★ ★ ★

When I knocked on the gate, the servant woman came immediately, as if she had been sitting on the steps waiting for someone. The expression on her face alarmed me.

"What's happened?" I asked.

"Don't know, baba," she said. "From the time Shehan baba came back, he has been in his room."

I wheeled my bicycle into the driveway and leaned it against a tree.

She followed me, saying, "I've only seen him once like this before and that was when his mother left." She sighed and shook her head. "What a calamity that was. But who can blame the lady? Husband was always out of the country on business. Never had time for his family. If not for me, I don't know what would have happened to the baba after his mother left."

I looked at her, puzzled, wondering why she was telling me all this. She asked me to come with her into the house.

When we got to the second-floor landing, I approached Shehan's door and listened. Inside I could hear him walking around. I knocked on the door and called out, "Shehan."

He stopped pacing.

"Shehan," I called again.

"What?" he finally said.

"Open the door."

"No. Leave me alone."

"What are you doing?" I said.

"Nothing."

"If you're doing nothing, let me in, then."

He was silent.

"Did that old woman ask you to come?" he asked.

"No," I said, "I came because I wanted to see you."

"Tell that woman to go away. Then I'll let you in."

I turned to the servant and asked her to go downstairs. She reluctantly agreed. She went halfway down the stairs and watched me. Shehan opened the door. His face was grimy from weeping. He still had his school clothes on, and his shirt hung out of his trousers. He closed the door behind me and bolted it, then gestured towards the bed for me to sit down. I did so.

"Shehan," I said after a moment, "I really need to apologize. I was so angry at you . . ." He raised his hand to say that he had already forgiven me. Yet he continued to look miserable.

"Now everything is okay, no?" I asked anxiously.

He shook his head. "I can't bear it," he said after a moment. "As long as you were there, I didn't mind being an 'ills and burdens.' But now that you're gone, I don't know what I'll do. I feel like . . ."

He stopped himself, and I could tell that he was on the verge of tears again. He moved his hand, as if willing himself not to cry. Then he went to the window and stood there for a long time, looking out at the playground across from his house. "I can't stand the constant punishments. If I don't get out of this, I think . . ."

He fell silent, and his expression was so serious that I felt afraid. I understood now why the servant woman had been so worried about him. She, who knew him so well, was aware that he had reached his limit.

★ ★ ★

As I cycled home through the rapidly descending dusk, despair began to grow in me. A despair that was fueled by my inability to relieve Shehan of his pain. I thought of all the times he had come to my aid, how he had rescued me from Salgado on my first day, how he had taken me to the British Council library. I was also reminded of the times he had been punished because of my failure to recite those poems and how he had borne his punishment without once blaming me for it. I felt that now it was my duty to find a way of getting him out of his predicament, though I couldn't think how to do it.

I was approaching the street that led to the Victoria Academy. On an impulse, I swerved my bicycle until I was in the middle of Galle Road, and then, when the traffic from the other side had momentarily cleared, I crossed and went down the street to the school.

When I got there, I stopped my bicycle. Beyond the railway lines I could glimpse the sea. The sun was an orange ball of fire as it sank slowly behind the waves. The sea had turned a coppery color, the tips of the waves brilliant amber glass. The light was changing over the Victoria Academy as well. The whole building was illuminated in a coral pink that swiftly deepened as the sun set. How peaceful and stately it looked. The balcony where Black Tie stood each morning, and where Shehan and I had spent many awful hours, now seemed cleansed in the rays of the setting sun. A few boys came strolling down to the gate, their cricket bats across their shoulders. As I gazed at this idyllic scene, the refrain from "The Best School of All" came to me: "For working days and holidays, / And glad and melancholy days, / They were great days and jolly days"—what foolish lines they were. Still, as I looked at the Victoria Academy, a voice in me said that this was how I would remember the school when I was no longer its captive. This was how my father must remember it, washed in the coral pink of memory.

No, I vowed to myself, I would never remember it like that.

I looked at the building again and I wondered how many boys like Shehan had passed through this school, how many Shehans had been its prisoner. I knew there must have been many. They were the ones no one spoke of, the ones past pupils pretended never existed. I gazed at Black Tie's balcony, now hidden in shadows, and I felt bitter at the thought that the students he punished were probably the least deserving. They were the ones who had broken his rules—no blinking, no licking of lips, no long hair—a code that was unfair. Right and wrong, fair and unfair had nothing to do with how things really were. I thought of Shehan and myself. What had happened between us in the garage was not wrong. For how could loving Shehan be bad? Yet if my parents or anybody else discovered this love, I would be in terrible trouble. I thought of how unfair this was and I was reminded of things I had seen happen to other people, like Jegan, or even Radha Aunty, who, in their own way, had experienced injustice. How was it that some people got to decide what was correct or not, just or unjust? It had to do with who was in charge; everything had to do with who held power and who didn't. If you were powerful like Black Tie or my father you got to decide what was right or wrong. If you were like Shehan or me you had no choice but to follow what they said. But did we always have to obey? Was it not possible for people like Shehan and me to be powerful too? I thought about this, but no answer presented itself to me.

These ideas about being powerful returned to me that evening as I was writing in my diary and also the next morning, when I went to school and saw Black Tie standing on his balcony.

Shehan was waiting for me at the top of the stairs that led to our classroom. I was surprised to see a happy glimmer in his eyes and the energetic way he ran halfway down the stairs to meet me. "Come and walk with me," he said and grabbed my elbow. When we were out in the quadrangle, he said to me, "I've thought of a really wonderful plan. I'm going to England to be with my mother." He grinned at me. "Good plan, no?"

I saw that behind his smile he was begging me not to question his idea. Yet it was so illogical and impractical that I felt I had to say something. "Shehan," I asked, "where will you get the money for the plane ticket?"

"I'll take it from my father," he said testily.

"So much money?"

"Don't worry, I'll find it."

"But will she let you come?"

"Of course she will," he said, but he didn't sound so sure. "Are you with me or not?" His face was beginning to darken.

"I'm with you," I said, halfheartedly.

Yet my acquiescence only made the expression on his face more grim, for he could tell that I didn't really believe he could pull it off. He was silent, staring across the quadrangle, his hands on his hips. As I watched him, I sensed the idea crumbling in his mind. The bell rang, and, without waiting for me, he hurried back inside. I followed slowly, hating myself for having let him down, hating the injustice of his predicament.

Black Tie sent for me in the second period. When I went into his office he was on the phone, and he pointed for me to stand in front of his desk. I noticed that the cane was not on it. I turned my head and saw that Shehan was out on the balcony again. Our eyes met for a moment, and then Shehan looked away. Black Tie put down the phone. "Okay, Chelvaratnam. Let's hear those poems," he said. Instead of reaching for his cane in the umbrella stand, he leaned back in his chair and waited. I began to recite the poems, and I was surprised how easily they came to me now that I was not under the threat of that cane.

When I was done, Black Tie put his fingers together and surveyed me. "Do you know the values these poems speak of?" he asked.

I nodded, even though I wasn't sure.

"Good. Remember them, because the way the school is going, these values may soon disappear." He glanced out at the balcony, a meditative expression on his face.

As I looked at him, I remembered what Mr. Sunderalingam had told me about the significance of the poems to Black Tie. On prize-giving day, next week, my reciting the poems was essential to Black Tie's speech. That was why he had changed his behavior towards me. It was not because he was fair that he had listened to Mr. Sunderalingam and removed the cane from his desk. Rather, it was because the poems were an indispensable part of his last hope of triumphing over Lokubandara. Without me his speech would fail and his efforts to save his position would come to nothing. A thought then presented itself to me, so simple I was surprised it hadn't come to me before. Black Tie needed me, and because he needed me, power had moved into my hands.

I looked at Black Tie and realized that any fear of him had disappeared.

When I left Black Tie's office, I walked down the corridor, thinking about my discovery. I considered the possibilities that lay before me. I couldn't refuse to recite the poems. Mr. Sunderalingam and Black Tie would force me to. Further, while trying to save Shehan, it was necessary that I didn't end up an "ills and burdens" again. I thought about pleading sickness. School would finish early on prize-giving day, and when I went home for lunch I could pretend to be sick. Yet, even as I thought of this scheme, I knew that unless I could produce a raging fever or something equivalent to it, my parents would insist on taking me to the prize-giving. Then I remembered the first time I had gone to recite the poems and the way I had confused them. A diabolical plan occurred to me. It was such a wicked idea I was shocked that I had actually thought of it. The plan was simple. Instead of trying to get out of reciting the poems, I would do them. But I would do them wrong. Confuse them, jumble lines, take entire stanzas from one poem and place them in the other until the poems were rendered senseless. Black Tie, who Mr. Sunderlingam said would write a speech based on these poems, would be forced to make a speech that made no sense. His attempt to win the cabinet minister to his side would fail, he would lose the battle to Lokubandara, be forced to resign, and that would solve things for Shehan.

As I waited for Shehan after school, I pondered over my plan. Part of me was scared and wanted to be relieved of it, of even thinking about it. Yet a stronger, sterner part of myself called me back not only to a sense of commitment but also to the memory of what Shehan and I had suffered at Black Tie's hands. It surprised me that I was thinking of doing something the bravest boy in my class would not dare. Where had the strength come from even to contemplate such an action? Then Shehan came in through the door, and as I looked at his face I realized I had made my decision. A feeling of numbness, of inevitability, seemed to come over me, as if my destiny had now passed out of my hands.

On the day of the prize-giving a week later, school finished early. Even Shehan and the other "ills and burdens" were allowed to leave. I had not told Shehan what I was going to do. I was afraid to put it into words, for I felt that if I did speak of it I would lose my courage to carry it through. I had, however, asked him if he was going to attend. I wanted his physical presence there to remind me of my commitment in case I had any last-minute doubts. He said he would come, but he'd watch from the second-floor gallery.

When Amma, my father, and I arrived at the auditorium it was crowded with parents and students. The murmur of voices and the rustle of saris created an air of expectancy and excitement. I walked down the central aisle with my parents, glancing up to my right at a gallery that ran the entire length of the auditorium. This gallery also served as a corridor for classrooms that were on the second floor. Shehan was not there.

My parents had now found their seats. A chair had been reserved for me next to Mr. Sunderalingam. Amma kissed me on both cheeks and wished me luck. My father put his hand on my shoulder and beamed at me proudly. As I made my way to the front, I turned to look at the empty gallery again. Mr. Sunderalingam was seated in the second row, behind the school's board of directors.

He patted the chair next to him and said, "Not nervous, are we, Chelvaratnam?"

"No, sir," I replied.

The stage had been decorated with coconut leaves and tall brass lamps whose lights were almost indistinguishable in the bright daylight that came in through the auditorium windows. The school choir stood at center stage, the choir teacher to one side of them. Mr. Sunderalingam opened his program and showed me the order of events. Once the chief guest arrived, the national anthem would be sung, followed by a presentation by the Sinhala Dramatic Society. Then it would be my turn to recite, and after that there would be the address by the principal. The program, with my name on it, made my recitation seem more real than it had been before. I felt a flutter of fear in my chest. Before it could turn to panic, I heard a hush sweep through the auditorium. I looked up the aisle. Black Tie and his wife were escorting the minister and his wife towards the front. Black Tie's head was bent courteously towards the minister, with whom he talked in a quiet tone. When they had taken their place in the front row, the choir began the national anthem and we rose to our feet.

When we were all seated again, the choir filed off the stage. A tabla player began to beat a rhythm, and a figure wearing a mask walked out onto the stage in time with the beat. Thus began the performance by the school's Sinhala Drama Society of the tale of Vijaya, the father of the Sinhalese nation, and his arrival on the shores of Lanka and his conquest of Kuveni, the Yaksha princess. I watched the figures leap about the stage in rhythm with the increasingly fast beat of the tabla, and I felt as if they were my heart personified, beating madly at the approaching moment when I would have to go up on that stage.

The tabla reached a deafening climax and the piece ended abruptly, like a life taken in midbreath. There was silence for a moment, and then the audience began to clap enthusiastically. I alone remained quiet, hating that the performance had finished, wishing that it would continue. The actors started to leave the stage, and Mr. Sunderalingam nudged me. I stood up unsteadily and started to go the wrong way. He took my arm and gently steered me in the right direction. As I passed, some of the teachers patted me on the back. I walked slowly down the side of the hall and then up the stairs to the stage. The curtains had been drawn following the actors' exit so that I would not be lost against the vast expanse of the stage.

When I reached the middle of the stage, I noticed that a microphone had been placed there. I stood looking at it, for a moment not realizing its purpose. The technician, thinking that I had not begun my recitation because the microphone was too high or low, came out and adjusted it slightly for me. I stood behind it and surveyed the expectant faces below me. Right in front of me was Black Tie and the minister, to my left Mr. Sunderalingam, and I could see my parents, not far back in the auditorium, looking at me proudly. Then I lifted my gaze to the gallery and saw Shehan leaning against the rail, watching me. He smiled. I took a deep breath and began my recitation. I kept my eyes fixed on the back wall, not looking at anyone, my ears attuned only to my voice as it mangled those poems, reducing them to disjointed nonsense.

Only when I was finished did I lower my eyes to the audience. Black Tie was looking down at his hands, his mouth slightly open. The minister had a bemused expression on his face. I didn't dare look at Mr. Sunderalingam or my parents. As I began to walk off the stage, I glanced up at the balcony. Shehan was staring at me in dismay and bewilderment. I came down the steps and made my way to my chair, squeezing past the teachers seated in my row, who seemed to recoil from me as if I carried a contagious disease. When I was seated, Mr. Sunderalingam leaned towards me and whispered kindly, "Never mind, Chelvaratnam. You did your best."

Black Tie had come to center stage now. He was silent for a long time, then he took a deep breath, and began.

"Ladies and gentlemen," he said, his voice cracking slightly. "Ladies and gentlemen, this young man who has just spoken to you was given the honor of reciting the words of a great poet. But he has taken it upon himself to defile a thing of beauty, wreak havoc on fine sentiments."

I could hear a rustle in the hall and people whispering behind me.

"He is a perfect example of what this school is producing," Black Tie went on. "The kind of scoundrel who will bring nothing but shame to his family and be a burden to society." His voice had reached a crescendo, but he had spoken too loud, for the microphone let out a sudden high-pitched squeal.

There was a titter of nervous laughter. The technician stepped out of the wings, but Black Tie waved him away and continued. "This young man is a prime illustration of what this country is coming to, of the path down which this nation is being led, of—" Black Tie suddenly broke off.

In front of me, the minister straightened up in his chair.

Black Tie was silent for a moment, then wiped his brow with his handkerchief, put on his spectacles, and took out his speech. He seemed to have regained his composure. He placed the pieces of paper on the podium, took a deep breath, and began to read.

"Honorable minister, ladies and gentlemen, those poems that you just heard so . . ." His voice faltered. ". . . rendered by a student of this academy speak powerfully of the values this school stands for, values that are now in jeopardy."

There was another titter of laughter. "In the poem, 'The Best School of All,' that we just heard, a few immortal lines ring even now in my ear, their message clear and succinct as only the words of a great poet can be."

Black Tie lifted his hand and quoted from the poem. " 'For though the dust that's part of us, to dust again be gone, yet here shall beat the heart of us—the School we handed on.' "

A few coughs could now be heard, the coughs of people trying to suppress their laughter.

Without looking up or acknowledging the disturbances, Black Tie continued his speech. "As I listened to those poems, I was reminded of my own youth as a student of the Victoria Academy. And I am wondering if those poems reminded you of your youth too."

The sounds in the auditorium grew louder, and I turned around and saw a few people leaving. I stared at Black Tie as the laughter and coughs buffeted his voice. He became silent now, staring at his speech. Gradually the auditorium became quiet. Everyone was looking at him, wondering what he would do next.

After a moment he picked up his pieces of paper and said, "Ladies and gentlemen, I now invite our esteemed guest to speak to you." With that, he introduced the minister, then turned and left the stage.

There was a smattering of applause as Black Tie came down the steps. I watched him as he took his seat. He looked tired and defeated.

I waited until the distribution of prizes began, and then, taking advantage of the movement of boys coming on and off the stage, I left the auditorium. I hurried down a corridor and up a set of stairs that led to the gallery. Shehan had seen me leave, and he was waiting for me at the top of the stairs.

"What happened?" he called out even before I was half-way up.

I didn't answer. Instead I bounded up the last few steps and then took his arm. I led him along the gallery and into a deserted classroom. I was panting now from climbing the stairs too fast. He looked at me searchingly as I recovered my breath.

"You know those poems perfectly. How could you mix them up like that?" he asked.

"Yes," I said, "I know them."

Then I began to tell him everything that Mr. Sunderalingam had told me about the importance of the poems to Black Tie's speech. As I spoke, his eyes widened in understanding.

"What made you do it?" he said to me almost in a whisper.

I didn't reply. Instead, I crossed to the window and looked out at the quadrangle below. As I gazed down at it, I recalled my first day at the Victoria Academy and how I had been so terrified of the older boys who were playing a game of rugger. That person seemed quite different from the one standing here. Even though barely two months had passed since that day, it seemed a long time ago. I turned away from the window. Shehan was waiting for a reply to his question.

"I did it for you," I said. "I couldn't bear to see you suffer anymore."

There was a look of surprise on his face, then understanding. He moved to me and I put my arms around him. From the auditorium below I could hear students' names being called out and clapping, but this seemed a distant reality compared to the rhythm of Shehan's breath against my neck and the warmth of his back under my fingers.

After a while, I became aware that the clapping had ended, and we heard a stirring of chairs as people stood up for the school song. Shehan and I moved away from each other with a sigh. We both knew that it was time to go down and face whatever had to be faced.

When we came out of the classroom, the school song had started. I walked to the gallery and stood there, looking down at the audience. My eyes came to rest on my parents. As I gazed at Amma, I felt a sudden sadness. What had happened between Shehan and me over the last few days had changed my relationship with her forever. I was no longer a part of my family in the same way. I now inhabited a world they didn't understand and into which they couldn't follow me.

Shehan was standing by the classroom door, waiting for me. The school song had ended now, and the audience was beginning to disperse. We stood for a moment, each lost in his own thoughts, then we began to walk together towards the stairs that led down to the auditorium.

Riot Journal: An Epilogue

⇌

July 25, 1983

6:00 A.M. Two hours ago the phone rang in the hall, waking us all. At first I thought that I was dreaming, but then I heard Amma and Appa's door open and I knew that I was awake. By the time I got to my door, Sonali, Diggy, and Neliya Aunty had already come out into the hall. Appa was on the phone, and from the expression on his face, we knew that something had happened. Finally he put the phone down.

"That was Mala," he said. Then he told us that there was trouble in Colombo. All the Tamil houses near the Kanaththa Cemetery had been burnt. We stared at him, unable to believe what he was saying. "Why?" Amma asked. Appa explained that it was because of the thirteen soldiers who were killed by the Tigers two days ago. The funeral was held last night and the mob at the cemetery went on a rampage. Appa tried to dismiss the whole thing. He told us to go to bed, that it was only a rumor, that there was probably some gang fight in a slum around Kanaththa which people were calling a communal riot. But I haven't been able to sleep. I have tried to read, but that is impossible, too. The only thing for me to do is write.

From the dining room, I can hear the murmur of Neliya Aunty's and Amma's voices and the clatter of plates and spoons. It is their attempt to provide some normalcy to the day. Yet all it does, this everyday sound, is make me realize how frighteningly different this day has been so far.

9:30 A.M. Sena Uncle and Chithra Aunty came to visit an hour ago. The moment we saw their faces we knew that the situation was serious. Amma invited them to have breakfast with us. They had been to the area around Kanaththa. The rumors are true. All the Tamil houses there are burnt, and the trouble has begun to spread to other parts of Colombo as well. Chithra Aunty started to say something more, but Sena Uncle stopped her and nodded towards us children. She became silent. After breakfast, my parents, Neliya Aunty, Sena Uncle, and Chithra Aunty went into Appa's study and closed the door behind them. Diggy, Sonali, and I crowded around the door, trying to hear what was happening, but they were speaking very softly. Sena Uncle said something, and Amma drew in her breath. "No," she said. "No. That can't be." Chithra Aunty said, "Shhh," and they spoke quietly again. When they came out, Amma and Neliya Aunty looked frightened.

Once Chithra Aunty and Sena Uncle had left, Amma called us into the dining room. "We're going to spend a few days at Chithra Aunty and Sena Uncle's house," she said.

This was not something we had expected. "Why, Amma?" Sonali asked. "Never mind why," Amma said. But then she felt a little sorry, for she said, "Don't worry, it's just a precaution. It's safer this way." Yet we knew she was lying. The situation must be very bad, for she has sent Anula away to stay with her aunt.

Amma said that we can only take a knapsack, otherwise it would look suspicious. We are supposed to bring a few clothes and one other thing that is important to us. I can't decide which thing to take. I have asked the others what they are taking. Diggy says he's not taking anything, but I noticed that some of his Willard Price books are gone. Amma is taking all the family albums. She says that if anything happens they will remind us of happier days. The picture of my grandparents is missing from Neliya Aunty's dressing table, and Sonali is taking two of her dolls, even though she doesn't play with dolls anymore. We are not using our own car because it is too small for all of us. Sena Uncle is going to return with his van.

Amma and Appa have phoned the other aunts and uncles.

So far, they are okay. Ammachi and Appachi's area is particularly bad. Some of their neighbors have offered to hide them in their house if anything happens.

The radio news is beginning again. We have listened to the broadcasts at 6:00, 7:30, and 8:45, but there is still no mention of the trouble. If not for the phone call and Sena Uncle and Chithra Aunty's visit, we would think that nothing was going on in Colombo. After the last broadcast, Appa looked at Amma significantly and said, "No curfew." From the way he said it, I assume that this has something to do with what Sena Uncle told him.

11:00 A.M. I have learned what Sena Uncle and Chithra Aunty told my parents. But I wish I had not found out.

I was in the garden trying to read when I heard the sound of Amma's and Appa's voices. Although I couldn't make out the words, just from the tone of Amma's voice I could tell that it was important. So I went and stood under the study window. "How can the government be doing this?" Amma was saying bitterly. "After all, we Tamils helped vote them in."

"We're not one hundred percent sure that they are behind the rioting," my father said.

"Of course they are. If not, why aren't they declaring curfew, and why aren't the police and army stopping the mobs?"

My father didn't respond.

"It has been planned in advance. Otherwise, how could the mobs get electoral lists so quickly?"

After that, both my parents were silent.

At first I didn't comprehend the reason for the electoral lists, but now I have thought about it and I understand. Since the mobs have electoral lists, they know which houses are Tamil and which houses aren't. This means that we have no chance of escaping if the mob comes down our road. And if they do, there will be no police to stop them.

12:30 P.M. The phones are dead, and for the first time I'm really frightened. Where is Sena Uncle? The van should have been here an hour ago. Has something happened to him?

1:00 P.M. The government has now declared curfew. Anyone caught on the road without a curfew pass will be shot on sight. I am so relieved, because this must mean that the government is not behind the rioting and that Sena Uncle and Chithra Aunty's story was wrong. After the announcement I could see relief on my parents' faces too.

Of course this means that Sena Uncle won't be able to pick us up. Appa says that it is all right. He didn't really want to leave the house in the first place, and since the government has declared curfew, the situation will soon be under control. Amma didn't agree. She said she would prefer to go to Chithra Aunty's house for the night.

3:00 P.M. The announcement of the curfew has not stopped the riots, and in fact the fighting has got worse. We have finally learned why Sena Uncle did not come for us.

About an hour ago we heard a bicycle bell outside. Then someone banged on our gate. The sound was so loud in the stillness that all the neighborhood dogs began to bark. Appa cautioned us to stay in the dining room. He went quietly down the hall and looked out through the drawing-room window. Then he signaled to us that it was all right. When we came to the gate, Appa was already outside talking to a man on a bicycle. He was a clerk from Appa's office. When he saw us, he stopped talking and looked at Appa, as if uncertain whether he should continue. Appa waved his hand and said, "They might as well know." I noticed that some of the other neighbors were watching from behind their gates. Appa turned to us and said, "Sena sent him. He had to abandon the van on Galle Road because some thugs stole all the petrol from it." Amma asked what they would want the petrol for, and Appa told the clerk to tell his story again.

Now Perera Aunty and Uncle, our next-door neighbors, came out of their gate and joined us. The clerk began to repeat his story. He told us that once he'd heard about the riots, he'd left the office. As he cycled towards Galle Road he saw that all the Tamil shops had been set on fire and the mobs were looting everything. The police and army just stood by, watching, and some of them even cheered the mobs and joined in the looting and burning. When he had finally made it to Galle Road, it was crowded with traffic going in all directions. Some motorists had abandoned their cars in the middle of the road and started to make the rest of the journey on foot. The pavements were no better, he said. They were packed with people hurrying home from work. Then, not far in the distance, he had heard a sound like a gunshot. Now the pedestrians began to scatter. When the pavement had cleared he had seen a terrible sight. There was a car in the middle of the road with a family inside it. The car was surrounded by thugs, and near it he saw Sena Uncle's van. The thugs were siphoning petrol out of it and pouring the petrol on the car. Sena Uncle stood by, watching helplessly. The clerk called out to him, and he saw him and came to the pavement. That was when Sena Uncle had asked him to take the message to us. Before he left, the clerk had taken one last look at the car. Even from where he stood, he could smell petrol. The family in the car were simply staring out at the thugs as if they didn't realize what was going on. Now one of the thugs began to ask around for a match. At this point the clerk had left. He had got on his bicycle and ridden away as fast as he could.

Ever since I heard this story, I have not been able to stop thinking about that family in the car. I thought I would go into the garden and sit on the swing for a little, but when I got there I didn't feel like it. Amma, Neliya Aunty, and Sonali were in the garden, tending to the rosebushes and anthuriums. I could tell that they, too, were trying not to think about what the clerk had said. Neliya Aunty says that there is nothing to do now but to trust in God and pray that we will be saved. Amma says that the best thing is to keep busy and hope for the best. But how can we hope for the best after hearing such a story?

Appa is in his study, reading the newspaper and waiting for the next news bulletin. Diggy is doing his exercises, and

I can hear the sound of the dumbbells every time he puts them down on the ground.

6:45 P.M. A little while ago, Amma and Appa asked us children to come into the dining room. Appa looked stern and serious, and Amma was very gentle. She explained to us that we have to be prepared if the mob comes. She and Appa have worked out an escape plan. She asked us to follow her onto the back verandah. In the back garden, I saw that our ladder had been placed against the side wall. If the mob comes, we are to climb up the ladder and jump over the wall into the Pereras' back garden. Perera Aunty and Perera Uncle will hide us in their storeroom. Even though Appa didn't think it was necessary, Amma made each of us go up the ladder so that we could get a feel for it. When I reached the top of the ladder, I saw that Perera Aunty and Uncle were watching us from the other side. Throughout the whole exercise, Amma kept saying that we were only doing this in case the mob came and that it was all a big "if." Yet I know that this is not so. I noticed that Amma has removed her thali and gold bangles. She must have sent them next door with her jewelry box. Appa also sent our birth certificates and bankbooks. They know that there is going to be trouble. Like me, they are certain that the mob will come. It's only a question of when.

11:30 P.M. This waiting is terrible. I wish the mob would come so that this dreadful waiting would end. No, I don't wish that. It is the last thing I want. Yet I know it's going to happen. There is no doubt in my mind. So wouldn't it be better if it happened sooner rather than later? Then we would be put out of this misery.

I am using my torch to write this. Everyone is supposed to be asleep, but I don't think anyone is. Appa is doing the watch right now, and I can hear him clear his throat from time to time. We have gone to bed completely dressed, even with our shoes on. Amma told us to wear jeans or something that was easy to move around in. Neliya Aunty, who always wears a sari, has borrowed a pair of Amma's pants. All the adults, too, have torches. In case of any trouble, one of them will wake us up. Without turning on any of the lights in the house, we must go into the dining room with our bags.

July 26

12:30 P.M. I have just read my last entry and it seems unbelievable that only thirteen hours ago I was sitting on my bed writing in this journal. A year seems to have passed since that time. Our lives have completely changed. I try and try to make sense of it, but it just won't work.

How quickly everything happened. I was lying on my bed, reading, and then I must have fallen asleep. Scared as I was, my body finally gave out. The next thing I knew, Neliya Aunty was shaking my shoulder. I opened my eyes and her torch was shining in my face. "Darling," she said, "it's time." She said it so gently that for a moment I thought it was time to get up for school. Then I heard the chants of the mob. I sat up in bed, and I must have got up too fast, because I fell off it. "Sssh," Neliya Aunty said.

I stared at her, unable to move. I tried to push myself up, but my legs seemed to have lost all their feeling. It was like a horrible dream. Neliya Aunty bent down and helped me up. I must have been crying, because I remember her saying to me, "Don't cry, child." Then we went into the dining room. The others were already there.

The chants of the mob were getting louder. Appa motioned to us and we followed him onto the back verandah. It was so dark outside that we could barely see ahead of us. The back garden looked menacing, and the trees and bushes seemed strange and unfamiliar. Even the verandah seemed alien. Amma shone her torch on the steps so we would not fall as we were going down into the garden. Appa was standing by the ladder. He indicated for Sonali to go up first, and he shone his light along the ladder. She began to climb to the top. By now the sounds of the mob had got even closer. "Faster," my father hissed at Sonali. She seemed to be climbing very slowly. Finally she reached the top and sat on the wall. After a slight pause, she jumped.

Now it was my turn. I was in such a hurry to get to the top that I missed a rung and nearly fell down the ladder. "Be careful," Amma whispered up at me. I had reached the top of the ladder now. I could see Perera Aunty and Uncle waiting for us on the other side. She had a kerosene lamp in her hand. From the top of the ladder I could see the glow of the mob's flares as they drew near. Perera Aunty beckoned to me urgently. I sat on the wall and, after looking fearfully at the distance between myself and the ground, I closed my eyes and jumped. Neliya Aunty was the next to come up the ladder, and then Amma. When Diggy came to the top, he sat on the wall and waited for Appa. Between the two of them, they pulled the ladder up the wall and threw it into the Pereras' back garden. Then they jumped down. We followed Perera Aunty into the house, going down a dark corridor to the kitchen. The servant was waiting in there, and Perera Aunty told her to hold open the door that led into the storeroom. We all crowded inside. It was a small room, and it smelled of raw rice and Maldive fish and other dry provisions. "I'm going to shut the door now," Perera Aunty said apologetically. My father nodded. She left the lamp on a shelf and went out of the storeroom, closing the door behind her. Now we were all alone.

There was a high window in the storeroom and we all looked up at it, as if through it we hoped to see what was happening. For some strange reason we could no longer hear the chants of the mob. Sonali crept close to me, and I put my arm around her. The first noise we heard was a crash and the shattering of glass. "Front door," Amma whispered. Then other sounds started. Cracking and banging and the dragging of heavy objects across the floor. I tried to place them, but it was impossible to tell where they were coming from. Then, through the storeroom window, we saw a spiral of smoke. "Fire," Neliya Aunty said in a panicked voice. "Oh God, they are setting the house on fire."

Soon the darkness of the night was broken by a golden light, as if the sun were rising. The light even came into the storeroom, illuminating our upturned faces. Then, gradually, the light subsided and the darkness returned. The mob had left by now, and there was a terrible silence, broken only by the sound of wooden beams giving way with a groan and crashing to the ground.

After a while we heard the storeroom door open. Perera Aunty and Perera Uncle came in. They just stood there looking at us, not knowing what to say. "They've gone," Perera Uncle finally said. My father nodded and stood up. "What's the damage?" he asked.

Perera Uncle shook his head. "I couldn't see."

"I should take a look," Appa said.

"No," Amma said, alarmed. "It's not safe. Wait till morning."

Perera Uncle and Aunty nodded in agreement. "You never know whether they'll come back or not," Perera Uncle said.

We heard the rattling of teacups in the dining room. "Come and have some tea," Perera Aunty said.

The sheer normality of her offer took us aback, yet when we were seated at the table with the hot teacups in our hands, the familiar taste of tea was comforting.

Once the sky had got lighter, we went to look at our house. The fire had completely died down by now. I stood at the gate, staring at the devastation in front of me. If not for the gate, which was still intact, I would never have been able to say that this had been our house. Many thoughts went through my mind as I stood there. The first thing that struck me was how much smaller the house seemed, now that most of the roof had caved in.

It was dangerous to go into the house, but we couldn't stop ourselves. I was struck by how uniform and characterless the rooms looked, with their debris of furniture and charred walls. They, too, seemed to have shrunk in size. I went to my room and looked around. As I examined the charred things on the floor, I was suddenly aware that records were not music but plastic, which had now melted into black puddles; that my books were mere paper that had browned and now came apart between my fingers. Legs, posts, and arms of well-known furniture, once polished smooth and rich brown in hue, now that they had cracked open revealed the whiteness of common wood. I observed all this with not a trace of remorse, not a touch of sorrow for the loss and destruction around me. Even now I feel no sorrow. I try to remind myself that the house is destroyed, that we will never live in it again, but my heart refuses to understand this.

While we were searching through the house, we heard a van stop. It was Sena Uncle and Chithra Aunty. They had finally been able to get some petrol and secure a curfew pass. We went to meet them. They stared at the house for a long time. Then Chithra Aunty began to cry. Amma went to her and tried to comfort her. There was something ironic about that. Amma comforting Chithra Aunty. Yet I understood it. Chithra Aunty was free to cry. We couldn't, for if we started we would never stop.

By then, the other neighbors had come to see the devastation. They were saddened by it, and a few of them said that when they looked at the house they were ashamed to say they were Sinhalese.

Before leaving, Amma, Neliya Aunty, and Sonali collected whatever had not been destroyed. In my room, I had thought to do the same but then left everything as it was. My father and Diggy, too, took nothing with them.

When we were leaving in the van, Mrs. Bandara from next door brought us some raw provisions. The other neighbors saw her doing this and they started bringing things too. Amma refused to take anything, because they have families to feed as well, but they were insistent. It was odd to see them standing at their gates and waving at us as we drove away.

3:00 P.M. We have just heard the news about Ammachi and Appachi's house. It, too, has been destroyed. Ammachi and Appachi are all right, however, and they are going to drive to Kanthi Aunty's house. She lives in Colombo Seven, and so far that area has not been affected at all. Sena Uncle said that Ramanaygam Road looks as if someone has dropped a bomb on it. So many houses have been destroyed that from the top of the road you can see clear to the railway lines and the sea. When I heard this I thought about childhood spend-the-days and all the good times we had there. These thoughts made me cry. I couldn't cry for my own house, but it was easy to grieve for my grandparents' house.

6:00 P.M. Something awful has happened. Amma and Appa called us into the drawing room a few minutes ago. Everyone there was looking very serious. Sena Uncle has received an anonymous phone call. The caller knows that we are here. He called Sena Uncle a traitor for sheltering Tamils and said that he and other "patriots" were coming tonight to kill us and burn down Sena Uncle's house. Sena Uncle tried to dismiss the call, saying that it was probably some crank, yet, all the same, he looked very worried. My parents want him to take us to one of the refugee camps that have been set up for victims of the riots, but he and Chithra Aunty will not hear of it. So once again we have an escape plan. Sena Uncle's mother lives next door, and there is a door in the side garden wall between the two houses. You can't really spot this door because it is hidden behind the dog kennel. If there is any trouble, we are to go over to his mother's house and she will hide us in the library, a room that is easy to miss unless you know the house well. Tonight we must sleep in our shoes again. I am tired of these escape plans. I'm tired of everything. I just want it all to end.

11:00 P.M. My hand shakes even though it's two hours since we had the scare.

We had just finished dinner when the doorbell rang. We looked at each other, not knowing what to do. Then Chithra Aunty signaled to Sena Uncle to go and see who was at the door. Appa told us to get our knapsacks. Sena Uncle came back and said that there was a group of men outside. The doorbell rang again. Chithra Aunty beckoned to us to follow her, and we went out into the side garden. Bindi, the dog, started to whine when he saw Chithra Aunty. She held out her hand so that he could lick it. While she was doing this, we went through the door into Sena Uncle's mother's garden. As we closed the door, I heard Chithra Aunty and their son,

Sanath, dragging the dog kennel in front of the door.

We had been in the library an hour when Sena Uncle came to fetch us. The men had gone away, he told us. He had spoken to them through the window. They said that they were collecting funds for a sports meet, and he gave them a hundred rupees.

It is obvious that something odd is going on, but what it is we don't know. Sena Uncle thinks that the phone call was made by the same men and that they have no intention of burning the house, it's simply a way of extorting money. Even though this is awful, I hope he is right. Appa and Amma are adamant that we must go to a refugee camp tomorrow, but Sena Uncle and Chithra Aunty refuse to even consider it.

July 27

7:00 P.M. Curfew was lifted for a few hours so people could buy food. Yet there was nothing to buy. A lot of the grocery stores are owned by Tamils, and they have all been destroyed.

We had an unending stream of visitors today. Despite the phones being dead yesterday, news seems to have got around about what happened to us. Although I am grateful that so many people care about us, at the same time I wish they wouldn't come. They only bring dismal and depressing news with them.

Only one visit brought me pleasure, for this afternoon Shehan came to see me. I had not seen him since the riots began. A whole cycle of life seems to have passed since the last time we met and lay on his bed, talking about what subjects we would take if we passed our O levels next year.

When I saw Shehan standing at Chithra Aunty's door, the reality of all that had happened hit me. Then I wanted more than anything else to hold him. But my family and some visitors were in the drawing room, so I shook his hand instead and asked him to follow me into the side garden, where we could be alone. Diggy, who was also in the drawing room, looked as if he was about to follow us, but Amma called out to him to leave us alone. This surprised me, because it was the first time that Amma had shown she was aware of Diggy's hostility towards Shehan whenever he visited me. Maybe, in the seven months I have known Shehan, Amma has come to accept him as a friend of mine.

When we were in the garden, Shehan told me he had gone to our house looking for me and was horrified when he saw the burnt remains. A neighbor had informed him about what had happened and where we were. I nodded, not really wanting to talk about it. Shehan must have sensed this, because he immediately began to tell me about a film that he wanted to see and how we could go for an afternoon matinee after school next week, if curfew is lifted. He was trying to cheer me up, and as I listened to him talk, something occurred to me that I had never really been conscious of before— Shehan was Sinhalese and I was not. This awareness did not change my feelings for him, it was simply there, like a thin translucent screen through which I watched him.

The phones are working again, and Lakshman Uncle called from Canada to find out how we were. He got the number from Kanthi Aunty, and he said that he had been trying to get through since Monday. Canadians have been watching the riots on TV, and they seem to know more about it than we do. It seems that there are demonstrations in Canada and England and India against the Sri Lankan government. When Appa had finished the telephone call, he was silent for a moment. Then he told Amma that Lakshman Uncle wanted us to come over to Canada as refugees, that this would be a good time to claim refugee status. I felt joyful at the thought of getting out of this country, and I could see hope in Diggy's and Sonali's faces too.

"Should we do it?" Amma asked.

Appa looked very thoughtful. "Let's watch the situation for a little longer and then decide," he said. "I have so many assets here. I don't want to just up and go like that."

Later, however, I heard Appa telling Amma that as soon as things quietened down, they would apply for passports for Diggy, Sonali, and me.

July 28

8:00 P.M. This day has been a terrible one for Appa. We heard that the hotel was attacked yesterday. It was severely damaged and most of the rooms were burnt. Fortunately there were no tourists there at the time; they had all been removed to the airport. Mr. Samarakoon and some of the staff tried to stop the mob, but it was useless. After he heard the news, Appa sat in the front garden, staring ahead of him. Amma went out to see if he was all right, and he said that he wanted to be left alone for a little while.

Appa finally came inside to hear the president address the nation. When the broadcast was over, he said that he wished he had stayed outside. The president expressed no sympathy for what we Tamils have suffered, nor did he condemn the actions of the thugs.

After the president's address, Appa went into the garden again and Amma followed him. I sat on the steps that led out from the French windows into the garden and listened to them. They were silent for a while. Then Appa said, "It is very clear that we no longer belong in this country."

Amma nodded.

"How could I have been so blind? Why didn't I see this coming? Now that I look back, it was obvious this was going to happen. I should have seen it, I should have known things would come to this."

"Don't blame yourself," Amma said. "It's difficult to see clearly when you're in the middle of something."

Appa shook his head. "But you saw it. You even warned me, but I refused to believe you." He turned to her. "How were you able to see it?"

Amma did not answer.

"When this is all over, we'll start to make plans for Canada."

I am glad he said that, because I long to be out of this country. I don't feel at home in Sri Lanka any longer, will never feel safe again.

July 29

10:00 A.M. The morning has hardly begun and already the visitors have started to arrive. How many times must we repeat the same story? The excitement of the riots is wearing off, and what happened to us has become dull from being told so many times. Ammachi and Appachi are the latest visitors. They say they have come to see how we are, but all Ammachi has done since she got here is moan about the loss of their house. Finally I got up and went away to write in this journal.

The reality of losing our house is slowly beginning to sink in, but what I feel is nothing like what I imagined. I expected to be sad and nostalgic for a part of my life that is now destroyed. But I only get irritated and lethargic. It's the little things, the comforts and luxuries, that I miss. The yearning for things like my records or my books or even the mat by my bed gnaws at me until I think I must have them this moment or I will die. Then I become angry and frustrated, because I can't have them. I am also beginning to feel claustrophobic, because with so many people in the house it is impossible to have any peace and quiet. I long to be with Shehan, and I am thinking of slipping out this afternoon to see him.

The loss of our house is also beginning to hit Amma. She has cried a lot this morning. She tries not to let us see her crying and goes to the bathroom. Still, we know what she is doing in there and that makes us feel terrible.

★ ★ ★

1:00 P.M. The riots have begun again. Just when we thought everything was going back to normal. We heard people running down our road, shouting that the Tigers had landed in Colombo, that they had come to avenge the Tamil people.

A few minutes ago the radio denied that the Tigers have landed in Colombo. So how did this story start? Was it merely a rumor to cause more trouble?

Appa has just finished talking to Kanthi Aunty on the phone again. Ammachi and Appachi left forty-five minutes ago in their car and they still haven't arrived at Kanthi Aunty's house. Where can they be? Neliya Aunty is praying in the drawing room with Amma. I should be praying too, but I can't. All I can do is write in this book.

Sena Uncle has gone looking for them.

The situation must be serious, because the government has declared curfew again.

August 2

So many things have happened over the last four days, I have not felt like writing until now.

Not long after my last entry, Sena Uncle returned. I was in Sanath's room and the door was open. From the silence in the drawing room, I knew what had happened. Then I heard Amma begin to weep, a long cry of despair. I just stood where I was, not knowing what to do. I couldn't bear to go into the drawing room and see Amma crying.

At first Sena Uncle didn't want to say anything, but Appa

pressed him until he finally told them what had happened. He had set out for Kanthi Aunty's house, following the route Ammachi and Appachi had likely taken. Shortly after he left, however, he noticed a crowd up ahead on the road and smoke rising into the air. The traffic in front of him was too congested, and, fearing the worst, he had got out of his car and hurried along the pavement. But he got there too late. The mob had set the car on fire with Ammachi and Appachi inside it.

Appa was silent for a while, then he said, "I must go. I have to see what happened." His voice was strange. "No," Amma said in a panicked voice. "You can't go. It's too dangerous." Now Appa began to shout, "It's my parents, for God's sake. It's my parents who are being burnt." Sena Uncle tried to calm him down but he wouldn't listen. Finally Amma yelled at him, "You have children to think of. If anything happens to you, what will become of them?" Appa became silent.

I knew that I couldn't stay in Sanath's room anymore. It wasn't right. I had to go into the drawing room and join them. My hands were sweating as I went towards the door. Everybody stared at me as I entered the drawing room, but I avoided looking at any of them. Amma turned to Sena Uncle. "What shall we do now?" she asked.

"We'll have to wait until the ambulance comes and takes the bodies away," he replied. "Until then, I'll go and keep watch over the car. Someone has to look out for"—he moved uncomfortably in his chair—"stray dogs and crows."

Chithra Aunty shuddered when he said this. I looked around me now. Appa sat in a chair, his legs sprawled out.

He stared at the floor and his jaw muscles tightened every now and then. Amma had smudges on her face. The knot on the back of her neck had come partially undone and a strand of hair hung down.

After Sena Uncle left, we all remained as we were, not knowing what to do. Finally Amma moved in her chair and said, "We should inform the rest of the family." Yet nobody made an attempt to get up and go to the phone.

Yesterday, we buried Ammachi and Appachi. It was a bright, sunny day, so different from what a funeral day should be like. Radha Aunty flew back from America for the funeral. It was peculiar to see her standing near the coffins during the service, her head thrown back in the way Ammachi used to do when she was upset about something and didn't want anybody to see it. We no longer have much to say to each other, but, as we followed the coffins towards the grave, she put her hand on my shoulder and kept it there.

The whole funeral had an unreal feeling to it. Even while they were lowering the coffins into the grave, I found it hard to believe that it was Ammachi and Appachi we were burying. I think that the other aunts and uncles felt the same way, for nobody cried at the funeral. We simply stood around the grave, watching the coffins disappear under the clods of earth that were thrown on them.

I find it impossible to imagine that the world will ever be normal again.

August 25

Today I received my passport. As I looked at it, I finally realized that we are really leaving Sri Lanka; that in two days we will be in a strange country. I thought about how, when we were young, Diggy, Sonali, and I would sometimes imagine what foreign countries were like. All those Famous Five books, and then *Little Women* and the Hardy Boys. We would often discuss what fun it would be to go abroad, make snowmen, have snowball fights, and eat scones and blueberry jam. I don't think that we ever imagined we would go abroad under these circumstances, as penniless refugees. We are going, not with the idea that something delightful awaits us, but rather with the knowledge that great difficulties lie ahead. First, Appa won't be coming for a while. He has to settle many things over here. The thought of not having Appa around is frightening. Amma didn't want to go without him, but he said that it was too dangerous for us to stay here, because we don't know when the next riot will break out. Second, we will have to live with Lakshman Uncle. This news makes me want to stay behind. It is bad enough living off Chithra Aunty and Sena Uncle, whom we know so well. But to be in a foreign country, living off the charity of somebody I hardly know, is terrible. Appa can't take his money out of the country because of government regulations. We are only allowed five hundred pounds each. The thought of being this poor scares me.

Today I watched a beggar woman running from car to car at the traffic lights, her hand held out, and I wondered if this would be our plight in Canada.

August 27

I have just returned from seeing Shehan. I can still smell his particular odor on my body, which always lingers on me after we make love. I remember the first time I noticed this. I had come home from being with him, and I was so nervous that others would detect it that, after putting my bicycle away at the back, I rushed to the shower. I smile to think about that, since now I am reluctant even to change my clothes for fear that I will lose this final memento.

When we made love for the last time today, it was nothing like I imagined it would be—almost passionless, uncoordinated and tentative, lacking synchronization. Like those afternoons when neither of us felt ardent, but, thinking that the other did, we would make our best effort. I had dreaded our parting so much that, for fear of the pain, I had withdrawn from him. I suppose he had done the same thing.

Afterwards, while we were putting on our clothes, I glanced up at the mirror and saw that he was watching me. For a moment our eyes met, then I turned away and continued getting dressed.

When I left his house, the sky had darkened and I could feel the moisture in the air. I had borrowed Sanath's bicycle for the afternoon, and as I cycled along Galle Road towards Sena Uncle's house, I had the nagging sense that there was something I needed to do but I couldn't remember what. When I passed Bullers Road, I knew what it was. I stopped my bicycle and wheeled it back along the pavement.

By the time I had turned onto our road, I could already feel a few drops of rain on my arms. The road was deserted.

From the top of it, I could see our house, its black walls and beams visible above the other houses. When I reached it, I pushed open the gate. Something was different from the last time I was there. The house looked even more bare, even more desolate than before. Then I realized what had happened, and I stared at our house in shock. Everything that was not burnt had been stolen. Whatever had remained intact, furniture, uncharred beams, doors, windows, even the hinges and the rain pipes, had been taken. How naked the house appeared without its door and windows, how hollow and barren with only scraps of paper and other debris in its rooms. I felt hot, angry tears begin to well up in me as I saw this final violation. Then, for the first time, I began to cry for our house. I sat on the verandah steps and wept for the loss of my home, for the loss of everything that I held to be precious. I tried to muffle the sound of my weeping, but my voice cried out loudly as if it were the only weapon I had against those who had destroyed my life.

Finally I could not cry anymore. I leaned back on one of the verandah posts, exhausted, and stared out at the garden. It looked so forlorn. The grass had grown, but in uneven patches, and the roses had lost most of their petals. The araliya tree was bare of its flowers. They, too, must have been stolen. I was struck then by a bitter irony. These araliya flowers would probably be offered to some god as a pooja by the very people who had plucked them, in order to increase their chances of a better life in the next birth.

I could hear the thunder in the sky now, and in the dust

on the driveway I could see the speckled pattern of raindrops. It was time for me to leave. I got up slowly and brushed the dirt from my trousers, then I went down the steps and picked up my bicycle. I wheeled it to the gate, staring straight ahead, not wanting to look at the house again. I didn't bother to close the gate as I left. There was no reason to protect it against the outside world anymore.

I began to ride up the road, and the rain suddenly started, falling in great torrents, as it does during the monsoon season. When I reached the top of the road, I couldn't prevent myself from turning back to look at the house one last time. For a moment I saw it, then the rain fell faster and thicker, obscuring it from my sight.

Glossary

aday an expression somewhat equivalent to "hey" in English
aiyo an expression used to convey many things, such as pain, sympathy, annoyance, etc.
akka older sister
almariah wardrobe
araliya frangipani
baba child; a term used by servants to address the children they look after
banyan undershirt, jersey
Buddu Ammo an expression of consternation; literally means Mother of Buddha
Burgher a descendant of the Portuguese or Dutch colonizers

karapi derogatory word for someone who is dark-skinned

karaya vendor

lamprais special preparation of rice and curry that is baked in a banana leaf

machan literally means brother-in-law; is used as a term of affection between male friends

Maldive fish a dry, salted fish

Manipuri a rich, embroidered sari material from Manipur in India

miris gala grinding stone used for chiles and spices

missie madam

mol gaha large pestle

mudalali merchant

mukkuthi nose ring

pala harams sweets and snacks that are prepared for festive occasions

palam popsicle

palu the part of the sari that falls over the shoulder

pittu dish made out of rice flour and coconut, steamed in the hollow of a bamboo shoot

pooja an offering to a god

pottu dot worn on the forehead by Tamil women

stringhoppers dish made out of rice-flour dough which has been pushed through a sieve, then formed into little circles resembling lace doilies, then steamed

tabla hand drums

takaran galvanized sheets of iron

thali necklace given to a woman by her husband when they are married and removed only when she becomes a widow

thatha father

vamban rascal

Acknowledgments

A first novel is often more of a group effort than is generally realized. I would, therefore, like to thank:

My family for their patience with me during the writing of *Funny Boy*. Especially my aunt, Bunny De Silva, for screening my calls and for keeping me well fed.

Fernando Sa-Pereira for his editorial advice and his belief in my abilities during the "formative years" in Montreal. Many of his invaluable suggestions are incorporated in this book.

Steve Pereira, Tony Stephenson, and Caesar Blake for their feedback on the initial drafts of this book.

Acknowledgments

Manel Fonseka for opening so many doors, even ones that I'd thought would be firmly shut.

Mr. and Mrs. Alles and family for their hospitality.

Ellen Seligman at McClelland & Stewart, with whom editing has been such a pleasure.

Dan Franklin at Jonathan Cape in London.

Will Schwalbe at William Morrow, for his enthusiasm and commitment to *Funny Boy*.

My agents, Lucinda Vardey in Canada and Carolyn Brunton in England, for believing so much in the book.

The Ontario Arts Council.